The Black Pilgrimage 2
Further Explorations in
Supernatural Fiction

The Black Pilgrimage 2
Further Explorations in Supernatural Fiction

Rosemary Pardoe

Shadow Publishing

THE BLACK PILGRIMAGE 2
FURTHER EXPLORATIONS IN
SUPERNATURAL FICTION

This edition © Rosemary Pardoe 2023
Cover photograph: The Museum Room from Rosemary Pardoe's Antiquary's Doll's House. Photograph by Darroll Pardoe. © Rosemary Pardoe 2023

All rights reserved. No part of this publication may be reproduced, stored in a retrieval system, rebound or transmitted in any form or by any means, electronic, mechanical, photocopying, recording or otherwise, without the prior written permission of the editor and publisher. This book is sold subject to the condition that it shall not by way of trade or otherwise be lent, resold, hired out or otherwise circulated without the publisher's prior consent in any form of binding or cover other than that in which it is published.

ISBN: 978-1-3999-4431-1
Shadow Publishing, Apt 19 Awdry Court, 15 St Nicolas Gardens,
Kings Norton, Birmingham, B38 8BH, UK
david.sutton986@btinternet.com

Original Appearances
G&S: *Ghosts & Scholars.* LWJ: *Lady Wardrop's Journal.*

Introduction

Part One: M.R. James and Jamesian-related Writings

"Tha hast conjured me": Dan Jones's *The Tale of the Tailor and the Three Dead Kings* (LWJ 74, Nov 2021)

"He was laughing in the church": Disembodied Voices in the Stories of M.R. James (LWJ 75, Jan 2022)

The M.R. James Murders: Nicola Upson's *Nine Lessons* (LWJ 53, Mar 2018)

M.R. James's Suffolk: Simon Loxley's *A Geography of Horror: The Ghost Stories of M.R. James and the Suffolk Landscape* (LWJ 76, Mar 2022)

Something happened in Felixstowe: Robert Lloyd Parry's *Oh, Whistle and I'll Come to You* and *Wits in Felixstowe* (G&S 34, 2018)

Michael Harrison 1907-1991 (G&S Newsletter 33, 2018)

Two Lesser-Known John Gordon Novels: *The Ghosts of Blacklode* and *The Midwinter Watch* (G&S 36/37, 2019)

"BE his Life Squeezed Away": Fritz Leiber's *The Pale Brown Thing* (G&S Newsletter 30, 2016)

The Return of Cindy Mars-Lewis: Phil Rickman's *Night After Night* (*A Ghostly Company Newsletter*, Spring 2015?)

Things that Go Bump in the Night: Roger Johnson's *In the Night - In the Dark: Tales of Ghosts and Less Welcome Visitors* (G&S Newsletter 21, 2012)

Part Two: The Rest

The Immortal William Palmer: Sebastian Baczkiewicz's *Pilgrim* (*A Ghostly Company Newsletter 79*, Autumn 2022)

The Real Thing Again (or perhaps not): Melissa Albert's *The Hazel Wood* and *The Night Country* (LWJ 55, July 2018; LWJ 66, May 2020).

"More Bones and Marrow for our Babies": Daisy Makeig-Jones's Fairyland Lustreware (LWJ 60, May 2019)

The Mystery and Magic of Rooftops: Helen Grant's *Demons of Ghent* (LWJ 62, Sept 2019)

"A Sense of Otherness": Folk Horror Revival's *Urban Wyrd* and *Harvest Hymns* (LWJ 63, Nov 2019; LWJ 58, Jan 2019)

"The Flame Still Flickers in the Fen": *Of Mud & Flame: The Penda's Fen Sourcebook* (LWJ 65, Mar 2020)

Not the F-word: Mackenzie Crook's *The Windvale Sprites* and *The Lost Journals of Benjamin Tooth* (*Waiting for You: A Detectorists zine 1*, 2020)

A Welsh Wild Hunt: Claire Fayers' *Storm Hound* (LWJ 70, Jan 2021)

The Mad World of Lionel Fanthorpe and Noel Boston: Shane P.D. Agnew's *John Spencer & Co (Badger Books) - Illustrated Bibliography* (LWJ 68, Sept 2020)

Windhollow Faire: Elizabeth Hand's *Wylding Hall* (LWJ 80, Nov 2022)

An Ineffably Strange Place: Mark Valentine's *Herald of the Hidden* and *Seventeen Stories* (G&S Newsletter 24, 2013; G&S Newsletter 25, 2014)

"A Sense of an Ancient Longing": Tom Cox's *Villager* and Zoe Gilbert's *Mischief Acts* (LWJ 79, Sept 2022)

Part Three: Ghosts & Scholars Columns

Lady Wardrop's Notes 1: Robert Macfarlane's *Ness* and Lois Austen-Leigh's *The Incredible Crime: A Cambridge Mystery* (G&S 38, 2020)

Lady Wardrop's Notes 2: The Portals of London website (G&S 39, 2020)

Lady Wardrop's Notes 3 (Part One): Possible Jamesian aspects of *Detectorists* (G&S 40, 2021)

Lady Wardrop's Notes 3 (Part Two): Did M.R. James read any of Lovecraft's stories? (G&S 40, 2021)

Lady Wardrop's Notes 4: Female ghosts in M.R. James's Stories and The Recurrence of Characters Named Mary (G&S 41, 2021)

Lady Wardrop's Notes 5: Dogs in M.R. James's Stories (G&S 42, 2022)

Lady Wardrop's Notes 6: Geographical locations in M.R. James's Stories (G&S

43, 2022)

Lady Wardrop's Notes 7: The Supernatural Consequences of HS2 (G&S 44, 2023)

Part Four: Introductions

Introduction: *The Ghosts & Scholars Book of Shadows Volume 1* (Sarob Press 2012)

Introduction: *The Ghosts & Scholars Book of Shadows Volume 2* (Sarob Press 2014)

Introduction: *The Ghosts & Scholars Book of Shadows Volume 3* (Sarob Press 2016)

Introduction (Extended Version): *A Ghosts & Scholars Book of Folk Horror* (LWJ 57, Dec 2018)

Introduction: *The Ghosts & Scholars Book of Mazes* (Sarob Press 2020)

Introduction: *The Ghosts & Scholars Book of Follies & Grottoes* (Sarob Press 2022)

Introduction: *The Angry Dead* (Cathaven Press 2021)

Part Five: Booklets

The Cropton Lane Farm Murders (2018)

"The Old Man on the Hill": English Hill Figures in Supernatural Fiction (2022)

English Hill Figures: Addenda (LWJ 82, Apr 2023; LWJ 77, May 2022; LWJ 80, Nov 2022)

Part Six: And Finally

The Wormwood Interview: Rosemary Pardoe (*Wormwood 38*, 2022)

Contents

Introduction 1

Part One:
M.R. James and Jamesian-related Writings

"Tha hast conjured me": Dan Jones's *The Tale of the
Tailor and the Three Dead Kings* 9

"He was laughing in the church": Disembodied Voices
in the Stories of M.R. James 15

The M.R. James Murders: Nicola Upson's *Nine Lessons* ... 23

M.R. James's Suffolk: Simon Loxley's *A Geography of
Horror: The Ghost Stories of M.R. James and the
Suffolk Landscape* 29

Something happened in Felixstowe: Robert Lloyd Parry's
Oh, Whistle and I'll Come to You and *Wits in Felixstowe* .. 37

Michael Harrison 1907-1991 43

Two Lesser-Known John Gordon Novels: *The Ghosts of
Blacklode* and *The Midwinter Watch* 51

"BE his Life Squeezed Away": Fritz Leiber's *The Pale
Brown Thing* 57

The Return of Cindy Mars-Lewis: Phil Rickman's *Night
After Night* 63

Things that Go Bump in the Night: Roger Johnson's *In
the Night - In the Dark: Tales of Ghosts and Less
Welcome Visitors* 69

Part Two:
The Rest

The Immortal William Palmer: Sebastian Baczkiewicz's
Pilgrim 77

The Real Thing Again (or perhaps not): Melissa Albert's
The Hazel Wood and *The Night Country* 83

"More Bones and Marrow for our Babies":
Daisy Makeig-Jones's Fairyland Lustreware 93

The Mystery and Magic of Rooftops: Helen Grant's
Demons of Ghent 101

"A Sense of Otherness": Folk Horror Revival's
Urban Wyrd and *Harvest Hymns* 107

"The Flame Still Flickers in the Fen":
Of Mud & Flame: The Penda's Fen Sourcebook 117

Not the F-word: Mackenzie Crook's *The Windvale
Sprites* and *The Lost Journals of Benjamin Tooth* 125

A Welsh Wild Hunt: Claire Fayers' *Storm Hound* 131

The Mad World of Lionel Fanthorpe and Noel Boston:
Shane P.D. Agnew's *John Spencer & Co* 135

Windhollow Faire: Elizabeth Hand's *Wylding Hall* 141

An Ineffably Strange Place: Mark Valentine's
Herald of the Hidden and *Seventeen Stories* 149

"A Sense of an Ancient Longing": Tom Cox's *Villager*
and Zoe Gilbert's *Mischief Acts* 159

Part Three:
Ghosts & Scholars Columns

Lady Wardrop's Notes 1: Robert Macfarlane's *Ness*
and Lois Austen-Leigh's *The Incredible Crime: A
Cambridge Mystery* 167

Lady Wardrop's Notes 2: The Portals of London
website 175

Lady Wardrop's Notes 3 (Part One): Possible Jamesian aspects of *Detectorists* 181

Lady Wardrop's Notes 3 (Part Two): Did M.R. James read any of Lovecraft's stories? 187

Lady Wardrop's Notes 4: Female ghosts in M.R. James's Stories and The Recurrence of Characters Named Mary 193

Lady Wardrop's Notes 5: Dogs in M.R. James's Stories .. 201

Lady Wardrop's Notes 6: Geographical locations in M.R. James's Stories 211

Lady Wardrop's Notes 7: The Supernatural Consequences of HS2 219

**Part Four:
Introductions**

Introduction: *The Ghosts & Scholars Book of Shadows Volume 1* 227

Introduction: *The Ghosts & Scholars Book of Shadows Volume 2* 237

Introduction: *The Ghosts & Scholars Book of Shadows Volume 3* 243

Introduction (Extended Version): *A Ghosts & Scholars Book of Folk Horror* 249

Introduction: *The Ghosts & Scholars Book of Mazes* 257

Introduction: *The Ghosts & Scholars Book of Follies & Grottoes* 263

Introduction: *The Angry Dead* 271

Part Five: Booklets

The Cropton Lane Farm Murders 283

"The Old Man on the Hill": English Hill Figures in Supernatural Fiction 319

English Hill Figures: Addenda 363

Part Six: And Finally

The Wormwood Interview: Rosemary Pardoe 375

Introduction

In 2018, David Sutton's Shadow Publishing produced *The Black Pilgrimage & Other Explorations*, a collection of my articles, essays, etc., on supernatural fiction. It covered my writings as far back as 1985. In 2022, I decided to start making a list of possible contents for a second volume, just to see how far away I was from being able to put together something about the same size as the first. I thought I might be a bit over halfway there. To my surprise, I discovered that in the five years since I'd finalised the contents of the original book, I'd already gathered pretty much enough for another. How could this be? Had I really been so prolific that what took more than thirty years the first time had now been accomplished in five? It didn't feel like it, but it must be the case.

One reason might be that, although I still write a column for *Ghosts & Scholars* magazine, I am no longer editing it. After forty years, in 2019 I handed it over to a series of guest editors, administered by Mark Valentine, who has done a marvellous job of keeping it going ever since. With all the extra time on my hands (looking back, *G&S* really was *very* time and effort consuming), clearly I was in need of another outlet for my creativity, such as it is - I hate writing but can't not write! Then there's the fact that my husband, Darroll, died at the beginning of 2021. He was a beautiful man and always proud of what I produced; prouder than me, if I'm honest. Somehow I feel that when I write, it honours his memory.[1]

So here we are. Readers of *G&S* and of Sarob Press's series of six *Ghosts & Scholars* books, as well as the 2021 Cathaven Press reprint of Mary Ann Allen's *The Angry Dead*, will be familiar with the items I've included in Parts Three and Four (my *G&S* column "Lady Wardrop's Notes" and my introductions for the books, respectively), although all have been revised and in one case the version here is nearly half as long again as the original. About half of the articles and reviews in Part One, "M.R. James and Jamesian-related Writings", are from *G&S*, but almost all of those in Part Two, "The Rest", are not. Of the two booklets in Part Five, one went out with *G&S* in 2022 but the other only had a print-run of 75 so will, I hope, be new to most readers of this book (it is, it's fair to say, a true crime investigation rather than anything supernatural, but there is a brief episode of the latter, plus an M.R. James connection).

I'm keen to give people value for money when it comes to inclusions they won't already have read, so around two-

INTRODUCTION:

thirds of the pieces in Parts One and Two combined are from *Lady Wardrop's Journal*, my little zine for The Everlasting Club. The Everlasting Club was started by me in 1993 and, as I explained in *The Black Pilgrimage* Volume 1, it was "the first and, so far, only Ghost Story APA (Amateur Press Association). Members produce small magazines containing articles, discussion and 'mailing comments', which are sent out to other members in a postal mailing every two months". Since then, the mailings have gone digital, but otherwise it continues as ever, with topics discussed revolving around supernatural fiction, but sometimes venturing further afield. Membership seems to stick at around a dozen, and we have had some well-known names in the past (still do), but anyone who feels they have something to say on the subject and is willing to pull their weight is welcome. The number of members being so small, I can guarantee that the pieces I've adapted from *Lady Wardrop's Journal* will be new to almost everyone here.

All of the following contents have been revised and in some cases expanded, especially with updated thoughts added in endnotes. I've tried to group related articles together, and also to avoid too much overlap, but a certain amount is obviously inevitable (most notably, quotes from a major article by Robert Macfarlane seem to turn up with remarkable frequency!). One or two inclusions predate 2018 and weren't in the first *Black Pilgrimage* purely because I accidentally missed them out.

You'll doubtless be expecting the bulk of the book to concern M.R. James and writers in the James Tradition, as in Volume 1. I don't think you'll be disappointed if that's what you're hoping for. There's plenty here for you. However, a glance at the titles of the articles in "The Rest" section suggests a much wider range of topics, and that's true too. But I've always said that, given a minute's thought, I can link almost everything back to MRJ. Don't be surprised to find that he crops up quite often in the most unlikely of places. How, for instance, can a piece about a book on Daisy Makeig-Jones's Wedgwood Fairyland Lustreware finish up with three perfectly relevant paragraphs on MRJ and *Ghost Stories of an Antiquary*? If you doubt that's possible, you really don't know what I'm capable of! When Robert Macfarlane wrote, in the aforementioned 2015 *Guardian* article "The Eeriness of the English Countryside", "We do not seem able to leave MR James... behind. His stories, like the restless dead that haunt them, keep returning to us...", I'm the supreme example of where this can lead. Let it be a warning to the rest of you!

--- Rosemary Pardoe

INTRODUCTION:

My thanks to David Sutton for once again being so keen to publish my stuff. And to Mark Valentine for patiently storing and looking over successive drafts. One day all this will be yours!!!

Note:

[1] This volume also honours the memory of all the *Ghosts & Scholars* contributors who have moved on to whatever world or mystery comes next: Michael Cox, Ken Cowley, Richard Dalby, John Gordon, Michael Halls, George Hay, Sheila Hodgson, Alan Hunter, Hugh Lamb, Joel Lane, Alan W. Lear, Roger Nicholson, Muriel Smith, Maureen Kincaid Speller, John Stewart, Don Tumasonis, Karl Edward Wagner, Elsa Wallace and Ron Weighell (I'm sure there are others). I suppose it's bound to be that, with a fanzine which has run for well over forty years, the list of such names will mount up, but in recent years there have been an increasing number added to it.

M.R. JAMES AND JAMESIAN-RELATED WRITINGS

"Tha hast conjured me"
Dan Jones's *The Tale of the Tailor and the Three Dead Kings*

When M.R. James's attention was first drawn to a medieval manuscript in the British Museum collection, his interest was piqued by what was written on the pages left blank by the main text. It was a series of supernatural tales, compiled by a monk of Byland Abbey in Yorkshire around 1400, and "strong in local colour". He transcribed the tales and saw them published, in the original Latin, in the *English Historical Review* 37 (1922), under the title "Twelve Medieval Ghost-stories". In a definite case of the pot calling the kettle black, he confessed: "The hand is not a very easy one, and the last page of all is really difficult; some words have baffled me" (those of us who have transcribed MRJ's own handwriting will know the feeling well!).

MRJ never did publish an English translation of the stories (although he included a few notes). He left that to others: the first appeared two years later, and more recently there have been several more, for example in Ash-Tree Press's *A Pleasing Terror* (2001) and S.T. Joshi's *The Haunted Dolls' House and Other Ghost Stories* (2006). There is also a brilliant website, www.anselm-classics.com/byland/about.html, which has all the original Latin texts, new translations, commentaries and an abundance of appropriate medieval illustrations. But *The Tale of the Tailor and the Three Dead Kings* by Dan Jones, published by Head of Zeus in 2021, is a bit different. Jones is a noted historian and has written several non-fiction books, mainly on the medieval period, as well as appearing in TV documentaries. He has taken by far the longest and best of the tales, Number II - "Concerning the extraordinary fight between a ghost and a mortal during the reign of Richard II" - and turned its two thousand or so words into a very short novel or novella. The back-cover blurb of this tiny but attractively-presented hardcover claims Jones has "resurrected this forgotten folk tale... and retold it for our time". This did not bode well as far as I was concerned: was he going to modernise it and reset it in the present day? Mercifully not. Jones puts it rather better in his introduction: "I have not tried to over-explain its eccentricities, and certainly not to analyse, but only to try and translate from the fifteenth-century original the compelling mood of horror and unease... this is a retelling. Yet at the same time I hope it conveys the marvellous spirit of the original".

This original tells how Snowball, a tailor, while riding along a local road between Gilling and Ampleforth, encounters a ghost which first takes the form of a raven throwing out sparks. After he fights with it for a while, it turns into a talking dog, speaking, like a literal ventriloquist, from its stomach not its mouth (Snowball sees right down into its intestines). The ghost tells Snowball that it was excommunicated for unspecified sins, and that he must find a priest to absolve it, and arrange 180 masses for its forgiveness; and then report back. When he does so after much effort, the spirit reappears as a goat and then as a huge, emaciated man, like the figure in a painting of dead kings. (MRJ notes: "I think the allusion is to the pictures of the Three Living and Three Dead so often found painted on church-walls. The Dead and Living are often represented as kings". A *memento mori* type fable.) The ghost tells of two other spirits with it there. One, which appears as a bullock or calf without eyes, ears or mouth, is not redeemable: in life, he was a layman who killed a pregnant woman. The other, a monk, appears as a hunter, and may be saved in the future by a person not yet born. Thanks to Snowball's efforts, however, the first ghost can now leave those two behind and go with thirty more spirits into eternal joy. It also explains to Snowball how he can make amends for his own (very minor!) sins.

 I must admit that I started reading Dan Jones's version expecting to dislike it, but I warmed to it within the first couple of pages. He sticks quite scrupulously to the original plot, while fleshing it out with succinct but descriptive passages which set the scene and give an idea of the Yorkshire countryside where the events take place; and adding conversations between the characters. He names some of the unnamed people such as the priests consulted by Snowball, including one whose sister died from the bite of a wild pig. There is humour here too, especially in relation to Snowball's horse Borin who, at one point, can be found eating clumps from the roof of a priest's house! The reason why Snowball in particular suffered the visitation of the ghosts is expanded upon, although late delivery of a neighbour's cloak, which he was repairing, doesn't seem too serious a crime. Deliberately not named is the sinner who became the chief spectre, nor his crime. This is in keeping with MRJ's note on the original that "Great pains are taken throughout to conceal the name of the ghost. He must have been a man of quality, whose relatives might have objected to stories being told about him". Possibly then he was a real person, known to the Byland monk.

Some of Dan Jones's expansions concern the physical appearances of the ghosts, and he dwells more upon their horrific nature. The goat manifestation has bloody wounds where its eyes should be: "birds had pecked the eyeballs out"; and the Dead King speaks "through a jaw that flapped from one hinge on the side of his skull". Sometimes these descriptions are a little too unsubtle, but that of the sinner who takes the form of a "baby calf" is almost poignant: "though it shook its bloated head and tried to low and cry and nudge Snowball for his help, it could not. It simply suffered in its dumb, blind, silent way" (serves it right, we might think, for murdering a woman and her unborn child).

Jones has an easy style which makes the text very readable without losing the feel that this is a medieval story. It's an extremely quick read: I'm not sure of the word count but it must be less than half a dozen times that of the original. I found it unexpectedly enjoyable, and if it alerts a new audience to the Byland tales, that can only be a good thing.

The book also includes a fairly lengthy note on the history of Byland Abbey, and how it would have appeared when the ghost stories were written; plus the original Latin text of Snowball's adventure. There is no English translation though, which might have been helpful to readers not familiar with it. The pleasantly chatty introduction explains something of the background to the Byland tales, and how MRJ first encountered them. Also Jones explains how *he* came upon the stories in MRJ's transcription for the first time (by mistake - what he was really looking for was an account of a revenant in Walter of Newburgh!).

The Tale of the Tailor and the Three Dead Kings (a confusing title, given than none of the ghosts are actually kings, but it does have a certain ring to it!) is just 96 pages long, in a hardcover book format of less than 8" by 5" (also available for Kindle). You'll have the whole thing done and dusted in under an hour. But it's a nice little addition to any Jamesian bookshelf.

"He was laughing in the church"
Disembodied Voices in the Stories of M.R. James

In 2021, and following a very favourable review of it in *Fortean Times*, I bought a copy of *Disembodied Voices* by Tim Marczenko (subtitled "true accounts of hidden beings"). I don't think it deserves such a good review, in fact, as it's overly credulous and very superficial, although it's occasionally thought-provoking. And I was happy to see that chapter one was headed with a line from my favourite supernatural story, Algernon Blackwood's "The Wendigo":[1] "That's about it, an' there's no misunderstandin' when you hear it. It calls you by name right 'nough". A later chapter is headed with the famous line from *Night of the Demon*, "It's in the trees! It's coming!", oddly not credited to the film but rather to Maurice Denham, the actor who said it!

The book did set me to wondering how many of M.R. James's tales include disembodied voices.[2] I'm defining disembodied as unexplained aural encounters specifically *not* accompanied by any visual appearances at the time (although associated visual phenomena might be seen on other occasions in the story). This is my list of quotes. It's not a hugely long one - such episodes only feature in a minority (about a third) of MRJ's tales - but I think it's significant that they're among the most memorable scenes.

Canon Alberic's Scrap-book

[While Dennistoun is being shown around St Bertrand-de-Comminges] ...one or other of the strange noises that trouble a large empty building fell on his ear. Curious noises they were sometimes. "Once," Dennistoun said to me, "I could have sworn I heard a thin metallic voice laughing high up in the tower. I darted an inquiring glance at my sacristan. He was white to the lips. 'It is he - that is - it is no one; the door is locked,' was all he said, and we looked at each other for a full minute."

[Later the sacristan reports to his daughter] "He was laughing in the church" - words which were answered only by a look of terror from the girl.

Lost Hearts

[According to Mrs Bunch, at the 'disappearance' of the gypsy girl] "...there was singing round the house for as much as an hour the night she went, and Parkes, he declare as he heard them a-calling in the woods all that afternoon."

[Parkes tells Mrs Bunch about noises (rats?) in the wine cellar] "I never laid no confidence in that before; but tonight, if I'd demeaned myself to lay my ear to the door of the further bin, I could pretty much have heard what they was saying."

Number 13

[Mr Anderson is in his room talking to the landlord of the Golden Lion when the occupant of the adjoining room starts to sing] It was a high, thin voice that they heard, and it seemed dry, as if from long disuse. Of words or tune there was no question. It went sailing up to a surprising height, and was carried down with a despairing moan as of a winter wind in a hollow chimney, or an organ whose wind fails suddenly. It was a really horrible sound...

...Suddenly the crying or singing voice in the next room died away, and the singer was heard seemingly to laugh to himself in a crooning manner.

A School Story

[One of the examples of the "lore of Private Schools" at the start of the tale] "Also there was the lady who, on locking her bedroom door in a strange house, heard a thin voice among the bed-curtains say, 'Now we're shut in for the night'."

The Rose Garden

[Mrs Anstruther tells how, as she was sitting reading in the arbour...] "All at once I became conscious that someone was whispering to me inside the arbour. The only words I could distinguish, or thought I could, were something like 'Pull, pull. I'll push, you pull.' I started up in something of a fright. The voice - it was little more than a whisper - sounded so hoarse and angry, and yet as if it came from a long, long way off..."

Casting the Runes

[After the paper with the runes blows into the fire, Henry Harrington's words to his brother are repeated by a voice which only John Harrington hears] "'Well,' I said, 'you can't give it back now.' He said nothing for a minute: then rather crossly, 'No, I can't; but why you should keep on saying so I don't know.' I remarked that I didn't say it more than once. 'Not more than four times, you mean,' was all he said."

The Stalls of Barchester Cathedral

[Several episodes from Dr Haynes' Diary]

Dec 6: The fact is (I may as well formulate it to myself) that I hear voices. This, I am well aware, is a common symptom of incipient decay of the brain - and I believe that I should be less disquieted than I am if I had any suspicion that this was the cause.

Jan 1: Last night, upon my return after midnight from the Deanery, I lit my candle to go upstairs. I was nearly at the top when something whispered to me, "Let me wish you a happy New Year." I could not be mistaken: it spoke distinctly and with a peculiar emphasis. Had I dropped my candle, as I all but did, I tremble to think what the consequences must have been.

Jan 15: I had occasion to come downstairs last night to my workroom for my watch, which I had inadvertently left on my table when I went up to bed. I think I was at the top of the last flight when I had a sudden impression of a sharp whisper in my ear "Take care."

Feb 27: I heard a light tap at the door, and a low voice saying, "May I come in?" (which I most undoubtedly did hear), I recollected the fact [that he was expecting his servant to come and pick up a letter], and took up the letter from my dressing-table, saying, "Certainly: come in." No one, however, answered my summons...

The following Jan 8: ...still whispering and whispering: what is it he wants to say?

Martin's Close

[Sarah Arscott's testimony following the death of Ann Clark] "...all the time I went on singing ['Madame will you walk...'], something louder and more bold-like. And as I was there all of a sudden I thought I heard someone answering outside the house, but I could not be sure because of the wind blowing so high. So then I stopped singing, and now I heard it plain, saying, 'Yes, sir; I will walk, I will talk with you,' and I knew the voice for Ann Clark's voice."

A Neighbour's Landmark

[The landscape suddenly changes for the narrator on his

pleasant country walk] There thrilled into my right ear and pierced my head a note of incredible sharpness, like the shriek of a bat, only ten times intensified - the kind of thing that makes one wonder if something has not given way in one's brain...

... And just then into my left ear - close as if lips had been put within an inch of my head, the frightful scream came thrilling again.

There was no mistake possible now. It was from outside. "With no language but a cry" was the thought that flashed into my mind. Hideous it was beyond anything I had heard or have heard since, but I could read no emotion in it, and doubted if I could read any intelligence.

The Malice of Inanimate Objects

[Mr Burton and Mr Manners, out for a walk, believe they have an explanation for a startling voice, but they are wrong!] As they turned a corner into the main street, a rather muffled and choky voice was heard to say "Look out! I'm coming." They both stopped as if they had been shot. [They think it's a nearby parrot in a cage but then realise that the parrot is a stuffed one]

The main thesis of Tim Marczenko's book is that there are beings who are trying to lure people away from safety by calling to them, often in voices resembling those of relatives and friends. "The Lure, The Trap, and The Lost" is the way he describes their technique. Most of MRJ's disembodied voices serve chiefly to terrify rather than to trap, but one tale does fit into Marczenko's category, and it does it perfectly:

A Warning to the Curious

[Mr Paxton is lured out to his doom by a voice or voices pretending to be that of his new friends. As a servant recounts...] "Why, I thought you gentlemen was gone out already, and so did the other gentleman. He heard you a-calling from the path there, and run out in a hurry, and I looked out of the coffee-room window, but I didn't see you."

Unlike MRJ's skillful and realistic inclusion of panic fear (in "A Neighbour's Landmark" and the unfinished "John Humphreys", for instance) and hypnogogic dreams (in "A View from a Hill" and "The Residence at Whitminster"), I don't think these aural disturbances necessarily have the ring of personal experience. I doubt whether MRJ ever actually heard disembodied voices himself (although plenty of otherwise 'normal' people do, according to Tim Marczenko's book). But his effective use of them in his stories can quite often supply what the Podcast to the Curious folk call a "Jamesian Wallop", with lines which stick forever in the memory.

Notes:

[1] Yes, I rate it even above anything by M.R. James, although its carelessly racist language (of its time!) is a worry.

[2] It's often the way that two people discover they're working independently on the same thing at the same time (as for instance with the two MRJ biographies by Cox and Pfaff, which came out so close together in the early '80s) - it must be something in the aether! So I wasn't entirely surprised, while finishing off this article, to discover that Tracy Hayes had also produced a paper on a similar subject: "Aural disturbance in the stories of M.R. James". I don't think it had been published at the time, but it later appeared in *Short Fiction in Theory & Practice* (Volume 11, Numbers 1-2) and I was able to read it then. According to the abstract: "Through the use of sound, and indeed the deliberate absence of sound, M.R. James, I would like to argue, is able to concoct in his stories an atmosphere of malevolence, in which his 'executors of unappeasable malice' (as Michael Cox describes them) are often heard rather than seen... James deploys alien soundscapes and aural disturbance to create sound as a tangible element within rich sonic tapestries that feature unique aural signatures and instances of acoustic chaos". Although the paper covers some of the same ground as my piece, Tracy Hayes mostly takes a more analytical, academic approach (I'm nothing if not *not* academic!), and she also deals with other sounds as well as human voices. As one might expect, there is no mention of Tim Marczenko's book.

The M.R. James Murders
Nicola Upson's *Nine Lessons*

When I was at Grammar School in Oxford in the 1960s, a lot of lessons became more relaxed during the final week or so before the summer holidays, and not too much formal teaching went on. Sometimes there would be trips out - to the Ashmolean Museum perhaps, or to Chedworth Roman Villa in Gloucestershire. Once, memorably, we went to the Cadbury Factory at Bournville and each left with a splendid tin of chocolate samples. One year, possibly when I was fourteen or fifteen, our history teacher handed out copies of Josephine Tey's *The Daughter of Time* (1951) for us to read in the course of the week. This is the book in which a present-day detective, confined to a hospital bed, spends the long hours trying to solve the historical mystery of what happened to the Princes in the Tower. Were they killed on the orders of that (supposedly) arch-villain Richard III, or did they suffer a different fate? The identical format, incidentally, was deliberately used by Colin Dexter in *The Wench is Dead*, in which Morse - stuck in a hospital bed (the same hospital where I was born!) with a bleeding ulcer - solves a Victorian murder case.

The Daughter of Time made a great impact on me

(possibly more than any of the 'proper' lessons ever did), and some years later it prompted me to join the Richard III Society for a while. I've never read anything else by Josephine Tey - not even her other famous book, *The Franchise Affair* - but I've always had fond feelings for her. I didn't know until recently, though, that she is the central character in a series of period detective novels by Nicola Upson. I didn't know, in fact, until the seventh in the series, in which M.R. James and his stories feature. *Nine Lessons* was published in 2017 and is described by the author thus:

> *Nine Lessons* will take you on an atmospheric journey from 1930s Cambridge to the bleak and desolate Suffolk coast, as Josephine and her friend, DCI Archie Penrose, investigate a series of audacious murders which hark back to the years before the Great War, when the famous ghost story writer, MR James, told chilling tales by candlelight to a handful of friends and scholars. Now, 25 years later, those men are dying, killed off one by one... MR James was one of two key strands of inspiration...[1]
>
> ... In December 1913 James failed to finish a new story. I found myself inventing reasons for this that were more sinister than pressures of time or college business. What if something terrible happened that

Christmas? What if, 25 years later, those men who gathered to be entertained start dying, killed off in ways that echo James's stories?

Nicola Upson contributed an article on MRJ, "An Evening's Entertainment (Past Masters)", to *Artseast* magazine in 2001/2, so she's not lying about being a long-time fan, even if she does cite her main reference sources as Michael Cox and Peter Haining. The first is essential, of course, but *Peter Haining*? (She must mean his *M.R. James: Book of the Supernatural* with all its multitude of terrible errors.) She has taken just a passing mention of a mundane event in Cox's *M.R. James: An Informal Portrait*, and used it imaginatively. The quote is on page 134, and records that, thanks to MRJ having taken over the reins of Vice-Chancellorship of the University in October, a year earlier than expected, "on one occasion at least, in 1913, Monty was unable to finish the story in time to read to his guests" at Christmas.

No one can accuse *Nine Lessons* of starting slowly. In Chapter One, we're faced with an especially unpleasant murder (unpleasant if, like me, you're a bit claustrophobic): an ex-chorister, an attendee (as we later find out) at MRJ's gatherings, is immured alive in a table tomb in a London churchyard. Near the tomb are three padlocks. DCI Archie Penrose, despite having been present himself at one of

MRJ's readings, isn't so much of a fan that he makes the immediate "Count Magnus" connection. Only later, when he's standing in a twin-bedded hotel room in Felixstowe, looking at the rumpled sheets on the spare bed and hearing about how the latest victim was chased over the groynes on the beach, does the penny drop. It turns out that there was a previous murder inspired by "The Stalls of Barchester Cathedral", and after the death based on "Oh, Whistle, and I'll Come to You, My Lad", there's one based on "The Tractate Middoth", together with an on-going thread relating to "The Mezzotint" and a big "A Warning to the Curious" climax at Aldeburgh.

What happened in 1913 to provoke this murder spree in 1937? And why was it triggered by MRJ's funeral the year before it began? Is it a kind of upmarket *I Know What You Did Last Summer* scenario (but without the great Muse Watson)? I'm afraid it pretty much is, but *Nine Lessons* is still a decent, solid whodunnit, with a nicely evoked setting. I'm less sure about the evocation of the period: I kept having to remind myself that it was 1937 and not 2017. The novel's use of MRJ's stories is quite clever, although Nicola Upson makes a number of careless mistakes when describing them: for instance, she says that "Oh, Whistle" is set in Seaburgh instead of Burnstow; and "The Mezzotint" at Cambridge instead of Oxford. But it all makes a change from those serial killer plots where the crimes are religion-inspired and revolve around the Seven Deadly Sins (*Se7en*), the deaths of the Twelve Apostles (*Messiah*), etc.

In some ways I think a reader not at all familiar with MRJ's tales would get more from *Nine Lessons* than those of us who, at some points in the plot, will be several steps ahead of the investigators. Even aside from that, though, I guessed the identity of the killer fairly early on (*spoiler alert*: I was following the rule that the nicest person is the one who did it!), and also that of the unrelated serial rapist. This was a disappointment, but then again I *do* read a lot of whodunnits and crime thrillers. I enjoyed the book enough that I then read another in Nicola Upson's series: *Fear in the Sunlight*, in which Josephine Tey meets Alfred Hitchcock at Portmeirion!

Note:

[1] The other source of inspiration was the real Cambridge Rapist who terrorised the city in the 1970s.

M.R. James's Suffolk

Simon Loxley's *A Geography of Horror: The Ghost Stories of M.R. James and the Suffolk Landscape*

I honestly don't know what to make of Simon Loxley's *A Geography of Horror: The Ghost Stories of M.R. James and the Suffolk Landscape* (*A Travel Guide*), which was published in 2021 by Lavenham Press. In some ways the author seems to have devoted too little thought and research to the subject and in other ways just too *much*. The first part of the book is a general overview of MRJ's life and stories. It's unexceptionable: reasonably thorough and with minimal (if slightly irritating) mistakes. It does, however, get on my nerves that he keeps dwelling on the 'fact' that, with a couple of exceptions, all of MRJ's better tales are his early ones: "we have the sense of James enjoying his mastery of styles of narrative but losing sight of his story's real purpose, which is to frighten us". Some will agree with that, but others (such as me) couldn't disagree more. Most of my favourite MRJ stories are amongst his later ones, and I don't know about you but I find the likes of "A Neighbour's Landmark" and "Rats" pretty darned scary! Also, the later tales leave the reader with more unanswered questions, which I love. I don't object to Loxley having a different opinion, but

I do dislike his assumption that it's a fact rather than an opinion.

Then we get to the separate chapters on Suffolk-set stories, and here I think he's stretched the category to breaking point by including "Count Magnus" and "Casting the Runes". He himself admits that there are no Suffolk scenes in "Count Magnus", the setting for the climax being over the border in Belchamp St Paul, Essex. And despite the fact that Lufford Abbey in "Casting the Runes" is clearly stated by MRJ to be in Warwickshire, Loxley believes it's only "technically" set in that county, and is actually inspired by Ufford Place in Suffolk. He provides no evidence whatsoever for this. The other five chapters, on "The Ash-tree", "Oh, Whistle, and I'll Come to You, My Lad", "The Tractate Middoth", "A Warning to the Curious" and "Rats", are better, although I'm as dubious of Loxley's Thorpeness identification for the setting for "Rats" as I was when Peter Haining first claimed it (with an entirely irrelevant picture of the House in the Clouds) in his *M.R. James: Book of the Supernatural*. These chapters, like the entire volume, are attractively laid out to include many full-colour photographs and old postcards showing the locations, along with maps and other accompanying material, much of which was new to me (there's no doubt that the book is a labour of love and has been put together with a lot of skill).

But, oh dear - the chapter on "A Vignette"! Yes, we've got the nice pictures and illustrations again, but it's clear that Loxley thinks he has hit upon an original interpretation of the story and (in the way of such hobby horses) he warps everything to support his case. Most of us know that "A Vignette" may have been based on a genuine experience of MRJ's Suffolk childhood, when he may have seen a terrifying face through a gap in the gate to The Plantation next to his home at Great Livermere. Since there are public footpaths across The Plantation, the chances are he saw a real person peering through the hole to look at the posh house beyond, and then (as was his way throughout life) he enjoyed building the experience up into something possibly supernatural. Loxley's theory, however, is that the story may reflect a repressed memory of a sexual assault on the young MRJ. Now, this isn't a new theory at all: I've seen it proposed elsewhere in pretty much the same terms as here, emphasising not just the face in the gate, but the villager who the narrator is surprised to see "standing still and looking after me" earlier in the story. I don't know *where* I've seen the suggestion before, but it's certainly not original to this book.

As evidence of something being 'off' about "A Vignette", Loxley quotes the lines at its end:

Are there here and there sequestered places which

> some curious creatures still frequent, whom once on a time anybody could see and speak to as they went about on their daily occasions, whereas now only at rare intervals in a series of years does one cross their paths and become aware of them; and perhaps that is just as well for the peace of mind of simple people.

And he comments: "This proposed parallel world of either creatures on another dimension, or a kind of 'faery folk' who inhabit our world but have become progressively more self-effacing as time goes on, is completely at odds with the supernatural manifestations in James' stories". Loxley does then concede that the "only time James explored this area was in... *The Five Jars*..."; and "'After Dark in the Playing Fields' is a late piece of whimsy that features a talking owl, which at a stretch might be included as a further example". At a stretch? The fact that he concentrates on the talking owl suggests that he's completely missed the link between the creepy quote from "A Vignette" and this famously disturbing one from "After Dark":

> You see - no, you do not, but I see - such curious faces: and the people to whom they belong flit about so oddly, often at your elbow when you least expect it, and looking close into your face, as if they were searching for someone - who may be thankful, I

think, if they do not find him. 'Where do they come from?' Why, some, I think, out of the water, and some out of the ground. They look like that. But I am sure it is best to take no notice of them, and not to touch them.

We're talking here of elementals or, indeed, "faerie folk", of a most sinister variety (one or two sinister ones can be found in *The Five Jars* too). There are strong hints of them also in a few of MRJ's other tales: I'm thinking, in particular, of Dr Abel's question to the Rector of Islington in "Two Doctors" as to:

what place... those beings now... hold in the scheme of creation which by some are thought neither to have stood fast when the rebel angels fell, nor to have joined with them to the full pitch of their transgression... It appeared... that he grounded himself on such passages as that of the satyr which Jerome tells us conversed with Antony; but thought too that some parts of Scripture might be cited in support. "And besides," said he, "you know 'tis the universal belief among those that spend their days and nights abroad, and I would add that if your calling took you so continuously as it does me about the country lanes by night, you might not be so surprised as I see you to be by my suggestion." "You are then of John Milton's mind," I said, "and hold that

"Millions of spiritual creatures walk the earth

Unseen, both when we wake and when we sleep."

"I do not know," he said, "why Milton should take upon himself to say 'unseen'... But for the rest, why, yes, I think he was in the right."

MRJ is referring to one of the most well-known Christian legends explaining the origin of faeries: as beings considered by God neither good enough for Heaven nor evil enough to join the fallen angels in Hell.

So the quote from "A Vignette" is not at odds with some of MRJ's other spectral personages at all. Loxley seems to have forgotten or not to know that MRJ, throughout his life, was fascinated by fairy tales and folk tales involving faerie beings. If anything, his interest in them may even predate his interest in ghost stories. He was a young boy when he wrote in his notebook: "I want to know what LEPRECHAUNES and CLURICAUNES are. They are a kind of supernatural beings but that's all I know about them..." (Michael Cox, *M.R. James: An Informal Portrait*, p.15). And by his mid-teens he was fascinated by Walter Map's medieval *De Nugis Curialium* with its various accounts of supernatural incidents, including the tale of King Herla who suffered the classic time distortion when taken away to the kingdom of faerie. That's not to mention MRJ's translations of Hans Andersen's and E.T. Kristensen's Danish tales and Jean-François Bladé's French *Tales from Lectoure*.

I see nothing in "A Vignette" to suggest repressed memories; what I do see is MRJ returning to the interest he had throughout his life in the mysterious hidden world of elementals and dark faeries. Some might wish that he had written more on the subject - I know I do.

Something Happened in Felixstowe
Robert Lloyd Parry's *Oh, Whistle, and I'll Come to You, My Lad* and *Wits in Felixstowe*

In 2005, Robert Lloyd Parry started to perform his one-man shows, narrating the stories of M.R. James in the character of the author. When he began, with *A Pleasing Terror: Two Ghost Stories by M.R. James* ("Canon Alberic's Scrap-book" and "The Mezzotint"), little did he, or anyone else, know that he would still be doing it nearly two decades on, having extended his repertoire to include numerous other MRJ tales. He has performed throughout the United Kingdom and beyond, always to enthusiastic audiences and reviews (several in *Ghosts & Scholars*). More recently he put some of his appearances on the Net and also released a number of DVDs and audio discs. I reviewed the DVD of *A Pleasing Terror* back in 2010, and described it as "scary when it should be scary, funny when it should be funny, and never less than compelling". By the time Robert turned up as MRJ in Mark Gatiss's 2013 BBC documentary *M.R. James: Ghost Writer*, I don't think I'm exaggerating when I say that, for a lot of us, it was impossible to imagine anyone else in the role.

It was in 2007 that Robert began presenting "Oh, Whistle, and I'll Come to You, My Lad" (along with "The Ash-tree"). The 2018 DVD of "Oh, Whistle" I'm discussing now was issued by Nunkie and ThomThom Productions, and was "filmed in one take by the light of a single candle at Hemingford Grey Manor" (making it slightly too dark for my taste), and Robert's performance is as good as ever. Occasionally I find the more dramatic scenes, such as the account of the boy who "seen it wive at me out of the winder", and some business with a table napkin during both the nightmare vision of the beach pursuit and the final attack of the demon, just a little *over*-dramatic. But this is a minor flaw (if it is a flaw at all); and I know that most people don't agree with me. It may be that it's less noticeable anyway, when there is a physical audience in attendance.[1]

The disc includes some very superior extras: a "rehearsed reading" of "Rats"; Patricia Hammond singing Robert Burns' eponymous poem; and, best of all, a new forty-minute documentary, *Wits in Felixstowe*, written, produced and fronted by Robert Lloyd Parry. Felixstowe is, of course, the Burnstow of "Oh, Whistle"; and the "Wits" of the title are not of the amusing variety, but rather those which one can lose. Filmed in Cambridge and Felixstowe, with Robert making a pleasantly non-pompous and relaxed presenter, it quickly becomes clear that this is not just another MRJ documentary. I knew that there was a connection between "Oh, Whistle" and the home of King's College ex-Bursar Felix Cobbold, but I didn't realise quite how close the connection was. It was to Cobbold's House, The Lodge at Cobbold's Point, on the edge of Felixstowe, that MRJ and various friends would decamp sometimes, between Christmas and the New Year (MRJ was there in 1892/3 and in 1897/8). The gorgeous Tudorbethan house still exists, although it is now split up into separate residences; and Robert points out (filming both outside and inside the building) that there is nowhere else in the town from which one can get exactly the view from the Globe Hotel's windows described in "Oh, Whistle". (Some writers have stated that the Globe was based on the Bath Hotel, but I don't know what evidence, if any, there is for that.)

It's all interesting but fairly uncontroversial stuff. However, Robert then moves on to make some new, well-reasoned suggestions connected with the 'fear of madness' which he perceives in a number of MRJ's stories. I was aware that MRJ's friend J.K. Stephen had lapsed into madness following some sort of accident. What I didn't know was that this happened while he was staying at Felixstowe, at Felix Cobbold's house, in December 1886. He suffered a blow to the head and there were various different accounts of how this happened. One was that his horse threw him after being startled by a *whistle* - admittedly, a train whistle in this case. Stephen seemed to have made a complete physical recovery, but his mental decline soon became evident and he died in a lunatic asylum six years later. Standing outside Stephen's lodgings in the busy centre of Cambridge, Robert gives an illustration of that madness by reading in full the horrendous women-hating poem "In the Backs", which is often cited by those who argue (unconvincingly) that Stephen might have been Jack the Ripper. It *is* horrible, but nothing could have shown Stephen's mental state more graphically, so I think it was right to include it (I do wonder what the numerous passersby in the street behind must have thought, though!). Robert is careful not to make overly bold claims but he wonders whether the connection between a whistle, Felixstowe, and a sudden, completely unexpected occurrence leading to madness (which Professor Parkins just managed to avoid, but Stephen didn't), could have led in some small way to the creation, ten years or so after Stephen's death, of "Oh, Whistle".

Wits in Felixstowe is a fully professional production and is the best documentary on MRJ I've ever seen; immaculately researched and visually enthralling with its combination of modern locations and old photographs.

I originally said at this point that "We need Robert to do more of these". I got my wish in 2019 when Nunkie and ThomThom produced a DVD of *A Warning to the Curious*.

As well as Robert's narration of that story, it contains a new documentary, *Dim Presences*. Here, he does for "A Warning to the Curious" what *Wits in Felixstowe* did for "Oh, Whistle", visiting not only Aldeburgh (Seaburgh) but also Cambridge, Bury St Edmunds and Eton. It's a more poignant film than the previous one, dealing with MRJ's reactions to the Great War (the manuscript of "Warning"[2] shows that he originally set it during the War), and the war memorial window in Eton College Chapel he helped design. If *Wits in Felixstowe* is the best MRJ documentary ever made (which it still is), then *Dim Presences* is the second best. I'll say again: "We need Robert to do more of these".

Returning to the *Oh, Whistle/Wits in Felixstowe* DVD, then, I can't recommend this highly enough. My only criticism is that there is no accompanying booklet. How good it would have been to have Robert's Felixstowe/Stephen arguments, with accompanying photographs, in print as well as on film.

Notes:

[1] Finally, in 2022 I was able to see one of Robert's live performances myself, during a sell-out event at Hawarden in North Wales. I witnessed for myself how he was able to hold the audience spellbound during his narrations of "Canon Alberic's Scrap-book" and "The Mezzotint". It's absolutely true what people say: the DVDs and Net appearances are great, but to see Robert live is something else.

[2] I lent Robert my photocopy of the "Warning" manuscript for the film, and it appears more than once. My annotations in red biro can clearly be seen. As I muttered to myself at the time, if I'd known when I wrote them that years later they were going to be on screen for all to see, I'd have written more neatly!

Michael Harrison
1907-1991

Michael Harrison (the pseudonym of Maurice Desmond Rohan, , and not to be confused with the science fiction and fantasy writer M[ichael] John Harrison[1]) was a prolific author whose subject matter ranged widely, including essays on Arthur Machen and H.P. Lovecraft, as well as books on spontaneous human combustion and mysterious vanishings. He is best known today for his crime and detective works, both fiction and non-fiction. He wrote a series of Sherlockian stories and is famed in Jack the Ripper circles for being the first person (in *Clarence*, his 1972 biography of Eddie, the Duke of Clarence) to suggest that M.R. James's troubled friend J.K. Stephen might have been the Ripper. Stephen (1859-1892) was a poet and a tutor to Eddie in the 1880s, but suffered a head injury in 1886 (see my article, "Something Happened in Felixstowe", above). Although it initially appeared that he had made a full recovery, he eventually became seriously mentally ill and was committed to an asylum in 1891. Some of his poetry seems savagely misogynistic (one poem involves the death of ten 'harlots'), but there is little or no other real evidence to link him with the Ripper murders. M.R. James writes briefly but kindly of

Stephen in *Eton and King's*, noting his "great brain... in the end stricken down".

Among Michael Harrison's claims to fame in the supernatural fiction world is that his non-fiction book, *The London that was Rome* (1971), was a major inspiration for one of Roger Johnson's very best stories, "The Soldier" (1990). *The London that was Rome* is a favourite nut book of mine, and like all the best of those, it may contain a kernel of truth. Its thesis is that the names of various places in London (particularly the church dedications) derived directly from former Roman buildings and locations on the same sites. Thus St Dionis Backchurch was on the site of a temple to "Dionysus Bacchus", and St Magnus Martyr is on the site of a temple to Magna Mater, the Great Mother Cybele. I'm not convinced by either of those, but a few other suggestions make a degree of sense. In "The Soldier", Roger Johnson cleverly invents a church named St Denis Mitre and proposes a kind of continuation on the site of the worship practised in the original Roman temple ("Mitre" being very close to the name of the soldiers' god in question).

But not too many people will be aware that Michael Harrison also wrote his own supernatural tales. On the Vault of Evil Message Board, in a thread on the *London Mystery Magazine*, James Doig reported that number 19 (1954) contained "quite a nice Jamesian short story" by Harrison, entitled "At the Heart of It". My thanks to James for subsequently sending me a copy.[2] "At the Heart of It" isn't entirely a lost tale. According to the on-line "FictionMags Index", it was reprinted in *The Magazine of Fantasy and Science Fiction* for June 1968. It was reprinted again in the Peter Haining-edited *The Necromancers: The Best of Black Magic and Witchcraft* (1971).

The story centres on Rufus Hopkins, a London bookseller whose "inexplicable death" in 1893 comes as the result of his curiosity and obsession with a book sought by a mysterious, dark-clad figure who frequents the cheap book boxes (but never buys anything) twice a year, on June 24th and October 31st. After several years, Hopkins speaks with the black-cloaked gentleman and discovers that the volume he is looking for is *Domus Vitae* by Edward Chardell, published in 1753. This Chardell, Hopkins learns, was associated with the Hellfire Club, and believed in some sort of transfer of life essence (into both animate and inanimate objects) on death. In a generous gesture, Hopkins tries to find the book and manages to acquire a copy to give to the stranger at his next visit, but meanwhile succumbs to the temptation to read it. He is horrified by the illustrations: "The frontispiece... showed a man and woman seated at a table in a rich, gloomy room; and with expressions of an animal lust writ on their faces, they were devouring the body of a child". In another picture, "Two babes (if one could call such horrors infants) were devouring the body of a cat". But it was "As though the villainy of the ghastly feast[s] was not in the alimentation itself but in the *reason* for it". Hopkins becomes convinced that the volume is incomplete, an "emasculated" edition: "often the bookseller had found himself trying to separate two pages, only to discover that the leaves were not fastened together"; and he commences to attempt to fill these gaps himself, only to destroy what he has written. But it's too late and his fate is sealed. The story reminds me a little of MRJ's "Lost Hearts" and also of Arthur Gray's "The Burden of Dead Books" from *Tedious Brief Tales of Granta and Gramarye*, but it's a bit nastier than either of those.

The rediscovery of "At the Heart of It" brought back a memory of another Michael Harrison story which I recalled reading in the late '60s: certain aspects of it had (if somewhat mangled by the years) stuck with me, for good or ill! After a deal of hunting, since the title is not at all what I expected, I finally identified it and tracked down a copy on the Net. "Some Very Odd Happenings at Kibblesham Manor House" was published in *Fantasy & Science Fiction* in the April 1969 issue and, unlike "At the Heart of It", seems to be original to that magazine. In 1990 it was reprinted for what may be the only time - in *The Eternal City*, an anthology of Rome-centred fantasy & SF, edited by David Drake, Martin H. Greenberg and Charles G. Waugh. Another reprint was due in *The Exham Priory Cycle*, one of Robert M. Price's ...*Cycle* series, but although it was announced in 2010 (and earlier) I can't find any evidence that the book ever appeared.

"Some Very Odd Happenings at Kibblesham Manor House" sounds like a title for a very Jamesian tale, and it begins in an almost stereotypically Jamesian manner. The narrator unexpectedly meets an old friend, Andy, the former owner of Kibblesham Manor House, who is much changed from when he last saw him. Andy has lost his sister and his parents in strange circumstances (the parents dead, the sister locked away), and the Manor House has been pulled down to be replaced by flats and a convent school. It seems that the house was erected on the site of a Roman building - not a villa as the narrator initially suggests, but a temple. Andy's sister, Verena, had done some amateur excavating and, as Andy explains: "she found something. She thought they were a pair of Roman nutcrackers, and in a way... that might have been one way of describing them. She cleaned them up with metal polish, and she got quite a polish on them..."

So far, so Jamesian, but then the story quickly becomes something that MRJ would never have written. The "nutcrackers" reference is the ironic clue, for the temple was dedicated to Cybele, and the "nutcrackers" were used by her priests in the process of the mutilations for which they were notorious. And these pincers seem to possess with similar urges those who handle them. In the case of Verena, she is haunted by dreams in which she is a priest anticipating that great sacrifice, and eventually becoming taken over and transformed by the goddess herself.[3] But an even greater atrocity than self-mutilation is required for that final state to be achieved, with horrific consequences for Verena's father: "To be castrated by one's own daughter... no wonder he was glad to die". Andy is not himself immune to the effects of the pincers and also seems not averse to spreading the curse. The narrator's doom seems certain as he is handed something: "I had unthinkingly accepted a pair of rust-stained forceps, the arms of which were set with tiny heads, amongst which I recognized those of some Roman gods".[4] There's nothing graphic about the way the story is told - most of the unpleasantness is only suggested - but there's something distasteful about the telling, nonetheless. As I said, the story is memorable for "good or ill", and I can't quite decide which it is.

A third supernatural tale by Michael Harrison appeared in *Fantasy & Science Fiction* in this same period: "Pull Devil, Pull Baker!" in the June 1969 edition. The website where I found "Kibblesham Manor House" also provided a text for this. It's not Jamesian as such, but concerns the vengeance wreaked through time on the descendant of a Norman knight who had tortured and killed a Jewish baker in 1298 while attempting to discover the location of a chest of money which he had buried. The baker's descendent, a dentist, is too decent a person to take the logical revenge available to him when the other man becomes his patient, but retribution still comes, in the churchyard of the lost London church of St Benet Sherehog. There is a certain amount of 13th-century tooth-pulling involved. What with that, and the subject matter of "Kibblesham Manor House", were I a Freudian I might begin to wonder about the state of Mr Harrison's mind!

Notes:

[1] Both Michael Harrison and M. John Harrison contributed to *The Magazine of Fantasy and Science Fiction* in the 1960s, adding to the possible confusion.

[2] James also sent me a scan of another Harrison story published in the *London Mystery Magazine*: "Twelfth Night" in number 27 (1955). This is a dull tale in which the ghost of Charles Dickens appears to the narra-

tor to regale him with an account of his disastrous love life. It's no surprise that "Twelfth Night" seems never to have been reprinted.

3 It was noted by "helrunar" on the Vault of Evil that Verena's transformation has echoes of Helen Vaughan's in Arthur Machen's "The Great God Pan".

4 There is a drawing of a set of Cybele's bronze forceps, identical to the ones described here, in Michael Harrison's seriously misguided, heavily Margaret Murray-influenced, *The Roots of Witchcraft* (1973), p.42. These were found in the River Thames in the 1840s. I reproduced the picture on the back cover of the *Ghosts & Scholars Newsletter 33*. In his foreword to *The Roots of Witchcraft,* Colin Wilson says of Harrison: "Having now read half a dozen of his exercises in historical detection - I am thinking particularly of The London That Was Rome - I am convinced that his inferences are usually pretty soundly based". This doesn't exactly enhance my opinion of Wilson's critical faculties, although he is careful to hedge his bets later in the foreword.

Two Lesser-Known John Gordon Novels
The Ghosts of Blacklode and
The Midwinter Watch

During February 2018's cold weather, one reporter, standing outside in the snow, said something along the lines of "it doesn't look like England". Of course it did! There aren't too many people who would disagree with the statement that Susan Cooper's *The Dark is Rising* is the supreme example of a midwinter children's/young adult's supernatural fantasy set in the snowy British countryside. It's far from the first, of course. Forty years earlier, in 1935, John Masefield wrote the much-loved and Christmas-set *The Box of Delights*.

These two books are examples of what is almost a snowy sub-genre in its own right (perhaps distantly related to such wintry fantasy fiction as "The Snow Queen" and *The Lion, The Witch and the Wardrobe*). Something of an expert on this setting was John Gordon, from his early *The Giant Under the Snow* (1968) to *Fen Runners* (2009: in which the central characters spend a lot of time skating on the frozen fens - something which the locals were doing in February 2018, for the first time in years). After his sad (if not entirely unexpected) death in 2017, I felt like reading something by

Gordon, but couldn't decide what. His Jamesian classic *The House on the Brink* was too familiar to me, so I looked for something new, and I had a surfeit of choice. Until I checked his bibliography on-line I hadn't realised just how out-of-touch I'd become with his output of novels and short stories. I picked two books, both set in the middle of winter: *The Ghosts of Blacklode* and *The Midwinter Watch*. It may be that you can't go *too* far wrong with a John Gordon book: while these are not Gordon at his very best, both are good reads.

The Ghosts of Blacklode is one of his later works, published in 2002 (*The House on the Brink* dates from 1970). It centres around three teenagers - Bill Brock, Charlotte (Charlie) Brundish and Harry Horobin. The story progresses as alternately seen from Bill's and Charlie's slightly different viewpoints, and the setting is somewhere in the fenland (as usual for Gordon). Bill and Charlie steal a small brass amulet shaped like a frog from the junk shop of Mrs Gosse, who pursues them, accompanied by a strange and supernatural figure like a sort of bipedal man-hound. Unbeknownst to Mrs Gosse, the amulet has special powers, which only seem to work when it is held by Bill or Charlie, and when they are in danger.

Four hundred years previously, Randal, the master of

Blacklode Hall, had been driven out, hunted down and killed by the pack of hounds of his uncle, Hugh of Wellbeck. The pack was headed by "Hugh's Hound", which was so enormous that - legend had it - it was "Hugh himself in dog shape". Mrs Gosse, who has summoned the hound, claims to be descended from Hugh of Wellbeck, and therefore that the Hall (now a museum, where Charlie's father works, and where the frog amulet's bird-shaped twin is found) is rightfully hers. Not just the Hall either, for there is the little matter of "Randal's Pledge", a mysterious (though I'd have liked it to be *more* mysterious!) six-line rhyme believed to contain clues to the whereabouts of Randal's treasure.

Randal, as "Ragged Randal", is said to haunt Blacklode Lane, the site of his murder. Early on, it becomes clear that there is some sort of connection between Randal and the teenagers, especially Bill. Daring himself to cycle down Blacklode Lane, Bill first seems to see an oak tree that moves and beckons to him, but on a later occasion he has an even more frightening encounter (here's where a bit of M.R. James's influence comes in - John Gordon could never quite avoid it). A frozen ditch by the side of the lane seems to bulge at one point "as though something down there was stretching itself, humping its back beneath the ice before raising itself upright". The figure that rises up is that of "a drowned man":

> The man stood among the reeds, his face too deeply shadowed for his eyes to be visible, but Bill knew the dead man's stare was directed at him. The bike was at his feet but he dared not stoop, and he backed away as the figure began to climb the bank. It stretched out a hand and he saw the tattered rags that clung to the bones of a thin arm as he stumbled further back and began to run... [Looking back he saw] The ghost of Ragged Randal was standing in the road and beckoning as if it wanted him to return.

And in another scene, quite reminiscent of *The House on the Brink* (and of a scene in MRJ's "John Humphreys" unfinished story draft), Bill looks out of his bedroom window and notices a lone fencepost in a snow-covered field. As he wipes the window to see it more clearly, it raises an arm and waves in time with his wiping.

The Midwinter Watch was published four years before *The Ghosts of Blacklode*, and I get the impression that it's intended for a slightly younger audience. I could be wrong, but the teenaged protagonists, Sophie, Jack and Simon, feel younger than Bill, Charlie and Harry. Out in the snow, they think they see a train arriving in the distance at the railway station near their village. But this can't possibly be, as the station is long abandoned and the rails pulled up. When Sophie, Jack and Simon get to the station they find a sole passenger has disembarked (except that he denies all knowledge of a train), and the money he gives them for helping with his luggage turns out to be an old ten shilling note - which ceased to be currency over thirty years before. Some people at the nearby Heron Hall seem to know who the stranger is.

A hundred years ago, the then owner of the Hall, Silas Heron, had lost his entire fortune in gold sovereigns in a robbery. The theft was blamed on a beggar, who is now said to haunt the area. Every year, around Christmas, this "Starveling Boy" ghost is reputed to knock at people's windows (echoes of the fate of Lord Saul in MRJ's "The Residence at Whitminster"), as he did in life, begging for food. It's Jack who first sees the ghost: "out on the smooth surface of the field, there was a movement... Something seemed to be keeping pace with him". Then: "over the churchyard wall a thin grey face was looking down on him". But the ghost is really only an adjunct to the main theme, which revolves around Silas Heron's skills as a clockmaker. One of his timepieces can somehow enable time travel via the old railway (I didn't understand the technicalities!), but this isn't the eponymous Midwinter Watch, which is lost and has even more power. The teenagers must try to find it and stop it falling into the hands of nefarious parties, and in doing so they also discover the truth of that century-old robbery.

My main criticism of both books is that the sum of the parts tends to be better than the whole. There are many excellent scenes, but the plots are both based around problems and mysteries which are a little too simply resolved. Nevertheless, there is much to like, and the more folkloric aspects of *The Ghosts of Blacklode* make that my favourite of the two.

"BE his Life Squeezed Away"
Fritz Leiber's *The Pale Brown Thing*

I've read and reread one of my favourite Jamesian novels, Fritz Leiber's *Our Lady of Darkness* (1977), more times than I'd care to count, but it must be at least a dozen. It begins with something stirring on Corona Heights, a "pale, brown" hill in San Francisco, California. Franz Westen, a supernatural fiction writer (one of the many autobiographical aspects of the book), is looking at the hill through binoculars when he sees a hooded figure moving about amongst the rocks. When he goes to investigate, he uses his binoculars to look back from the hill at his apartment window, and a "pale brown shape" leans out of it and waves at him. This is far from the only direct reference to an M.R. James story - see my *Ghosts & Scholars* article "*Our Lady of Darkness*: A Jamesian Classic" reprinted in *The Black Pilgrimage* Volume 1. The events that ensue involve Westen's "Scholar's Mistress" (the pile of books, shaped roughly like a woman, which he keeps on his bed - Leiber had one too[1]), and the discovery of a journal written by Clark Ashton Smith (who I assume needs no introduction to readers here). Hidden within that journal is a mysterious curse: "...when the weights are on at Sutro Mount (4) and Monkey Clay (5) [(4)

+ (1) = (5)] *BE his Life Squeezed Away*". Leiber's theory of "paramentals", created from the very essence of cities (seen in an early form in his 1940s tales, "Smoke Ghost" and "The Hound") comes to the fore. And one of the best fictional books ever invented, *Megapolisomancy: A New Science of Cities* by Thibaut de Castries, plays a central role.

There was another (presumably slightly earlier) version of *Our Lady of Darkness*, also published in 1977: the novella, *The Pale Brown Thing*, which appeared in the January and February issues of *The Magazine of Fantasy and Science Fiction*. Would it be unfair to assume that this was nothing more than a lesser, shorter version of *Our Lady*? In 2016 Brian Showers' Swan River Press, with the first-ever reprint of *The Pale Brown Thing*, gave us the chance to discover whether this assumption is correct or whether "the two texts should happily exist side by side, each worthy of exploration". These words are from the seven-page afterword ("Story-telling, Wonder-questing, Mortal Me: The Transformation of *The Pale Brown Thing* into *Our Lady of Darkness*") by Leiber expert John Howard, who also notes that Leiber said: "...the two texts should be regarded as the same story told at different times. If Franz's story is longer in *Our Lady of Darkness*, the reason is that he recalls more the second time he tells it". Or, as John puts it: "If *The Pale Brown*

Thing is... Franz Westen telling the story for the first time, then the longer version, *Our Lady of Darkness*, is the story as told again later, expanded and amplified, with the addition of much 'secondary' matter of all kinds".

The main difference between *Our Lady* and *The Pale Brown Thing* is that there is less descriptive background in the novella, so San Francisco is not quite so powerfully brought to life (in *Our Lady*, as John Howard says, Leiber develops the city "into a character in its own right, rather than as simply the background for the story"). There are fewer 'secondary narratives' and the subsidiary characters are not so fleshed out (at one point, fifteen pages of anecdotes recounted by some of Franz's neighbours in the apartment building are missing, for instance). I regret the former a little more than I do the latter. I also regret the slight trimming down of some of Thibaut de Castries' back story as it relates to his connections with the circle of San Francisco writers such as Jack London and George Sterling; and of some of the other literary references (although all the MRJ allusions are present in both texts). In many cases it is de Castries' 'dark mistress' whose presence is minimised, while the related quotes from and references to Thomas De Quincey's "our Lady of Darkness", *"Mater Tenebrarum"* (from *Suspiria de Profundis*), don't appear at all in *The Pale*

Brown Thing. Clearly they were an afterthought of Leiber's, but one which adds an important new layer to *Our Lady*. Unfortunately, the one aspect of *Our Lady*, which I could do without - Leiber's obsession with slight, gamin, near-jailbait girls (to be found in a number of his writings, in fact) - is present almost in its entirety in the shorter narrative.

There is little or nothing in *The Pale Brown Thing* that is not also in *Our Lady*, and I don't think any fan of *Our Lady* will like the novella *quite* as much as they do the novel. But if I had never read *Our Lady*, I suspect I would love *The Pale Brown Thing*. Swan River's edition would be a valuable volume to have in that case, but even those who compare *The Pale Brown Thing* unfavourably with *Our Lady* will want the book, especially with John Howard's fine, if all too brief, afterword (I doubt whether anyone knows more about the subject than he does); and his scrupulous line-by-line listing of the differences between *Our Lady* and *The Pale Brown Thing*. "Thibaut de Castries: Revenant", the more personal foreword by Donald Sidney Fryer (who features in both versions of the story as the flamboyant "Jaime Donaldus Byers" and knew Leiber well), adds further value. Sidney Fryer examines a possible source for Thibaut de Castries (Adolphe de Castro, a revision client of Lovecraft's), and also considers the similarities and differences between Byers and Fryer (referring to himself irritatingly in the third person). I like his summation of *Our Lady* as reflecting "and amiably so, the Hippie Period that flourished in 'the City' during 1965 through 1975, and then lingered in some form or fashion for some yet further time".

As always, Swan River Press has produced a lovely-looking book (nicer than any edition of *Our Lady*, which has not been well served by cover artists), with wrap-around dust-jacket art by Jason Zerrillo, based on part of the illustration for *The Pale Brown Thing* from the cover of *Fantasy and Science Fiction*, but much moodier. At the risk of seeming to be too picky, I would point out that both of these show the "Thing" leaning out of the window of a traditional San Francisco Victorian rowhouse. It makes for an atmospheric picture, but it's nothing like Leiber's/Westen's apartment block at 811 Geary where the central events are set. Within the dust-jacket a kind of secret secondary illustration (a bonus feature which Swan River has made its own), on the boards of the book itself, depicts Westen's Scholar's Mistress. Thank goodness Leiber's own Scholar's Mistress never came to life - as far as we know!

Note:

[1] For photographs of Leiber's/Westen's apartment, including the beginnings of Leiber's "Scholar's Mistress", see *Locus 378* (July 1992) and Don Herron's *The Literary World of San Francisco and its Environs* (1990).

The Return of Cindy Mars-Lewis
Phil Rickman's *Night After Night*

B ack before Phil Rickman's Merrily Watkins series of supernatural/crime novels really took off, he wrote a couple of books under the Will Kingdom pseudonym. *The Cold Calling* (1998) and *Mean Spirit* (2001), both 'earth mysteries fiction' (to coin a phrase), featured a different cast of characters to the Merrily novels. Most notable among them was Cindy Mars-Lewis, a Welsh transvestite, ventriloquist, shaman. I know what you're all thinking: "how on earth could M.R. James have forgotten to include one of those in any of his ghost stories?" In fact, Cindy is arguably Rickman's best creation, and he[1] was much missed, not only by me. Some years ago I asked Phil if there was any chance of Cindy returning, and to my joy he didn't entirely rule it out. But I had more or less given up hope.

Happily, thirteen years on, in *Night After Night* (2014), Cindy did return and in fine fettle. The events revolve around Knap Hall near Winchcombe in Gloucestershire. It's a place with a dark past, from possible connections with Katherine Parr in Tudor times, through vilely evil goings-on in the eighteenth century, to much more recent deaths. Is the house haunted by these events, or did it *cause* them? Is there a connection with the nearby (real) long barrow, Belas Knap? These are among the questions which may or may not be answered when a television crew takes over the house to film a week-long reality show, a sort of combination of *Celebrity Big Brother* and *Most Haunted* called - wait for it - *Big Other*! The idea is to gather together a group of seven celebrities, not exactly at the peak of their careers, but known either for their scepticism or for their belief in the supernatural. What will they experience in the house and how will they interact? What secrets will be revealed? Which 'side' will win the argument? Well, it's clear where the author's sympathies lie (mine too!): he has no qualms about including some less than favourable asides referring to Richard Dawkins and Brian Cox.

Among the celebrities, in the 'believers' camp, is our Cindy, but he's been brought in by the director as a kind of *agent provocateur*, should nothing dramatic happen. As far as that's concerned, he's not really needed. Strange figures are seen both by the celebrities and by the crew (eerily, at one point, a ghostly man passes through one of the false walls and appears on the side where a camerawoman is filming), and odd things occur. The central character of *Night After Night*, Grayle Underhill, is another witness to the phenomena. Grayle was formerly a writer for a New Age magazine (she, like Cindy, is from the Will Kingdom books), but she's now taking a break from slumming it in the mainstream press to work as a researcher on the show. Quite early on, Grayle has an almost "Rats"-like encounter in a room empty apart from a four-poster bed: "She can only see, through eyes she wants to close and can't, not four bedposts but five, and the fifth is a man with his arms by his side, a thin shadow joining him to the blackness above..." For spookiness this scene is beaten by a diary entry, in which a recent former resident of the house recounts a dream she had about one of the (real) grotesque carvings on the outside of Winchcombe church:

> ...I saw this little thin figure coming down the nearly dark street towards me, and when it got close enough it was one of THEM with those horrible round stone eyes with the holes in them and its tongue sticking out... [I]t was... dancing like an old-fashioned puppet, and it had a full body, a male body, and I saw that it was naked and... you know, I knew exactly what it wanted to do to me.

That starts very Jamesian and then veers off into territory where MRJ would never have gone, I'm sure you'll agree!

With *Night After Night*, Phil Rickman was on terrific and terrifying form. At more than five hundred pages it's a chunky read, to say the least, but it never for one moment lost my interest. I recommend it highly.

In the original version of this review, I said that I didn't think Phil Rickman had been quite on top of his game in the last couple of Merrily Watkins books before *Night After Night*: I wondered whether maybe he was running out of places to go with his characters there or maybe he just needed a break from them. It turns out that I was right with my second guess. Phil did return to Merrily Watkins two years later, with *Friends of the Dusk* (2016), quickly followed by *All of a Winter's Night* (2017). My article on them is in *The Black Pilgrimage* Volume 1. With its Kilpeck location (where MRJ and the McBrydes sometimes worshipped) and dark Morris, *All of a Winter's Night* is one of the very best of all the Merrily novels (and possibly my favourite). More recently, and following a long delay due to Phil's serious illness, the sixteenth book in the Merrily series appeared. *The Fever of the World* (2022), which centres around William Wordsworth and a poem he wrote as a young man after visiting the Wye Valley area, is flawed and somehow doesn't entirely hang together for me, although I found much to enjoy. Not least is this very Jamesian description of two ghosts: "Rags... They were like rags being blown. Grey cloth... cloth flapping about. One appeared to be wearing a cap of some kind and one had hair blowing out from its head. Like the husks of things". Lines worthy of MRJ himself, I think. Sadly, nothing more is made of these ghosts and, in common with a lot of the book, threads are left dangling.

Note:

[1] "He" is the pronoun by which I referred to Cindy in this piece when it first appeared. Personally I would be more comfortable with "they", and I considered changing it for this reprint, but Cindy is "he" throughout the book so, out of respect for the author and the character, "he" it stays.

Things that Go Bump in the Night
Roger Johnson's *In the Night - In the Dark: Tales of Ghosts and Less Welcome Visitors*

This large, paperback collection of stories, poems and other fiction by Roger Johnson was released by MX Publishing in 2011. It gathers together material mostly produced between 1983 and 2006, with a few earlier items and a handful of previously unpublished tales. It is divided into three sections: "Things that Go Bump in the Night" (Tales from the Endeavour), "Things from Beyond" and "More Things in Heaven and Earth...". The second section contains eight broadly Lovecraftian stories (and a poem), some of which are really rather good, with sinister, often Essex-based settings, a couple of fine Dunsanian fantasies, and a take on HPL's "The Nameless City" that is better than the original. The six items in the third section are a miscellany of less categorisable pieces, ranging from the horrific "Love, Death, and the Maiden" (original title "Mädelein") to the not terribly successful early attempts at humour in "Oddities Investigated: Tales from a Hero's Casebook".

But it is the fifteen stories in "Things that Go Bump in the Night" which would be of particular interest to *Ghosts & Scholars* readers as they are almost all, to some degree at least, in the M.R. James tradition. Seven of them - "The

Melodrama", "The Prize", "The Scarecrow", "The Watchman", "The Interruptions" (originally published as "The Dog"), "The Wall-Painting" and "The Searchlight" - are reprinted from *G&S* and other Haunted Library publications. "The Scarecrow", as I explained at the time in *G&S 6*, was a rejected entry for a ghost story competition run by *The Times*, which may not seem like something to be proud of until one considers that another reject was Ramsey Campbell's disturbing "In the Bag". Along with several of Roger's other tales, "The Scarecrow", after its initial appearance in the small press, went on to be reprinted in a *Year's Best Horror Stories* volume.

The Endeavour in question is an Essex inn and the yarns are, in traditional manner, told by people frequenting that establishment. 'Traditional' is definitely the operative word. In his review in *G&S 33* of the previous book of Endeavour tales - Sarob Press's *A Ghostly Crew* (2001) - David Longhorn said: "...if I have one quibble with this ghostly crew it's that they are largely time travellers from an earlier epoch". It's a fair criticism and anyone seeking cutting-edge modern supernatural fiction here is going to be disappointed. The usual themes are all present and correct, especially curses, revenge from beyond the grave, and objects or places with scary guardians; and yet Roger Johnson is very capable of ringing the changes and bringing originality to well-worn formats. Thus, for instance, we have "The Prize", in which a treasure hunt of the Kit Williams *Masquerade* type goes badly wrong; and "The Melodrama", in which an actor in a theatrical performance of the Murder of Maria Marten in the Red Barn has something to hide in his own past and is dogged on stage by a "figure... of an almost terrifying thinness". One of my favourite Johnson tales (possibly his best), "The Wall-Painting", appeared originally in the Haunted Library's *Saints and Relics* (1983). It has a good Jamesian church setting (as does "The Watchman" incidentally) and a wall-painting that is not at all what it seems: St Tosti, the human figure in it, is accompanied by another ("as it might be the shadow of a dog or a wolf") which appears to change in a manner deeply troubling to those who see it. There is also horror far more cosmic than is usually found in a Jamesian tale, a horror that deals in infinity and disappearance: never have the words "There's no door here" been used more terrifyingly.

Although I think most of the best inclusions in the "Things that Go Bump in the Night" section are reprinted from my publications (and I don't believe this solely because I'm biased!), another huge favourite of mine is "The Soldier", from the Richard Dalby-edited *Mystery for Christmas*

(O'Mara 1990). The setting is the City of London, and Roger has worked up a plot centred on the theories of Michael Harrison in his book, *The London that was Rome* (1971).[1] Harrison's idea was that some of the street names and dedications of the medieval churches in the city were based on the gods and deities worshipped since Roman times on the sites (St Magnus Martyr equals Magna Mater; St Dionis Backchurch is Dionysus Bacchus; and so on). It's one of the best nut books I've ever read (I am a connoisseur of such!) and so superficially credible that I want to believe there might be some truth in it, though the rational fragment of my mind and my tolerable knowledge of church history/ecclesiology tell me it's highly unlikely. Clearly Roger was equally drawn to the concept, and the result, in "The Soldier", is a tale of a nineteenth-century innocent, told in his own words with much left out. The alarming truth, I think, becomes clear to the reader fairly early on (the mysterious church which young Wenlock discovers is St Denis Mitre - think about it), but there's a satisfying twist in the tail.

There are weaker stories in the book (two of the Endeavour tales based on real local Essex events/folklore, "The Breakdown" and "The Pool", are prime examples), but few if any in the first and second sections are not worth reading, indeed rereading. I regret the omission of an introduction, but Roger provides each tale with an afterword, which fills the gap to some extent. I really enjoyed renewing my acquaintance with George Cobbett and his fellow drinkers at the Endeavour. Roger is a fine, literate writer who knows how to put together both a good sentence and a good plot. This would be enough in itself to encourage fans of Jamesian fiction to buy *In the Night - In the Dark*, but the touches of something extra that make a few of the stories stick disturbingly in one's mind, and one's nightmares, for years to come are surely enough to convince all but the most anti-traditionalist of doubters.

Note:

[1] My apologies for returning to *The London that was Rome* more than once in this book - it *is* rather special (not necessarily entirely in a good way).

THE REST

The Immortal William Palmer
Sebastian Baczkiewicz's *Pilgrim*

A few years ago, I treated myself to the two CD box sets of BBC Radio 4's wonderful *Pilgrim* plays by Sebastian Baczkiewicz,[1] which began in 2008. Box One contains series 1-4: sixteen 45-minute stories in all. Box Two contains series 5-7: thirteen stories. The episode titles in Series 1 are all taken from John Bunyan's well-known pilgrim hymn; Series 2 titles are descriptive; but later episodes are almost all named atmospherically after their settings, e.g. "Gallowstone Hill", "Bleaker Lake", "Lindey Island", "Bayldon Abbey" and "Crowsfall Wood". Series 7 (2016) was supposed to be the last, but at Christmas 2018 there was a new two-part story, "The Winter Queen"; and in October 2020 another two-parter, "The Timbermoor Imp". There's no reason that there shouldn't be more, for:

> Of all the tales told on these islands, few are as strange as that of William Palmer. Cursed, apparently, on the road to Canterbury in the spring of 1185 for denying the presence of the other world by the King of the Grey Folk - or Fairy - himself, and compelled to walk from that day to this between the worlds of magic and of men, and subsequently

known in all the strange and wonderful lore attribut-
ed to the mysterious William Palmer, as Pilgrim.

In other words, the tales of the immortal William Palmer, former stonemason and creator of gargoyles, could go on forever. I don't think Sebastian Baczkiewicz could ever completely let him go: Palmer has apparently even insinuated himself briefly into one of Baczkiewicz's other, unrelated radio plays.

The above quote, after an initial scene, introduces each one of the *Pilgrim* episodes. There's also a description of them, which seems to have been used in the BBC's publicity. It sums them up quite neatly:

> What if all the myths and folktales of these islands were true? And what if they were not only true but present now in our world? All the spirits, existing, as they have always existed, in the gaps between tower blocks, in the shadows under bridges, in the corner of our vision...

William Palmer, played to perfection by Paul Hilton, travels throughout modern Britain encountering legends and supernatural beings too numerous to list in full. Included among them are such things as changelings; werewolves and werefoxes; spirits of lakes, woods, wells and stones; a dragon; a man slowly and grotesquely turning into a hare; a sleeping giant; Joseph of Arimathea; and, of course, various representatives of the "grey folk", some - but not all - working on behalf of their King. There are threads running through each series, but every episode also contains a stand-alone tale. In one story, a drowned church is filled with angry ghosts; in another, two people foolishly raid an old tomb, that of the "last of the seven chieftains"; and in a third, a burial mound is occupied by the "Goat Lord" who lures and entraps people through time. William Palmer spends much of Series 5 searching for the "Radiant Boy", a family's harbinger of death, who has been scared away, resulting in the family being stuck in a kind of limbo, unable to die (forced immortality is inevitably a repeated theme in these tales).

Among Pilgrim's recurring 'opponents' ('enemies' is too simplistic a word to describe them) is Puck, who steals away and marries Palmer's elderly, dying daughter, Doris. Doris agrees to the arrangement to avoid seeing her father being pursued by a kind of Wild Hunt. Another opponent is Mrs Pleasance, otherwise known as Birdie. She, among others, is trying to get hold of the *Abaeron*, a (stone) 'book' of great power originally owned by Merlin, "the drowned mage", and eventually briefly possessed by Palmer. I don't think it's overtly stated, but it's clear that Mrs Pleasance is actually Merlin's bane, the enchantress Nimue. In Series 6, the villain (a real villain this time, a betrayer of William's trust) is a human corrupted by power gained through alchemy; there's another magician who escapes danger into a landscape painting; and a treacle mine! This series also contains perhaps my favourite episode of all: in a field with an old Ferris wheel built by him, "Ouldmeadow Jack" dances every Midsummer to keep the residents of a nearby barrow "warm".

In 2019 Sebastian Baczkiewicz was interviewed for the first volume (*Spirits of Time*) of Folk Horror Revival/Wyrd Harvest Press's two-volume *Urban Wyrd* (see my article, "A Sense of Otherness", later in this collection). The conversation was entitled "Reclaiming the 'f' word", the word in question being "fairy". Of his reasons for creating *Pilgrim*, he explains:

> For a long time, I'd wanted to do something about myths and legends and the enormous wealth of folktales that every single corner of this country has... I became, and still am, very interested in those stories. How they've evolved and how they touch a kind of older reality, or an older, stranger and quite mysterious tradition that goes back centuries and centuries.

Notice there the reference to "a kind of older reality", which relates to my idea that some works of genre fiction are "the real thing" and many not (on which subject, more shortly). He continues:

> I think the thing is that people are more aware that there is an older beat to this country... that seems to be darker and stranger and exciting and mysterious and charming and beguiling... It's not necessarily pleasant or reassuring... it's actually quite frightening, but it's definitely mesmerising and it makes people feel connected to something that somewhere got lost...

For those who've not yet encountered *Pilgrim*, I hope I've given an idea of why the plays are so marvellously strange and magical: they are "mesmerising" indeed. It's the combination of real folklore with lore from Sebastian Baczkiewicz's imagination, merged in such a way that *all* of it feels like an older, deeper and more authentic reality. There's never been anything else quite like *Pilgrim* - it's a work of inspired, and very personal, genius.

Note:

[1] I believe all episodes are now available for download on BBC Sounds.

The Real Thing Again (or perhaps not)
Melissa Albert's *The Hazel Wood* and *The Night Country*

I've written previously about "The Real Thing": those books and stories that don't seem *just* to be telling a story but to be expressing something far truer, deeper and stranger about the world. Examples I've given in the past (and which I adapted for the article called "The Real Thing" in *The Black Pilgrimage* Volume 1) have been Alan Garner's *Boneland*, Megan Lindholm's *Wizard of the Pigeons*, Lindholm and Steve Brust's *The Gypsy* and Terry Pratchett's *The Wee Free Men*. To those I could add the first three of Robert Holdstock's Ryhope Wood sequence, *Mythago Wood*, *Lavondyss* and *The Hollowing*; a number of Mark Valentine's tales such as "Sea Citadels", "As Blank as the Days Yet to Be" (which I reprinted in *The Ghosts & Scholars Book of Mazes*) and "Herald of the Hidden"; and Sebastian Baczkiewicz's *Pilgrim* radio plays.

With Melissa Albert's first novel, *The Hazel Wood* (2018), I thought I had found another addition to the list. This had an enthusiastic review in the *Guardian* so I decided to give it a try, as there was a copy in the library; I suppose I was expecting something along the lines of *Mythago Wood*. Is it? Well, yes and mostly no! The central character in the story is

Alice, a seventeen-year-old living in New York as the tale begins. She and her mother, Ella, have spent their lives running from one place to another, always pursued by bad luck and unexplained events. Years before, Alice's grandmother, Althea Proserpine, had written a book of the blackest of black fairy stories, *Tales from the Hinterland*. It developed a cult following which only increased on the coming of the Web, with message boards discussing the author and the unknown whereabouts of her home, Hazel Wood, into which she and her daughter had withdrawn completely, following the death of her second husband there. The stories, with titles such as "The Door That Wasn't There", "Jenny and the Night Women", "Alice-Three-Times" and "Twice-Killed Katherine", are also examined at length by her fans on the message boards and in blogs. This is despite the fact that copies of the book are almost impossible to come by, even on the Net; appallingly expensive when they do turn up; and not available in any reprint or on-line version (not so unusual, in my experience - remember my writing in the first *Black Pilgrimage* about the ever-elusive *Hobby Horse Cottage*?). A film of the book also disappeared without trace; and one particular fan and blogger, who managed to locate Hazel Wood, returned severely changed and damaged, while the person she was with didn't survive

Early on in *The Hazel Wood*, Ella receives a letter telling her that Althea has died, and soon afterwards Ella is kidnapped, apparently by some of the denizens of the Hinterland. Most of the rest of the book superficially resembles all those stories, from *Tam Lin* (which is mentioned) to *The Wee Free Men*, about the rescue of a relative or lover from Fairyland. It's a rather peculiarly-plotted book, but in a good way, for it seems to take the form of five separate sections, each within a different sub-genre. The first section is urban fantasy, in which Alice and her scholarly fanboy friend, Ellery Finch, are pursued through New York by a series of weird and sometimes dangerous figures. The second section is a road trip narrative, as Alice and Ellery drive through upstate New York in search of the Hazel Wood, where they are sure they will find (and attempt to rescue) Ella. They realise that the town of Birch, where there have been several unexplained murders over the years, might be a good candidate. But a dreadful tragedy strikes when they reach it.

The third section is the one that most resembles *Mythago Wood*, and deals with what happens when Alice finds the "Halfway Wood" itself. It's a terrible place, occupied by people from some of Althea Proserpine's tales (just as Ryhope Wood is occupied by Robert Holdstock's "mythagos"). Alice only survives because she has in her pocket a comb, a bone and a feather, which a man whom she seemed to recognise had left on the table in the New York coffee shop where she had been working. In the fourth section, Alice discovers and enters her grandmother's house in the middle of the Wood, and her narrative becomes a surreal nightmare, with rooms changing as she walks through, corridors becoming endless, fleeting figures including her mother at various different ages, and such images as: "a fairy-tale bed, hung to the ground with tattered curtains. Where they were at their sheerest, I could see the shape of someone lying motionless inside... I didn't want to see what lay on that bed". Then, opening a door, Alice sees her grandmother, and listens as Althea tells a young Ella a fairy story that goes some way to explaining how the wall between the worlds had been breached. When Althea turns her attention to her granddaughter, however, Alice learns something that turns her world upside down.

I won't say anything about the fifth section, except that many more figures from the Hinterland and from our world appear, some more sinister than others. The Briar King is an especially good and archetypal one ("Then I recognized it - his stink, of rot and ruin with a wild green heart"). There are also two interludes in the early sections, where Ellery Finch retells a couple of the stories from *Tales from the Hinterland* - "Alice-Three-Times" and "The Door That Wasn't There" -

and they really are very dark indeed.

When the Hinterland and its residents enter our world, things become terrifying. Take, for instance, the appearance of "Twice-Killed-Katherine" in New York:

> "Do you see that girl? ... Look at her scar. And her hair. And - oh, my god. Do you see what she's holding? ... It's a birdcage. It's what Twice-Killed Katherine carries..."
>
> A man in a heavy gray overcoat was walking down the street toward her... Before he could get too far, she opened the birdcage.
>
> The thing that came out of it was canary-shaped, but it wasn't a canary. It was small and darting and looked like it had been hole-punched out of shadow. It unfurled its wings wider and wider, till it was the size of a hawk.
>
> It went for the man... the thing latched onto his neck. He went down noiselessly, and the creature dropped heavily onto his chest. It stretched its wings so we couldn't see exactly what it was doing... I looked back at the girl... the expression on her face was worse than anything. It was a kind of... selfish ecstasy.

The Hazel Wood is a remarkable book - I'm tempted to add

"for a first novel", but it would be remarkable at any point in a writer's career. It's loved by almost everyone who has read it (judging from the reviews on the Net), though it seems that a minority of readers can't take the changes in sub-genre as the plot develops. Anyone expecting a straightforward modern fairy tale will be especially disappointed, I think. I'm not too sure about the fact that it's been optioned for a film version though. Will it work as a film? I think I'd rather not find out - I almost hope that, if it *is* made, it might disappear without trace, just as the film of *Tales from the Hinterland* did.

Melissa Albert's next book was set to be *Tales from the Hinterland* itself (which I believe has now been published), so that was the next one I was expecting from her. What I *wasn't* expecting was a sequel to *The Hazel Wood*. But at the start of 2020, this is what appeared, in the form of *The Night Country*. Alice is back in New York, trying to live a normal life, and to avoid getting drawn into the lives of the other characters, or "ex-Stories", from the Hinterland. For, in escaping from the Hinterland in *The Hazel Wood*, Alice has created some sort of fracture through which all the other characters having been moving (deliberately or inadvertently) into the real world. Meanwhile the Hinterland is dying.

Ex-Stories in New York are dying too - or, rather, being murdered/sacrificed. Alice survives an attempt on her life, but others are not so lucky. From each of the bodies a part is being removed (a foot, a hand, a tongue), and the manner of their deaths makes some of the ex-Stories suspect Alice. Meanwhile her bookish not-boyfriend Ellery, who in *The Hazel Wood* had chosen to remain in the Hinterland when Alice escaped, is experiencing its fracturing and trying to return to his own world (Ellery is not an ex-Story, and it seems that others like him are trapped there).

Reading *The Night Country* caused me to cool slightly towards *The Hazel Wood*, and I'm no longer sure I'd count it as the "Real Thing". In fact, after about twenty pages of *The Night Country*, I seriously considered not bothering to continue. I did, in the end, as Alice's quest for the murderer interested me enough to want to know whodunnit, and I was also keen to see whether Ellery (always the best and most likeable character in both books) finally escaped and caught up with Alice again.

The Night Country, I suppose, started at a major disadvantage as I read it in the middle of my periodic reread of Rob Holdstock's Ryhope Wood series. Superficially, there would seem to be a similarity of theme between the two authors' work. Albert's ex-Stories and Holdstock's mythagos both derive ultimately from people's minds (which doesn't mean they're imaginary). But the ex-Stories are from the mind of one non-human person (albeit they are often archetypal in nature), while the mythagos are from the myths, legends and fears of humanity over the many thousands of years of its existence. They go much deeper and resonate much more strongly; sometimes they are recognisable, at other times they feel as though they *should* be recognisable, could we but remember.

In his wise introduction to the 2014 reprint of *Mythago Wood* (the first in the series), Neil Gaiman writes: "It seems to me that the marvel of *Mythago Wood*, and the stories that followed it in the Ryhope Wood sequence, is that Rob created something that seemed, in retrospect, to have been there the whole time. Like a sculptor who takes his tools to an oddly shaped log and seems to do almost nothing to it, but now we see the dragon that was waiting there to be revealed the whole time. It was obvious, but we could not see it". Or, as Rob Holdstock himself says in his afterword to the 2015 reprint of *Lavondyss* (the second in the series), quoting Ralph Vaughan Williams (who appears in that book) on the folk tune "Dives and Lazarus": "I had that sense of recognition. Here was something which I had known all my life, only I didn't know it". These quotes express, a good deal more eruditely, my feelings about the "Real Thing". I originally thought this was the case with *The Hazel Wood*, but now I wonder.

Don't get me wrong, I enjoyed *The Night Country*, and it's certainly well-written - once I got into it, it held my interest. Partway through, it goes up a level and there are some marvellous scenes, especially during Ellery's surreal escape from the Hinterland, as he passes through such places as a magician's library and - in particular - an incredible shop on a Dickensian street, in which magical artifacts from fairy tales are bought and sold (mercifully not as Harry Potter-ish as it sounds). But coming straight after I reread the mind-blowing final forty or so pages of Rob Holdstock's *Lavondyss*, Melissa Albert's creation seemed rather superficial and lightweight by comparison.

"More Bones and Marrow for our Babies"
Daisy Makeig Jones's Fairyland Lustreware

I used to vow that I would never spend more than thirty or forty pounds on a book. I largely stuck to this until fairly recently: I think the most expensive non-small-press book I'd bought was one about John Pugh's *trompe-l'oeil* murals, which cost me around £30, give or take. It was then released in a paperback edition and has since been available much more cheaply. Still, I don't really regret my purchase: I've looked through the book (dreaming of exploring the world of some of the murals) so often that a paperback would probably have been a false economy; I'd have worn out two or three copies by now.

But this vow had, until early 2019, prevented me from getting a book which I'd long lusted after, but which had never shown up for sale on the Net (old or new copies) at a price of less than three figures. Then the first lot of royalties for *The Black Pilgrimage* Volume 1 came in, and they were more than I'd expected. So finally I managed to talk myself into breaking my vow - just this once (maybe!). *Wedgwood Fairyland Lustre: The Work of Daisy Makeig-Jones* by Una des Fontaines (1975) is the only full-scale book on that subject, and copies are very rare. The cheapest on the Net I could find was £100 exactly (still only a tenth the going rate for the most modest pieces of fairyland lustreware itself), and the next cheapest was at least a third more, with other prices soaring to ridiculously huge amounts. So I chose the £100 copy and, as it turned out, I picked well: the book, when it arrived (very swiftly), was nearly brand new and in pristine condition. And it's lovely!

Daisy Makeig-Jones (1881-1945) produced her fairyland lustreware for Wedgwood between 1915 and 1931, at which point it went out of fashion, and I get the impression that Wedgwood was pleased to have got rid of her as she wasn't the easiest of people to work with. But what she created was - almost literally - magical. In a range of lustrous, gorgeous colours, her vases, plates, bowls and plaques depict strange scenes and landscapes, peopled by weird-looking fairies, goblins and other less explicable creatures from folklore, myth and imagination. These beings are quaint, often amusing, always strange but never twee - she was no Mabel Lucie Atwell. The designs have titles like "Woodland Elves", "Elves in a Pine Tree", "Candlemas", "Fiddler in Tree" and "Elfin Palace". There is another entitled "Ghostly Wood". It's inspired by *The Legends of Croquemitaine*, a French book of 1863, with an English translation published in 1866, illustrated by Gustave Doré. This describes the exploits of Charlemagne and his knights, Mitaine being a bold young girl who was squire to one of those knights. Her enemy was the eponymous Croquemitaine who lived in the "Fortress of Fear". In 1921, Wedgwood published an illustrated booklet[1] to accompany Daisy Makeig-Jones's designs, in which she explained and recounted the tales depicted on them. Of "Ghostly Wood" she said:

[This is] part of the Land of Illusion which had to be traversed by Mitaine before she reached and conquered the Fortress of Fear. It was an awesome place to cross... trees, which in the distance had the appearance of a fairy cloud of pinkest blossoms, dripped blood as she approached and shrieked and howled in an eldricht *[sic]* manner. Other trees, which seemed quite ordinary afar off, when looked at closely, resembled dried and blasted trunks, with demons' heads in place of leaves; while bats and elves hung on their branches. Above, in the topmost boughs, their nests made of dead men's bones, sat the Owls of Wisdom, crying "Twhit Twhoo, all fools too, more bones, more bones and marrow for our babies". Drifting everywhere were the spirits of those who had failed to reach the Fortress - wailing, holding the flaming candle of their souls, and doomed with the Fairy of the Desert in the form of a hideous toad, and the Yellow Dwarf, to dwell in the Land of Illusion, misleading and making fearful the craven traveller, until 3000 times 3000 years shall have passed away... The vase also shows the White Rabbit, more than a trifle scared by these apparitions, hurrying across the earth to guide the immortal Alice to Wonderland...

Is that weird enough for you? The design is indeed one of her oddest, and depicts a very sinister and crowded wood with a procession of those wailing spirits, all cloaked and hooded in white, being menaced by one of her most oft-repeated figures, a "bird-like creature with prominent eyes and the wings of a bat" which she named "the Roc". A Google image search has revealed that she adapted both of these images from Doré. By contrast, Alice's White Rabbit is a cute, almost Disneyesque creature.

At the end of the book is a fascinating section on some of Daisy Makeig-Jones's influences, for she was a great copier (not just of Doré): her talent wasn't so much in inventing her own characters as in taking the creations of other artists and illustrators and adapting them to her own imagination, in landscapes of stunning colours. The influences noted here are Edmund Dulac, Kay Neilsen and (particularly) H.J. Ford. Most people who have heard of Ford (1856-1941) will know him from his gorgeous and often highly detailed illustrations for Andrew Lang's *Colour Fairy Books* - he was the sole illustrator for the last ten. Keen M.R. James fans, however, might know him better for his work in MRJ's *Old Testament Legends* (1913): ten beautiful full-page pictures depicting such scenes as "How Satan deceived Eve in the River", "Satan departs, vanquished by Job at last", and "Ephippas and the Demon of the Red Sea bring the great pillar to Solomon" (the latter, accompanying MRJ's retelling of *The Testament of Solomon*, is perhaps the best of a superb lot).

Two things I hadn't realised until I read the short biographical paragraph on Ford in *Fairyland Lustre* is that he had six brothers, one of whom was MRJ's long-time friend, Lionel Ford. It was Lionel Ford who wrote of MRJ: "He was the centre of our group [of undergraduates at Cambridge], never seeking people out, but letting people find him, and then with apparently endless time at their disposal". The second thing I had completely forgotten but rediscovered when looking up the single reference to H.J. Ford in Michael Cox's *M.R. James: An Informal Portrait* (p.139). In 1903, when publisher Edward Arnold was getting together the contents of *Ghost Stories of an Antiquary*, and before he realised that MRJ badly wanted his beloved friend James McBryde to illustrate the book, Arnold wrote to MRJ:

> We are thinking whom we can suggest as illustrator, but it is not easy to find anyone whose style would match those [stories] you sent us. H.J. Ford might do, but he is expensive; probably he would charge £4.4.0. a drawing. Should you feel disposed to pay for them? We do not as a rule do more than incur the cost of reproduction, but we might contribute something if desired.

The four drawings which James McBryde produced for the book before he died have become so central to the way we think about it, and they clearly meant so much to MRJ, that it almost feels blasphemous for me to say this, but I wish MRJ *had* forked out the money for Ford instead. Pleasant enough though McBryde's drawings are (but lately I've made no secret of the fact that I think his wife Gwendolen was the better artist), I would love to have seen what Ford could have done with MRJ's stories. The result would surely have been magnificent.

Note:

[1] *Some Glimpses of Fairyland.* I've since acquired quite cheaply a 1972 American facsimile reprint of this booklet: "Reprinted for Members of the Buten Museum of Wedgwood", Merion, Pennsylvania. I was surprised (and pleased) to see that Daisy Makeig-Jones begins by quoting

Algernon Blackwood: "For all the World is a child that goes past your window crying for its lost fairy land".

The Mystery and Magic of Rooftops
Helen Grant's *Demons of Ghent*

It was 2019. They'd been moving around all the books in Chester central library, for no accountable reason except, perhaps, that they were trying to kill off the library altogether to make additional space for the more lucrative parts of the building (the - ahem! - 'award-winning' Storyhouse) - cinema, theatre, restaurant, etc. While wandering round desperately searching for the crime fiction, which was no longer situated in the quiet, comfy area, I came upon what I now realise was the Young Adult section. And I was immediately struck (as which of us wouldn't be?) by a book with the beguiling title, *Demons of Ghent*. To my joy, when I took it off the shelf, I found that it was by our very own Helen Grant, author of stories in *Ghosts & Scholars* and the Sarob Press *G&S* books. Only when I got it home did I discover that it's actually the second in a trilogy, with the overall title *Forbidden Spaces*. It's typical of me to read book series out of order. I speak as one who started Charles Stross's Lovecraftian 'Laundry Files' series with the then most recent of the over-half-dozen books; and as one who, as a child, reread C.S. Lewis's *The Last Battle* at least twice before realising that there were numerous other previous Narnia books.

Anyway, I wasn't going to take *Demons of Ghent* back unread because of this! I'm glad I didn't. There's nothing wrong with a novel being classed as Young Adult, but in this case it seems to be only because the central characters are teenagers. Veerle De Keyser has moved to Ghent from a village near Brussels, after the apparently devastating events in the first book in the trilogy. She hears that people in Ghent are dying, some of them by falling from the rooftops of the city's historic buildings, though their deaths are judged to be suicides. But Veerle learns of rumours connected with an old Ghent legend: that the rooftops are frequented by demons - demons with a task which they have carried out for hundreds of years, since being invoked by the painter of Van Eyck's famous "Adoration of the Lamb" in Sint-Baaf's Cathedral (I saw the painting myself when visiting Belgium in the 1970s).

In a possibly foolish move given the above, Veerle pals up with a pleasant young man, Bram, who just happens to be a nightclimber: one of an informal group of people in the city who enjoy secretly clambering up to the tops of the buildings. The accounts of the pair's various climbs are exciting enough on their own, without the added frisson of their first being attacked and then witnessing the death on an adjoining roof of one of their fellow explorers.

Someone or something is stalking the roofs and streets, but what or who? Helen Grant is extraordinarily adept at walking that fine line between a possible supernatural and a very human evil - or is it a bit of both? I can't offhand think of another author who does it better. It's true that we, the readers, know a little more about what's going on than the protagonists do (since we see some of the events through the killer's eyes), but not enough to come to any specific conclusions on this question for some time. I won't give the game away, but I will say that it kept me guessing more or less until (and beyond) the end. And it helps that one really does care what happens to the central characters, while the setting is atmospherically evoked. I've since read the first book (*Silent Saturday*) and the third (*Urban Legends*) in the trilogy and enjoyed them both. Helen Grant's more recent (adult) novel, the Scotland-set *Too Near the Dead*, is even better.[1]

I'm fascinated by rooftops and their mysteries, doubtless because they seem like an entirely different world to what is going on beneath. When I watch - say - a city marathon or bike race on TV it's always to see the aerial shots of the roofs as the competitors pass. And when I watch the film of the Beatles performing on the top of the Apple building in Savile Row, it's always the goings-on on nearby roofs that grab my attention (some of those office-workers do *not* look safe!). Any fiction with that theme attracts me straight away: one of the first I remember reading was Christopher Fowler's pre-Bryant & May *Roofworld*, which has the added attraction of being set in London, still a city of many mysteries (despite the fact that so much has been done to destroy those mysteries by people who only care about making money for themselves and their cronies). There are echoes in *Demons of Ghent*, of course, of the famous Cambridge nightclimbers. I suppose many/most cities have them, but Cambridge is most famous for them thanks to a couple of books on the subject. One of these, *Cambridge Nightclimbing* by 'Hederatus', even inspired me to tackle my own piece of related fiction in the form of Mary Ann Allen's apocalyptic "The Cambridge Beast", where the climbers encounter something scary on the roof of King's College Chapel. Mary Ann does love her apocalypses - she tells me her favourite poem is Yeats's "The Second Coming"! ("The Cambridge Beast", for those who want to follow it up, was included in her collection *The Angry Dead*, revised and reprinted by Cathaven Press in 2021 - see my introduction to it later in this book.)

Oddly enough, despite the fact that Helen Grant's terrifying story "The Lost Maze", in *The Ghosts & Scholars Book of Mazes* (2020), goes for a vertically *entirely* different location (down instead of up!), there is a paragraph in *Demons of Ghent* - an account of one of Veerle's dreams - which reminded me strongly of the basic set-up in that story. I checked this with Helen and she confirmed that both were inspired by an actual recurring dream of hers. I once had a similar dream but I'm very glad indeed that it wasn't a recurring one - I'd be scared to go to sleep.

Note:

[1] I commented on this novel in The Everlasting Club in 2022, saying: "...if Helen were known as a mainstream rather than a genre author, *Too Near the Dead* would have been taken up for serialisation on the radio or maybe sold for TV dramatisation by now".

A Sense of Otherness
Folk Horror Revival's *Urban Wyrd* and *Harvest Hymns*

In 2019, Folk Horror Revival/Wyrd Harvest Press published a huge two-volume set with the overall title *Urban Wyrd*. The two subtitles are *Spirits of Time* and *Spirits of Place*. As with previous FHR books, like *FHR: Field Studies* and *Harvest Hymns* (see below), *Urban Wyrd* contains a collection of articles, reviews and interviews by a wide range of authors, so the quality inevitably varies. "What is Urban Wyrd?" you cry, and even after seeing the pocket definition in the front of each book you may still be struggling:

> A sense of otherness within the narrative, experience or feeling concerning a densely human-constructed area or the inbetween spaces bordering the bucolic and the built-up or surrounding modern technology with regard to another energy at play or in control; be it supernatural, spiritual, historical, nostalgic or psychological. Possibly sinister but always somehow unnerving or unnatural.

I see what they're getting at, although it's vague enough that it can cover almost anything slightly strange or disturbing in a human-dominated urban, suburban or borderland location (and actually, I like my definition better!). In all, the two volumes contain close to a thousand pages, and I think they could have been improved by being trimmed down to 600 or 700, or alternatively the editors could have gone entirely the other way and easily extended to three volumes. Astonishing literary omissions include Ramsey Campbell, Fritz Leiber and Christopher Fowler, whereas Lovecraft's "At the Mountains of Madness" gets a full-length article (is it *really* "urban wyrd" - there's a city, yes, but not a "human-constructed" one). Many skimpy mini-articles, on potentially good topics like *The Prisoner*, *Candyman*, *Q The Winged Serpent*, China Miéville, *Invasion of the Body Snatchers* and Russell T Davies' superb *Years and Years*, serve no real purpose. You can find better in numerous places on the internet.

On the other hand, among the longer articles are some excellent ones. I'd single out in particular "A Tandem Effect: *Ghostwatch*" by Jim Moon; "Voices of the Ether: Stone Tapes, Electronic Voices and Other Ghosts" by James Riley; and (the best piece I've ever seen on this subject) Grey Malkin's "The Burryman of South Queensferry: The Past Within the Present". Among the interviews, there are several gems. *Fortean Times* fans will remember Bob Fischer's well-received article of a few years ago on "The Haunted Generation" (which has since become a regular *FT* column). Here he talks further of that "generation of kids that grew up somewhere between the mid-1960s and the mid-1980s, and became profoundly affected by a feeling that I can only describe as a kind of 'cosy disquiet'. It came from the TV and films and books of that era, which were frequently infused with supernatural and paranormal themes..." The admirable John Linwood Grant discusses his interest in and publications on occult detectives; and Chris Lambert's disturbing interview with Professor Phillip Hull contributes to the ongoing Black Meadow mythos.

Chris Lambert also provides my favourite section of the books, "Reclaiming the 'f' word": a conversation with Sebastian Baczkiewicz, the writer of the *Pilgrim* radio plays (the 'f' word is fairy, in case you were jumping to conclusions there!). Baczkiewicz's motivation for writing *Pilgrim* is exactly as I'd hoped it would be:

> For a long time, I'd wanted to do something about myths and legends and the enormous wealth of folktales that every single corner of this country has... I became, and still am, very interested in those stories... I think the thing is that people are more aware that there is an older beat to this country... that seems to be darker and stranger and exciting and mysterious and charming and beguiling. For want of a better word, it's 'soul'... It's not necessarily

pleasant or reassuring... It's not necessarily a pretty vision, it's actually quite frightening, but it's definitely mesmerising and it makes people feel connected to something that somewhere got lost...

Unfortunately there's one final downside to *Urban Wyrd*: a number of the articles are by academics, and in the general nature of such things, they spend a long time and use a lot of academic language to say practically nothing. Take, for instance, "The City that was not There: 'Absent' Cityscapes in Classic British Ghost Stories" by Anastasia Lipinskaya. This is part of its (questionable) initial summary paragraph:

> This article deals with the problem of "absent" cityscapes in classic ghost stories... Such stories... rarely show public spaces. Probably the 'absent' city in ghost stories is a result of... the author's intention to construct a closed private space for the contact with supernatural forces inserted into the modern sociocultural reality but not destroying it.

Among the examples she cites is MRJ's "The Mezzotint":

> ...in the so-called antiquarian gothic... one single room or even one artefact like a picture or a book is enough. In *The Mezzotint* the transitional zone [where the natural meets the supernatural] is actually an old landscape engraving which mysteriously

comes alive...

The other significant characteristic of this space is its limited size, especially interesting if we remember that the story is set in London. We actually see only a room in a library where the protagonists watch the mysterious engraving like a window into some other space and time.

Wrong and wrong! The events in "The Mezzotint" take place in Oxford ("another University"), not London; and they don't happen in a library but in college rooms. In fact, only two of MRJ's stories are set primarily in London: that's the Old Bailey trial of George Martin in "Martin's Close" and most of "Casting the Runes" (notably the famous British Museum scene). The city also features in scenes in a couple of other tales: the book auction at the start of "The Diary of Mr Poynter", and the climactic scene in Poschwitz's office in "The Uncommon Prayer-book".

But if, as Anastasia Lipinskaya asserts, "for a classic ghost story a limited, closed zone of contact with the supernatural is perhaps a necessity", her proposed explanation doesn't hold much water, especially with reference to "The Mezzotint":

...in ghost stories it is often next to impossible to understand whether something extraordinary actually happens or is it just the product of someone's imagination... or driven by illness, for example... In this context we can suppose that showing ghosts in vast public spaces like cityscapes is problematic for it would demand... [a] world where ghosts and other potentially dangerous forces are real and there is no chance to dismiss them as an illusion.

I'd have thought the presence of multiple witnesses in "The Mezzotint" rules out any sort of non-supernatural explanation (except maybe an unlikely mass-hallucination). MRJ's own, far more sensible (and more simply expressed!) view on the subject can be found in his introduction to *Ghosts and Marvels* (1924): "It is not amiss sometimes to leave a loophole for a natural explanation; but, I would say, let the loophole be so narrow as not to be quite practicable".

Harvest Hymns Volume I: Twisted Roots and *Volume II: Sweet Fruits* are a pair of 2018 paperbacks from Folk Horror Revival on the subject of folk horror in music, past and present respectively. Each volume consists of around forty articles, interviews and reviews by various authors, and as with *Urban Wyrd*, the quality varies. So does the material covered, ranging from the Child Ballads to Black Widow's *Sacrifice* (which I recall writing about in my old fanzine *Seagull*, many, many decades ago!); from Kate Bush and Maddy Prior to The Fall and Dr John. Overall, the good pieces easily outweigh the not-so-good if you're interested in the subject, and there are many gems to be found, along with the occasional reference to M.R. James throughout.

So, for instance, Trees' 1970 album *The Garden of Jane Delawney* is described as having "an air redolent of M.R. James's ghost stories". I don't know about that, but the title track has to be one of the strangest and most sinister songs ever written - I'm not sure whether even the writer of the track, band member Bias Boshell, knows what it's about, but there seems to be a murder involved. That's certainly true of another on my list of most sinister songs: Comus's furious (wish-fulfilment?) "Drip Drip". Both this and a third from my list, Kate Bush's "Experiment IV", are also discussed in Volume One. If you haven't seen the video for "Experiment IV", incidentally, with its scientific experiment gone wrong and creation of a banshee-like creature, you really should check it out.

In Volume Two, the musicians featured include The Hare and the Moon, Ghost Box, and the contributors to the multimedia sense-of-wonder project that is The Black Meadow, which "explores the mysteries surrounding the Black Meadow on the North York Moors. A place of inexplicable occurrences, strange traditions and disappearances". (And a place which doesn't exist - or does it?) There are omissions - not surprising and perfectly forgivable when the subject is so wide ranging. It's a little disappointing that The Triple Tree's MRJ-inspired *Ghosts* doesn't get coverage, and Emily Portman's *The Glamoury* album rarely gets recognised as folk horror, perhaps because it's so superficially sweet and fey (one track, "Hide", a grotesque but empowering tale of supernatural vengeance, is yet another to add to that list of most sinister songs ever written).

One interview in *Sweet Fruits* is specifically about an MRJ adaptation: "'Who is this who is coming?' - scoring M.R. James" is an interview by Jim Peters with Tristin Norwell, the composer of the score for the BBC's appalling 'reworking' of "Oh, Whistle, and I'll Come to You, My Lad" in 2010. I admit I have no memory at all of the music: I think I was so horrified by the whole thing that it was the least of my worries. But in his review in *G&S Newsletter 19*, Dan McGachey gave his opinion in no uncertain terms: "...eerie, often atonal music, reminiscent in places of the radiophonic whining and ringing used to such good effect in the classic 1970s version of *The Signalman*, crops up frequently, making otherwise mundane scenes appear portentous, so that the few instances of genuine supernatural activity lose much of their impact". Tristin Norwell may well be a fine composer but it's clear that he has no more respect for MRJ's story than did Neil Cross, the writer of the 2010 version. Asked by the interviewer "Did you reference the original M R James story when you... were creating the soundtrack?" Norwell's reply begins: "Unlike 90% of other scores where I score from the script, often before it's been cast, the *Whistle...* script was only referenced for the cue; the credits roll. And arguably this was actually Rabbie's tune..." So not really an answer at all, and it almost looks as though he was unaware of MRJ's original, referring as he does more than once to the 2010 *Whistle* being a "remake" of Jonathan Miller's 1968 version.

Still, don't let this put you off - all of Folk Horror Revival's publications are well worth getting and all are very reasonably priced.

"The Flame Still Flickers in the Fen"
Of Mud & Flame: The Penda's Fen Sourcebook

I've often said that, in my opinion, *Penda's Fen* (BBC1, 1974) is the best one-off play/drama ever to appear on TV. Directed by Alan Clarke (who has never done anything else similar, and confessed that he didn't really understand it), it was written by David Rudkin, who later produced the even odder (and partly Jamesian) *Artemis 81*, and is known to M.R. James enthusiasts for his flawed but interesting dramatisation of *The Ash Tree* (1975) in the BBC's "Ghost Stories for Christmas" series. In 2017, a conference on *Penda's Fen* was held in London, and a book containing a collection of the papers presented was promised to follow from the excellent Strange Attractor Press. It seems to have taken a bit longer than they expected to put the book together, but it was worth the wait: *Of Mud & Flame: The Penda's Fen Sourcebook* (edited by Matthew Harle and James Machin) finally appeared in late 2019 and contains not merely the papers from the conference but other articles, a foreword and brief afterthought by David Rudkin, interviews with two of the main actors, and the complete, revised screenplay. It's a chunky, well-illustrated volume.

For those who haven't seen *Penda's Fen*, here is a brief

summary (or not so much a summary as an idea of what it's about). Set in the lovely scenery east of the Malvern Hills in Worcestershire, near the village of Pinvin (the Penda's Fen of the title, named after King Penda of Mercia), the central character is Stephen Franklin, the teenaged son of the Rector. Unlike his father, who seems to be quite unorthodox in his views, Stephen begins as a reactionary - he despises a local leftwing writer (Arne, Rudkin's semi-autobiographical character), and hates everything which doesn't represent the status quo and the 'purity' of the English race. But he is an outsider at his private school, and the play explores his slow discovery of his own mongrel nature - he learns that he is adopted, of mixed race, and he also accepts his homosexuality. Meanwhile, the landscape in which he lives has its own secrets, some of them mythic and others more modern: there is some sort of underground government experimental facility, fatal to anyone who gets too close (this is a theme explored more fully in *Artemis 81*). In the introduction to the booklet accompanying the 2016 BFI DVD release of *Penda's Fen*, Sukhdev Sandhu gives a nice description of the play's message:

> [it suggests] that radical questions and alternative answers are present not out there in universities, museums or sanctioned citadels of learning, but

closer to hand, on the ground beneath our feet. Penda himself becomes a symbol of heretical nationhood, of pre-Christian identity, of an imaginative wildscape which has the potential to redeem us from the lies and orthodoxies of state knowledge.

Among the many memorable scenes, these are a few of my favourites. There is the disturbing scene when Stephen dreams that a stone gargoyle demon from his father's church is perched on his bed. And the shocking hallucination which he experiences while practising Elgar's *The Dream of Gerontius* on the church organ: first, he sees a vision of the pierced crucified feet of Jesus (or is it?) in the organ mirror, and then the floor of the church nave splits all the way along and the camera shot moves down into it. Another great, more cerebral scene occurs when Stephen discusses Manichaeism with his father, who seems to harbour some subversively Gnostic views for a Church of England clergyman (and had been writing a book, now abandoned, entitled *The Buried Jesus*, in which he "sought to establish how the Gospel originals have been malevolently tampered with"). When Stephen, while sheltering in a ruined building from a rainstorm, meets the ghost of the elderly Elgar (an actual ghost or another hallucination?), it's quite touching and sad. In the magnificent and inspirational final scene, Stephen flees from the forces of Mary Whitehousian darkness, and meets Penda himself, the last pagan king in England (who died in 655 CE). Penda tells him (and this feels even more timely today):

> Your land and mine goes down into a darkness now; and I, and all the other guardians of her flame, are driven from our home, up out into the wolf's jaw. But the flame still flickers in the fen... Cherish the flame, till we can safely wake again... we trust it to you, our sacred demon of ungovernableness... child be strange, dark, true, impure and dissonant. Cherish our flame.

Of Mud & Flame is split into several sections. Aside from the introductory matter and the screenplay, there are six items in "Part One - Frames of Reference" (putting *Penda's Fen* into its chronological, literary and artistic context); five in "Part Two - Figures in Landscape" (more wide-ranging and personal responses); five in "Part Three - Deep England" (the historical and geographical background); and four in "Part Four - Penda's Poetics" (poetic and musical aspects). There is so much to take in that I'm just going to have to pick out some particular highlights, bearing in mind that there is the inevitable mixture of excellent commentary/background and academic pointlessness (though less of the latter than you might expect), along with some surprises such as a bit of fanfic featuring a character who has only a couple of scenes in the play!

David Rudkin's "Mongrel Nation: A Foreword" briefly but atmospherically evokes the Malvern Hills ("To this day... I hear rise from the landscape some massive Elgarian harmony - not a specific quote, but some amorphous chord in the head that is essentially him, in its brazen exultation that is also the cry of an anguished soul"). I'd previously encountered Gary Budden's envigorating writing on his adoption of the term "landscape punk"[1] - here, his "Gnostic Anarcho-Punk Anti-Pastoral Visions" looks at the concept in relation to *Penda's Fen* ("Watching the film gave me one of the most important feelings a person can experience: the shock of recognition"). Budden shares with Rudkin himself the opinion that the play isn't folk horror. Adam Scovell, one of the major writers on folk horror, considers this question in "And in the Soil, there be Mirrors: *Penda's Fen* and Folk Horror", concluding that: "I doubt it truly matters... [but as in both] the antidote to the fallacies of Englishness has always lain in wait under the soil, ready to be exhumed".

J.R.R. Tolkien and Francis Brett Young come to the fore in "Penda's Mercia: The Past in the Present" by Carl Phelpstead, with photographs of modern Mercia by his brother

Ben Phelpstead; part of a project to explore the "ways in which memories of the past give meaning to modern landscapes" in the works of various writers. "Stephen and Women" by Carolyne Larrington examines the troublingly stereotypical portrayal of the few women in *Penda's Fen*. In "Gasping for the Silbury Air: Notes on the Music of *Penda's Fen*", John Harle questions whether the right decisions were made when balancing the score, with Elgar so predominant and music as a whole so rarely used on the soundtrack. The fact that only eleven minutes of music feature, of which a mere seven-and-a-half minutes are of Elgar's *Dream of Gerontius*, surprises me as music seems to dominate the proceedings so much (I wonder - is the same true of *Artemis 81*, in which music again seems so central?).

Tom White's fascinating "*Penda's Fen*: Geoffrey's Archipelago" connects the play with Geoffrey of Monmouth and his twelfth-century *History of the Kings of Britain*: "one of the few sources of information on Penda". But White doesn't confine himself only to Geoffrey, going on to discuss further examples of "romantic historiography" ranging from Bede to historians in the nineteenth century with their subtle idealisation of "racial purity", the legacy of which is sadly "still clear to see".

M.R. James gets three listings in the index (yes, there is a decent index!). One, in Roger Luckhurst's "Always Historicise? *Penda's Fen* in the 1970s", is just a passing mention in relation to Robert Macfarlane's *Guardian* essay, "The Eeriness of the English Countryside". In "Making Space for the Shadows: *Penda's Fen*, Katabasis, Tradition and Legacy", David Ian Rabey describes Rudkin's (not very successful) 2016 theatrical version of "Oh, Whistle, and I'll Come to You, My Lad". A little more extensive are Craig Wallace's comparisons between *Penda's Fen* and the BBC's *The Ash Tree/A Warning to the Curious* in "The 'Old, Primeval "Demon" of the Place Opening Half an Eye': *Penda's Fen* and the Legend of the Sleeping King". He concludes: "Rudkin, like the medievalist James, engages with the past… appropriating medieval culture to excavate England in the present".

Excavation: that's the main theme which *Penda's Fen* and MRJ's stories have in common, but it's also the major difference. In MRJ, the digging down to hidden things is invariably ill-advised and ends badly. They are best left hidden. In *Penda's Fen*, that delving provides revelations, both interior and exterior (Stephen's discoveries about himself and the landscape he lives in, respectively), which are valuable and enlightening.

Note:

[1] Although, as far as I know, it was Hookland's David Southwell who first coined the phrase, it was Gary Budden who popularised the "landscape punk" term, as a less pretentious name for some forms of psychogeography. He is also responsible for one of the best examples, his *London Incognita* (2020), which I recommend to anyone interested in the subject. It's a compilation of his short stories about London, its buildings, its underground (literal and metaphorical), and its spirits, good and bad. They include previously published tales and novellas like "Judderman", who is something between a *genius loci* and one of Fritz Leiber's urban paramentals; and "We Pass Under", which concerns the Judderman's female counterpart, the Commare.

Not the F-word

Mackenzie Crook's *The Windvale Sprites* and *The Lost Journals of Benjamin Tooth*

While discussing *Detectorists* and *Worzel Gummidge* with a friend, I described their author/director/starring actor Mackenzie Crook as "some sort of gentle genius as a writer". At that point I didn't know he'd already shown evidence of that "gentle genius" a few years earlier. In 2011, to be precise, he wrote and illustrated a children's book entitled *The Windvale Sprites*. The first I heard of it was when it was mentioned by someone in the *Detectorists* Facebook group, and I immediately hurried to get hold of a copy. It's a sweet read.

Following the famous storm of 1987, young Asa Brown finds the body of a dead being, blown into the garden pond from the nearby moor. At first sight it looks like a dragonfly, but it soon becomes clear that it's something much stranger. A fairy, for want of a better word. Although there *is* a better word: a sprite:

> It had big eyes. Huge black eyes that were all pupil. It was skinny like a stick with extraordinarily long legs that were bent back unnaturally. Its slender arms ended in delicate hands and fingers that tapered to fine points... Asa saw, with amazement,

that sprouting from its shoulder blades were four, slender, transparent wings. An intricate network of veins divided each like a stained-glass window.

Asa buries the body in the nearby Cottingley Woods (a reference to the infamous Victorian case of the Cottingley Fairies photographs). He wonders to start with whether he's the only person who didn't know fairies existed, and if there is some sort of conspiracy to hide the truth from him. But soon he realises that no one else believes in them, or none of his contemporaries, at any rate. An excursion out to the moor results in a fleeting encounter with another fairy, injured in an attack by a hobby.

There was a man, Benjamin Tooth, a local, eighteenth-century "alchemist, inventor, astronomer, astrologer, scientist", who did believe in fairies, or rather sprites (not "the F-word... It is vulgar and unscientific"), and wrote about them in his papers. The papers were thought lost or destroyed, but thanks to a series of fortuitous events, Asa discovers them. Among them is a map of the moor, marking the places frequented by the sprites. Armed with this, he sets out to camp on the moor, with the aim of capturing a specimen. Capturing beings from the faerie realm is rarely a good idea for either the captured or the captor, but Asa Brown is at heart a kindly, nature-loving soul (like Mackenzie Crook himself). When he reads more in Benjamin Tooth's papers, learning how cruelly Tooth treated the sprites, and then discovers that they are in trouble, he knows he has to help. There is a missing, hallowed object they need to reclaim. The climax to the novel could have been truly horrific, but Crook's gentleness and humour turn the initial horror to sadness.

The Windvale Sprites feels as though it comes from a different age, or a different decade anyway - not so much the 2010s as the 1970s, when so many strange books and TV series shaped a British generation. It's a charming, sometimes spooky, sometimes humorous read (e.g. the elderly librarian whose deafness results in her shouting and persistently being shushed by the library's punters); and the slightly primitive but effective illustrations enhance it nicely. Why is *The Windvale Sprites* not more well known? I've sometimes asked that same question in relation to M.R. James's fairy story novel, *The Five Jars* (1922), which Crook's book reminds me of, just a little. Crook's sprites, however, are more consistently effective, while James's are marvellous when they're bad fairies, but pretty terrible when they're good: then they are nothing more than mischievous little public schoolboys (MRJ, of course, was an Eton scholar and later Provost of the College).

Unlike the kind-hearted Asa Brown, Benjamin Tooth was seemingly a very nasty piece of work, thinking nothing of catching, killing and dissecting a multitude of sprites in order to 'study' them and gain world fame and fortune. It's satisfying that his ambitions finally bring him a suitably pathetic comeuppance (and no world fame!), as revealed in *The Windvale Sprites*, but Mackenzie Crook evidently didn't feel he had quite finished with him. In 2013, Crook published a prequel to *The Windvale Sprites*. The parenthesised subtitle of *The Lost Journals of Benjamin Tooth (Scientist, Botanist, GENIUS, age 11)* clearly indicates that even at this early age (starting in 1768), Benjamin Tooth was way too full of himself. Having such a potentially unsympathetic character as the main focus of a book, especially a first-person-narrated book, is always difficult, but Tooth's total confidence in his own importance and superiority is endlessly amusing. Dare I say that it's almost endearing?

The Lost Journal is the lesser, and less genuinely fey, of the two volumes, but there is still plenty of enjoyment to be had, as we learn more about Benjamin's early life, including some of the episodes which were mentioned in passing in *The Windvale Sprites*. How and when did Tooth discover the sprites, for instance? The first inkling of the answer comes in the form of a mysterious 'young' man, Farley Cupstart, whom Benjamin first meets on the moor. Cupstart is seeking the sprites for his own reasons, and there is something in the Tooth family home which he badly wants, enlisting Benjamin's (unwilling) help to find it. This is the first incident that sets Benjamin on the path which turns him into the cruel figure depicted in *The Windvale Sprites*. Others follow, some funny, some strange, some absurd (a brief interlude involving a nifty bit of ghost trapping comes into that last category!). By the time the journal ends (in 1780, the content overlapping with the papers discovered by Asa Brown), Benjamin Tooth has passed from a naturalist's fascination with the sprites, through obsession and eccentricity, onto something much darker (and just possibly out the other side).

One remaining point struck me as I read these two books: that there are echoes of a couple of themes which Mackenzie Crook would return to in *Detectorists*. The first is the sprites' tendency to steal and hoard shiny things, including "coins, some of them gold, dating back to Roman times" - just like the secret Romano-British hoard of the magpies in the third series of *Detectorists*. There is treasure to be found in, or beneath, the countryside. And the second is the image of the derelict cottage. In *The Windvale Sprites*, it belonged to Benjamin Tooth and hides an unpleasant secret in its cellar. I hope Mackenzie Crook's character, Andy, wasn't fated to find something similar in the cellar of Tatterdown Cottage, following his auction purchase in the final episode of series three of *Detectorists*.[1]

Note:

[1] Years later, in the 2022 Christmas Special, it was revealed that Tatterdown Cottage had burned down, so we may never know.

A Welsh Wild Hunt
Claire Fayers' *Storm Hound*

Very early one morning in the summer of 2020, I was lying in bed listening to a repeat of the Arts programme on BBC Radio Wales (Chester is, after all, a border town), and they were discussing the nominees for the English language Tir na n-Og Award. There are three annual Tir na n-Og Awards, the other two being for Welsh language works. The English one is given for a children's book with "an authentic Welsh background". A couple of the nominees sounded quite interesting and I was especially intrigued by one, which, it was revealed at the end of the programme, had won the prize (I think it's £1000 - not to be sniffed at, but this isn't the Booker!). The book was *Storm Hound* by Claire Fayers (Macmillan), and I ordered a copy later that day.

What dog-lover could resist the central premise? Storm (of Odin) is the youngest member of the Wild Hunt of folklore fame, and during his first Hunt he finds to his horror that he is "having a little trouble keeping up". He falls to earth near the Skirrid Mountain (so this is yet another fantasy/supernatural story set in the Black Mountains area of Wales - I'm losing count). Storm discovers that he is now no bigger than a small, black puppy, with some at least of a puppy's instincts. Adopted by twelve-year-old Jesse, who has just moved to Abergavenny with her father and younger brother, there is much humour in his attempts to merge his Wild Hunt urges with his puppy status. For instance, he is shocked to find that, when he is taken to Obedience Classes, it's the dogs who are expected to learn obedience, not the humans.

But two groups of people are searching for him. There are three professors (the last remnants of the Invisible College), who want to kill and dismember him for his magic: apparently every part of a Wild Hunt hound has some particular magic power. And there is a middle-aged woman with a young boy of Jesse's age, a boy who is actually a shape-shifted hare. The motives of the latter pair are less obvious, although the fact that the woman is called Ceridwen and the lad Morfran, two names from Welsh legend, gives a hint that there is something mythic going on. Everything reaches a climax on Skirrid Mountain when the Wild Hunt returns. Storm has a choice to make...

The book *Storm Hound* most reminds me of is Barbara Sleigh's *Carbonel*, about the young girl Rosemary and her encounters with the secret world of the cats.[1] A contributory factor to this feeling is undoubtedly that one of the best characters in *Storm Hound* is the next-door cat, the elderly and curmudgeonly Nutmeg:

> *Don't bother me, stormhound. I've watched the Wild Hunt pass by in the dead of night. It doesn't impress me.*
>
> Storm's bottom hit the grass in surprise. *Are you sure we're talking about the same Wild Hunt? Odin's Hunt. The Hunt of Arawn. Hounds and horses from the Otherworld riding through storm clouds?*
>
> The cat stared at him through narrowed eyes. *I am a cat - descended from gods. I don't need to run in a pack and snap at lightning to feel important.*

This is also, for me, reminiscent of some of the grumpier of M.R. James's cats in his fairy novel *The Five Jars* and his letters to the McBrydes and Sibyl Cropper.[2]

I think *Storm Hound* is aimed at roughly the same age group as *Carbonel* - maybe eight to eleven - but as is usual with the best of such books, it can be enjoyed by readers of any age. Reviews on the Net seem to give it uniformly five or at worst four stars. I mostly agree, except for two reservations. It loses half a star because I didn't feel it had a strong sense of place. And it loses another half star because it's a book with 'a message'. Personally I prefer my children's fiction free from messages (as with Mackenzie Crook's two novels and, for that matter, *Carbonel*). In *Storm Hound*, the message is that the most important thing is 'home': Storm learns it in the end, and Jesse learns that she still has a home (or homes) despite the fact that her parents have split up. It's a little heavy-handed, to be honest. But to counter that (which might have soured the conclusion of the book for me), there is a good, unashamed, tear-jerker of an ending (a happy one) for a lesser canine character who had featured in one of the early scenes.

Notes:

[1] I wrote about Barbara Sleigh's *Carbonel* and *Kingdom of Carbonel* (1955/1960) in *The Black Pilgrimage* Volume 1 ("Early Reading: Dogs, Cats and Hobby Horses"), saying: "I loved [them] for their portrayal of a whole separate magical world (of cats) within our world".

[2] The former in *Letters to a Friend* (1956); the latter in "Letters to a Child", *Cornhill Magazine 160* (Nov 1903), reprinted in *Ghosts & Scholars 3* (1981) and on the *G&S* website.

The Mad World of Lionel Fanthorpe and Noel Boston

Shane P.D. Agnew's *John Spencer & Co (Badger Books) - Illustrated Bibliography*

In 2020, following a mention on the Vault of Evil message board, I bought myself a copy of *John Spencer & Co (Badger Books) - Illustrated Bibliography: Volume 1: Comics, Science Fiction and Supernatural,* self-published by Shane P.D. Agnew. Badger Books were the publishers of the periodical *Supernatural Stories* (1954-1967, 109 issues), famous for including literally hundreds of stories by the great Lionel Fanthorpe, many under various pseudonyms. Most, though not all, of Fanthorpe's pseudonyms were made up from letters contained in his full name (Robert Lionel Fanthorpe), such as Pel Torro, Bron Fane, Peter O'Flinn, Trebor Thorpe and, my favourite, Oben Lerteth (I think he must have been getting desperate for variations by then!). So at the time, readers might have been confused by the inclusion of ten stories by Noel Bartram or Bertram, the letters of which can be made from Fanthorpe's name with the exception of the final 'm'. If they thought that Bartram/Bertram was yet another pseudonym they would have been correct, except that the man behind the penname wasn't Fanthorpe but his friend Noel Boston. (I don't know whether it still does, but at one time the Fanthorpe Wikipedia entry included Noel Bertram among Lionel's pseudonyms, and that mistake has, of course, been copied by other sites.) Now things will have become clearer to those of you with a passing acquaintance with the James Gang list of Jamesian authors.

"Noel Boston: Master Antiquarian" was the title of an article by Mike Ashley in *Ghosts & Scholars 5* (1983). In it Mike tells how Boston (1910-1966) became friends with the Fanthorpes while he was vicar of Dereham in Norfolk. In one of Lionel's later non-fiction works it's claimed that Boston told him he had seen the Holy Grail. Was he having him on? Perhaps not, as Boston was a member of a number of obscure societies and orders. He also wrote several non-fiction books, especially reflecting his interest in history, antique guns and music, such as *The Musical History of Norwich Cathedral* and *Church and Chamber Barrel-Organs*. Four of the ten Boston tales in *Supernatural Stories* first appeared in his *Yesterday Knocks*, published locally in 1953 and soon to become "all but unobtainable". None of the ten are, as Mike notes, exactly Jamesian, for: "Although they follow a Jamesian motif by way of an antiquarian's investigations, they break one of James's fundamental creeds in that the ghosts are not malevolent". Several have an ecclesiastical setting, such as "The Brass Tombstone" ("basically a non-supernatural detective story, involving the identifying of the original church from which some brasses... had been taken") and "Right Through My Hair" ("the phantom body of a suicide still hang(s) in the Triforium of Losingham Cathedral"). *Yesterday Knocks* was also the title of a 2003 volume from Ash-Tree Press, which reprinted all eleven of Boston's tales in one place for the first time (the eleventh was in the original *Yesterday Knocks* but not in *Supernatural Stories*). I imagine this volume is almost as hard to find as the 1953 book, although there is a Kindle edition.

For several years I had a genuine phobia about disembodied hands (films like *The Beast with Five Fingers* and *Dr Terror's House of Horrors* were no-go areas for me). I can date this quite specifically to the time, presumably in or soon after 1961, when my cousin Bob lent me a copy of *Supernatural Stories 51*, which was published in that year. The lead story in the issue was "The Grip of Fear" by a pseudonymless Fanthorpe, and it was about a disembodied hand. I understand that Fanthorpe was sometimes given the front-cover illustration and expected to write a story around it. Here, I don't think he quite succeeded as the magazine's cover depicts a woman being menaced (a frequent subject of these covers!) by a gigantic hand. Somehow a gigantic hand isn't anything like as scary as a normal-sized one. It's possible that my memory is at fault (I was only ten in 1961) and there *was* an enormous hand in the tale, but I only remember a skittering human-sized one. Issue 51 is deeply significant to me for another reason: it contains Noel Boston's "The Brass Tombstone" (aka "P Aia Johns Blak"), which was my very first encounter with an antiquarian weird tale. The memory stuck with me until, a few years later, I was introduced to the works of M.R. James and thought, "hello, I've read something like this before".

John Spencer & Co (Badger Books) - Illustrated Bibliography: Volume 1: Comics, Science Fiction and Supernatural has now provided me with everything I needed to know (aside from the texts of the actual tales) about that edition of *Supernatural Stories.* Every issue of the magazine, and the other genre periodicals and novels published by John Spencer, has an entry, with a list of contents, a note of the cover artist, and a reproduction of the cover. The reproductions are small (approx 2" by 1.5") but very well printed and in full colour; tag-lines and subtitles can be easily read with a magnifying glass. The covers are a fascinating study in their own right. So are the story titles: probably in most cases these titles are better than the actual stories, but who wouldn't want to read "The Voice in the Wall", "The Nine Green Men",

"The Thing from Boulter's Cavern", "The Carnival Horror", "The Eldritch Chair" and "The Midnight Museum", to name but a few of Fanthorpe's 381 (yes 381!) contributions. Who for that matter, wouldn't want to know what "The Drud" is? I wondered if it was a typo for "Druid" but seemingly not, as the word appears on the cover. Presumably it's the bat-lady depicted there, with the tagline, "The victim was so obviously trapped. Why did he smile?" We might well ask!

In addition to the main part of Shane Agnew's book, there are various indexes and spreadsheets including two lists of actual authors' names and pseudonyms with numbers of stories for each year; an alphabetical index of story titles; and another of titles listed alphabetically by author. Once one can get over the fact that the authors are ordered under first names (silly!), and that titles beginning "The" all appear under "T" (actually not as awkward as it sounds; you just have to think of them as an index *within* an index), these are all invaluable. There is also a short but informative introduction on the history of John Spencer and Badger Books. I wish all bibliographical reference works were as thorough, complete and largely typo-free as this. I didn't get the planned second and third volumes, which were going to deal with John Spencer's crime, spy, westerns, romance and war publications, but I'm glad I bought this first one. Even for those not wanting to use it for reference, it's just a great book to browse and to look at (but maybe not always admire!) the pictures.

Windhollow Faire
Elizabeth Hand's *Wylding Hall*

After reading an enthusiastic review by Katherine Haynes in the summer 2022 *A Ghostly Company Newsletter*, I decided to buy a copy of Elizabeth Hand's *Wylding Hall*, a gorgeously presented book from PS Publishing (2015). I enjoyed it very much, although there are some slightly worrying inconsistencies and errors, and it does sometimes have a sort of secondhand feel to it, as though the writer had got all her information from books rather than succeeding in getting inside the heads of the people at the time that the novel is set (i.e. early 1970s, during the acid folk wave). In her "Author's Note", she says that one of her main sources of information was Rob Young's *Electric Eden: Unearthing Britain's Visionary Music*. That's a book I love, but it has been criticised for its superficiality and inaccuracies (I'd also criticise it for the weakness of its binding - my copy is falling apart).

The story revolves around a folk rock group, Windhollow Faire, gathered together by their manager in a country house, Wylding Hall, after the tragic death of one of their members. It's told bit by bit by each surviving member and others, giving their version of events to an American documentary filmmaker. A room filled with dead, beakless birds is discovered and this is only the beginning of the strangeness. One of the group, Julian Blake, is prone to walking alone in the wren-haunted woods, despite warnings from the locals. He writes a song cum spell and when he performs the final version at the village pub, it appears to invoke a mysterious pale girl who he takes to his room. That night they both disappear, never to be seen again (his vanishing isn't a spoiler - it's mentioned right from the start). Apart from these strange events, which develop in a suspenseful and atmospheric way, I wonder if readers have realised just how much of the story is based on fact. Elizabeth Hand adds in her "Author's Note" that the novel is "inspired in part by numerous real-life musicians and song-writers" but that the members of the group, Windhollow Faire, are all fictional. Yes and no! Mostly fictional, yes (I'm not questioning the originality of her plot), but their inspiration is clear.

Windhollow Faire is Fairport Convention. Reviewers have noted this connection, and Elizabeth Hand has said as much herself in interviews, but I haven't seen a review which has looked into just how close the connection is. There may well be some reviews that do, in which case nothing here will be new, but anyway these are my thoughts. My husband Darroll was a true Sandy Denny obsessive and had all her records both with and after Fairport, the albums where she guested on tracks (e.g. Led Zeppelin's "The Battle of Evermore"), radio sessions, the two biographies (one of which was never officially published, I think due to legal wrangles with her family), and a book that attempted to solve such mysteries as the identity of the North Star Grassman (subject of my favourite Sandy solo song). So I became kind of embedded in the world of Fairport and maybe this gives me a reasonably individual point of view.

The line-up of Windhollow Faire includes Lesley Stansall, the hard-drinking singer with the amazing voice, brought into the band to replace the previous singer who was told she no longer fitted into where they were going with their music. Lesley is Sandy Denny, hard-drinking until the end, an incredible voice, and brought into Fairport to replace Judy Dyble in exactly those same circumstances (Fairport's Richard Thompson writes: "Judy... did not have the vocal strength to sing over a band that was becoming more muscular"). Judy Dyble lived to sing another day, but Windhollow's ex-singer Arianna died soon after being given the news that "the rest of the band wanted to head in a different direction, musically", falling or jumping from the window of Julian's flat.

The other members of Windhollow Faire are more fictional and don't have quite such direct links with Fairport.

Julian's "whispery" voice is based more on Nick Drake than on Richard Thompson's devastatingly powerful baritone, but Will Fogarty's visits to the library of Cecil Sharp House must be inspired by Fairport's Ashley Hutchings who "started frequenting the archives at Cecil Sharp House and researching different versions of the great ballads" (sleeve notes to the CD of *Liege & Lief*). Windhollow's producer/manager, Tom Haring, is based loosely on famed producer/manager Joe Boyd (whose stable also included Nick Drake). Julian's fascination with "magick with a K, astrology... Palmistry... Casting Spells" is an echo of Fairport fiddler Dave (Swarb) Swarbrick's interest in "all that sort of stuff...". According to Richard Thompson, "The strange carving of a doll-like effigy on the back cover of the *Liege and Lief* album... always gave me the creeps. (It) belonged to [Swarb], and was probably used for magical purposes at some point". It is indeed an odd, primitive-looking thing. In *Electric Eden*, Ashley Hutchings is quoted as saying that it was "found by Swarbrick under a pile of leaves in a churchyard".

After the death of Arianna, Tom Haring decided that Windhollow Faire needed to re-group (as it were!) and the ideal way to do this would be to rent an old house in the country, Wylding Hall, where they would stay for the summer. Wylding Hall (in Hampshire) is Farley Chamberlayne (again, Hampshire). Joe Boyd likewise rented Farley Chamberlayne in 1969, following a tragic death in Fairport. In their case, however, it wasn't the female singer but their drummer, Martin Lamble, killed when the band's van was involved in a motorway crash (Richard Thompson's girlfriend also died). What came out of Fairport's stay at Farley Chamberlayne was the magical *Liege & Lief*, their best album (in my and most people's opinion), and one which defined and pointed the way for the folk rock of the time. A few years ago it was voted the best-ever folk album. What came out from Wylding Hall was an eponymous album which "topped out at number seven" in a millennium survey of best albums of all time (ahead of Oasis - not difficult, in my opinion!).

My favourite track on *Liege & Lief* is "Tam Lin", the Scottish folk ballad based on the legend of a fairy kidnapping and the rescue of the hapless victim from the thrall of the Queen of the Fairies. But there is no rescue for Julian Blake. I said above that *apart from* the supernatural events at Wylding Hall, a lot of the novel is quite close to the reality of Fairport. I'm not even sure that that *apart from* is entirely true. Although there were no mysterious disappearances of band members at Farley Chamberlayne, there were plenty of weird goings-on, which don't seem entirely divorced from those at

Wylding Hall. Swarb's esoteric interests extended to sessions with a Ouija board and on one occasion, as Richard Thompson writes: "we summoned the Fairy Queen from the song, and she did not seem to be a happy camper. The energy in the room was utterly strange and superhumanly violent".[1] Ashley Hutchings in *Electric Eden* says: "There was a special feeling in the house... also a lot of hidden magic and weirdness on that album". Compare that with the "very, very weird vibe" at Wylding Hall, and Julian's wish for "the album itself to be a kind of spell".

Wylding Hall is not exactly a ghost or horror story, although it has its horrific scenes, one of them a bit Jamesian ("And now I could hear another sound - a kind of slithering, like something being slowly dragged up the steps. Or something dragging itself"). It is a tale of the dangers of becoming involved with the world of faerie. Who or what was that mysterious pale girl who appeared on the cover of the *Wylding Hall* album but wasn't seen by anyone at the time the photograph was taken? Other snaps taken in quick succession on the day show her first appearing at the back by the woods, then coming closer and closer to Julian (rather in the way of Gawdy in M.R. James's "The Mezzotint"). In the closest, she is frankly pretty terrifying, with one surprising detail I found unexpectedly disturbing. If that's what fairies look like, I don't want to meet one! Mistaken early on for a ghost by a visiting journalist, the girl only becomes manifest to the rest of them after the completion of Julian's invocation in the village pub a week *after* the day of the photographs (it's not clear when Julian himself had seen her for the first time).

What is the significance of the long barrow in the nearby woods, which is much bigger and higher than its physical form appears to be? Barrows, of course, are often reputed to be entrances to the land of faerie. What might be discovered if the barrow were excavated? Julian was fascinated by space and time; and time is famously distorted in faerie. Years later, a Neolithic passage grave is found under the oldest part of Wylding Hall during renovations, and among the artifacts in it is Julian's wristwatch. There is almost an echo here of Arthur Machen's identification of races of ancient humans with fairies. Then we have the apparently relatively recent local survival of the Boxing Day custom of Hunting the Wren (probably inspired by one of the inclusions on the *Liege & Lief* sleeve). How does that fit in with the bird-haunting of Wylding Hall, and what does a local "geezer" at the pub mean when he says, "That's what you get hunting birds out of season"? I'm not sure. But remember that legend has it the tiny wren is a fairy bird (the specific legend that it is an evil fairy woman may have been invented for the novel - I'd never heard of it before).

PS Publishing have shown a nice attention to detail with the moody dust-jacket illustration for *Wylding Hall*. By David Gentry, it is based around a photograph of a house that looks very like Farley Chamberlayne. I'm not saying I think it *is* Farley Chamberlayne, but it's definitely a house of a similar type. In a good way, reality and fantasy have become almost indistinguishable.

Note:

[1] All of the Richard Thompson quotes here are taken from his 2021 autobiography, *Beeswing: Fairport, Folk Rock and Finding My Voice 1967-1975*. I don't know whether Fairport's Ouija board summoning of the Fairy Queen is recorded elsewhere previously (it's not in *Electric Eden*). If not, it can't have been an inspiration for *Wylding Hall* as that was first published six years earlier, but it's a spooky coincidence.

An Ineffably Strange Place
Mark Valentine's *Herald of the Hidden*
and *Seventeen Stories*

Fans of Mark Valentine's fictional writings had a good year in 2013. First, Brian Showers' Swan River Press published his *Selected Stories*, then Tartarus Press released *Herald of the Hidden & Other Stories*. Finally, in December, Swan River produced *Seventeen Stories*.

Among current weird and supernatural fiction authors, Mark Valentine has established a position as one of the most original and interesting. He rarely sets out to horrify, but rather to awe and mystify, even to inspire; an aim he usually succeeds in achieving. He is most known, perhaps, for writing (with John Howard) the sequence of tales featuring The Connoisseur, "aesthetical detective extraordinaire". But before The Connoisseur, there was Ralph Tyler, occult detective; an ostensibly ordinary sort of chap, living in a dowdy flat, without private means or particular psychic abilities, and based in Northamptonshire ("that still sometimes secretly lovely shire"), where Mark was brought up. His friend, who accompanies Tyler "on his researches into the stranger, darker incidents of provincial existence", narrates these tales. The Ralph Tyler stories appeared in various small press magazines in the '80s, particularly *Dark Dreams*, edited by

Jeff Dempsey and David Cowperthwaite. The first of these tales, "The Grave of Anir", was written in 1983 when Mark was twenty-four years old, and published in 1984 in *Dark Dreams 1*; the last (until the new ones in this book) around 1995. Jeff and David's Crimson Altar Press was also the publisher of a small booklet of the tales, *14 Bellchamber Tower*, in 1987. In *Herald of the Hidden and Other Stories*, Tartarus Press has collected together all ten Ralph Tyler tales, seven of them reprints and three previously unpublished (of which two are newly written). The book also contains six mostly early stories not in the Tyler series.

In Mark's introduction, he enthuses nostalgically and infectiously about those '80s small press journals: "however quaint these publications may now look, they are coated with a magic glamour for me... The smell of the ink, the texture of the paper, bring back to me the camaraderie and the excitement of those early days". I hope no one here harbours the belief that the good small press magazines back then had lower standards than the professional presses of the time.

Although M.R. James is not a stated influence on Ralph Tyler's adventures (Arthur Machen, Algernon Blackwood and William Hope Hodgson are), there are a few stories with distinct Jamesian aspects. In "St Michael & All Angels", for instance, the restoration of a church is disrupted by a winged figure - not one of the angels, but some sort of "giant bat" of truly terrible visage, which is the unearthly product of a twelfth-century feud. An archaeologist disappears while searching for "The Grave of Anir", a gigantic son of King Arthur. Legend has it that, just as the Rollright Stones can't be counted correctly, so Anir's grave can't be measured, varying from nine to fifteen feet long.

"The Folly" is haunted by the spirits of creatures who suffered at the hands of the hunting and shooting fraternity (this is better polemic than H.R. Wakefield's attempts at the theme). The obscure clue to the identity of the imperious white lady who manifests on "Madberry Hill' is in the title. "The Ash Track" is imprinted with the aftermath of a tragic death, and another (more intriguingly) haunted road is the location of "The Hermit's House". Once again, the clues are in the story's title, but so well hidden that I had no idea what was to come. In "The Heritage of Fire", an old house and its Japanese ornamental garden are being restored as a 'Heritage Hotel' (with all the horrors that implies), but something elemental in the garden doesn't like it. A lesser tale is "William Sorrell Requests...", which appears to feature summonings from beyond the grave, but the explanation is less sinister (if no less odd).

"The Almanac", one of the new Ralph Tyler stories, concerns an obsessive almanac maker and a house troubled by a large "restless blank sheet" of his paper, with "glimpses of a mouth and of eyes glistening". Is this his spirit (a less original writer would leave it at that) or something much more abstract? We must draw our own conclusions. The second of the two new Tyler tales is "Herald of the Hidden" (though, with the necessary name change, it could just as easily be in the Connoisseur sequence). This is Mark on absolutely top form, conjuring up the essence of the hidden matter of England. In a beautifully evoked Northamptonshire forest setting, strange lights are seen and UFOs are suspected, but the explanation is nothing so prosaic, combining near-cosmic strangeness with the mysteries of heraldry in a way which only Mark would think of.

The other, non-Tyler stories are varied, a couple of them quite slight. "The Guardians of the Guest Room" is a minor and not very Valentinian tale of an unpleasant man's comeuppance from some unexpected furnishings; while I'm afraid the cricketing setting and traditional ghost of "Twilight at Little Brydon Cricket Club" were always going to be off-putting for me. "Go to the West", on the other hand, is a short but effective fable dealing with the perils of dabbling too deeply into alchemical secrets - and of mishearing the title phrase! The ending is terrifying. "Tree Worship" I love for its quintessential paganism, in a satisfying account of the clash between the spirit of the woodland (and of the pagan year) and the residents of an 'executive estate'. The protagonist of "Woken by Candlelight" is not so much woken physically as spiritually by a chance purchase in an antiques shop: a cliché of a plot transformed into something that bit deeper. And the more recent "Their Special Glee" finishes off the volume on a high note: it's very probable that a village's most disturbing resident is not the old lady who makes it her business to look out for wickedness, and not the imps which are the village's mascots, but someone else entirely…

Mark Valentine would be the first to agree that his early stories are less sophisticated than his later creations, but he's right when he says in his introduction that they "have a certain gusto, almost a fierceness. There's a real sense of a young author trying to put a lot of intensity into their work". The tales are polished, original, quite funny at times, and already have some of the magic. But everything which is good about them got better and better over the ensuing years, as can be seen in the masterly "Herald of the Hidden".

The *Seventeen Stories* in the eponymous Swan River collection (sixteen reprints, most of them hard to find, and one new tale) are divided into five sections, all with beguiling titles: "Three Singular Detectives", "Four Curious Books", "Three Strange Places", "Three Odd Societies" and "Four Haunted Figures". The reader seeking something in the Jamesian line will probably zero in on the "Four Curious Books", and, sure enough, one of these is "An Incomplete Apocalypse" (from Tartarus Press's anthology *Dark World: Ghost Stories*), in which a medieval manuscript is found in a country house in Northamptonshire. The illuminations in this Draycott Apocalypse are extraordinarily "strongly imagined" except for a figure with a missing face, opposing the Old Serpent of Revelation. The dragon has a faint air of melancholy and disappointment about it, but this might not always be the case! "The Last Post" concerns an edition of William Fryer Harvey's *The Beast with Five Fingers* and the dangers of misreading(?) a bookseller's catalogue. If Harvey's story is Jamesian then "The Last Post" is too. I suspect there are also autobiographical aspects to it: I'm sure Mark and I aren't the only people who, when listening out for the post, hear the familiar "rattle of [the] letterbox and the scuffle on the doormat" only to find nothing there.

The other two "Curious Books" are different. "The 1909 Proserpine Prize" is an annual prize for the book "that most skilfully went into the dark and emerged with something of the light". The nominees for 1909 include works by Algernon Blackwood, Bram Stoker, M.P. Shiel, Marjorie Bowen and William Hope Hodgson, but it's another volume that has certain ways of influencing proceedings. In "The Seer of Trieste", a scholar visits that city in search of lost writings by Richard (*Arabian Nights*) Burton, but finds that the "spirit of Trieste" has a reality which has influenced other authors too.

Jamesians might next choose to try either the "Three Strange Places" or "Four Haunted Figures" sections. Half of the latter could well be familiar, for "Yogh" comes from *G&S Newsletter 23* and "Fire Companions" (a sequel to MRJ's "Two Doctors") is from the first *Ghosts & Scholars Book of Shadows*. "The Antioch Imperial" has a fine antiquarian setting - an ancient church sited possibly where Christianity first came to Britain. But the latest visitor isn't Joseph of Arimathea... The theme of this succinct tale is a favourite of mine but it would spoil it if I went into more detail. By contrast, "You Walk the Pages" may be the closest Mark has ever got to modern urban horror.

The first of the "Three Strange Places" is the Isle of Axholme, just west of Scunthorpe in Lincolnshire. In "The Axholme Toll" - possibly the best story in the book - this area (no longer an actual island) is evoked in all its magical oddness. What is behind its particular air of "deep-buried differentness"? Mark builds up the atmosphere superbly with historical and folkloric background, all of which is authentic, and the final possible explanation doesn't disappoint. Another inland 'Isle', that of Ely in the Fens, is the setting for the terrifying "The Fall of the King of Babylon". Mark doesn't often do horror, let alone were-beasts, and for my peace of mind I'm glad of it! Since I have a phobia of eels, this is a tale, superb though it is, that I shan't be rereading. After these, the third story in this section was almost bound to be a let-down, and "The Other Salt", set in marshland on the Atlantic coast of France, is certainly slighter, but its final revelation is nightmarish.

The tales in "Three Singular Detectives" are all further episodes in the lives of the creations of earlier authors, and all are set in the late nineteenth or early twentieth century. In "The Adventure of the Green Skull", Sherlock Holmes has another case; in "Prince Zaleski's Secret", M.P. Shiel's eponymous character foils a plot (with a cameo from a thinly-disguised Aleister Crowley); and in "The Return of Kala Persad" (the one new story in the book, inspired by Headon Hall's *The Divinations of Kala Persad and Other Stories*, 1895), a sinister dream of snakes turns out to be something unexpectedly wondrous.

Finally, there are the "Three Odd Societies". "The Tontine

of Thirteen" is Mark's individual take on the 'Everlasting Club' theme; while a lost musical composition by an obscure composer is performed "Without Instruments" to an audience of his admirers. "Morpheus House" is a gorgeous invention, set up in the Edwardian era "for the purpose of collecting and cross-referencing dreams". Correspondents send in reports of their latest ("a cockatrice,[1] a stilt-walker... a stuffed humming bird that spoke... an angel from Lemuria"), which are duly filed away in oak drawers. But is this the right way to treat dreams?

The world is an ineffably strange place, filled with wonder and hidden or lost things. So are Mark Valentine's stories. There's scarcely a weak one in this book and some are Mark on top form, which is very good indeed ("The Axholme Toll" and "Morpheus House" especially). Swan River Press's production and design values are excellent, as usual, offering a dust-jacket design and a different hidden picture on the book's covers. In this case the dust-jacket, with Egyptian-looking door-knocker, masks an atmospherically decaying wall with broken plaster exposing some old brickwork. One feels that just beyond the edge of the cover is a door. A door leading who knows where?

Note:

[1] In 2017, Mark returned to the subject of cockatrices in one of his finest stories: "As Blank as the Days Yet to Be" (which I reprinted in *The Ghosts & Scholars Book of Mazes*).

A Sense of an Ancient Longing
Tom Cox's *Villager* and Zoe Gilbert's *Mischief Acts*

> *Myth is an opportunist. It's there waiting for us, and when we need it most, someone will finally notice it.*
> --- from the future 'lecture' at the end of *Mischief Acts*

Two new novels I read in 2022 have several things in common: they are *Villager* by Tom Cox (Unbound) and *Mischief Acts* by Zoe Gilbert (Bloomsbury). Both are episodic, and sections of them could be taken out and considered as separate short stories, but in both one character's influence looms over the events in each section. In *Villager* it's a fictional psych folk singer from the 1970s called RJ McKendree, and in *Mischief Acts* it's Herne the Hunter and his Wild Hunt. Both books revolve around their settings, *Villager* so much so that parts of it (among my favourite parts, in fact) are narrated by the *genius loci* of the landscape itself, a not-quite-real Dartmoor (that "just happens to be in the same place on the map"). In *Mischief Acts* it's the old Great North Wood of south London. And both make important points about environmental destruction, all the better for their restraint and integration into the plot. Both novels also range through time from centuries ago to years in the future (*Mischief Acts* takes it chronologically, *Villager* doesn't).

There is a old folk song, "Little Meg", of which RJ McKendree wrote a version, and which appears to be some sort of inherited memory of an ancient girl buried ritually out on the moor thousands of years ago. To balance the darker, sadder bits in *Villager*, there's plenty of humour, and the spirit of "Meg" features in one of the funniest sections: on a local Message Board, the participation of "Megan Beaker" causes much confusion. I don't think the others on the Board ever realise exactly who and how old she is, despite the fact that the clues are there. Of "old broadsides and ballads", Megan comments "The lyrics are mostly wrong". And at one point, when they are discussing the origin of the place-name Totnes, supposedly named after someone called Totta, Megan's comment is "I know who Totta was. I met her and she was a supercilious prick".

Those who have read Tom Cox's *21st-Century Yokel* will know that he is an M.R. James fan. But as with his earlier collection of supernatural short stories, *Help the Witch*, there is nothing Jamesian as such in *Villager*, and not really any ghosts unless you count Megan Beaker on the Message Board. And yet it is haunted. Some of the characters sense echoes of past residents: "sometimes it felt like voices were speaking to him through the stone. A woman. He said she watched him sometimes". And perhaps there are physical residues too: dog hair , a doll in the wall, a credit card lost on the moor...

I'm at a loss to know what else to say about *Villager*: I love it too much to put into words (or more words than these!). After finishing it I went straight back into a second read (and a third since then): that doesn't often happen to me. Tom Cox had been hoping and intending to write a novel - *this* novel - for many years. It's his first. It won't be his last, although it'll be hard for him to improve on *Villager*.

As for Zoe Gilbert's *Mischief Acts*, I liked this one a lot too, and I've read some sections of it more than once. At times it seems a little pretentious (Tom Cox is *never* pretentious), particularly in the last section, "2073: Horn Dance", which would have been improved by not being arranged and spaced oddly for no obvious reason. But some of the separate poems and 'stories' are excellent, especially "1877: Nullius in Verba", in which the central character, the very unsympathetic Walter Ship, watches (and tries but fails to photograph) a tiny fairy harlequinade in the woods (folklorists link Harlequin via Herlequin with Herne). Or *is* it? Is it instead, as the members of the scientific society he hopes to impress conclude, an example of Charles Bonnet Syndrome, where people, usually ill people or those losing their sight, see tiny figures in odd costumes (Ship had recently suffered a head injury)? Zoe Gilbert seems to expect the reader to accept that explanation, and yet... and yet... What is Charles Bonnet Syndrome anyway? (I first read about it in *Fortean Times*.) Just because it has a name and a neurological diagnosis, it doesn't mean we know exactly what it is. Could they really have been fairies after all?

And what of the other figures Walter Ship sees? The "scruffy black terrier", which he notices several times in the house and thinks must belong to the maid, doesn't seem to exist for anyone other than him. There are echoes here of H.F. (Gerald) Heard's "leprous black fox" in his 1950 novel *The Black Fox*, not to mention the cat ("there *is* no kitchen cat"!) in "The Stalls of Barchester Cathedral", the MRJ story that undoubtedly inspired Heard's underrated book. In both of these, the figures are manifestations of the guilt felt for a murderous act, and I wonder if the same is true of *Mischief Acts*. Did Walter Ship's friend really just *fall* from a hot air balloon?

Mischief Acts ends with a 'lecture' from the future, "The Birth of Myth", which neatly draws together all the threads of the various sections, and incidentally cites MRJ's translation of Walter Map's *De Nugis Curialium* in a footnote on the Wild Hunt and King Herla (a "singularly silly story"). It all comes back to MRJ in the end.

I don't normally bother to read back-cover blurbs, but I did notice one on *Villager* because it's another link between Tom Cox and Zoe Gilbert. Gilbert provides a quote which ends with a great line: "*Villager* left me with a sense of an ancient longing that is hard to shake off". So right. I've felt that sense of longing - even of need - for some time. I wish I knew how to deal with it.

GHOSTS & SCHOLARS COLUMNS
LADY WARDROP'S NOTES

Lady Wardrop's Notes 1

Robert Macfarlane's *Ness* and Lois Austen-Leigh's *The Incredible Crime: A Cambridge Mystery*

In 2019, Penguin published *Ness* by Robert Macfarlane (text) and Stanley Donwood (illustrations), described by the publisher as "Part-novella, part-prose-poem, part-mystery play". The Ness in question is Orford (near M.R. James's Aldeburgh, Suffolk), as is indicated by this quote from the book: "Listen to the silence of the merman who *would not talk, e'en when tortured & hung up by his feete*". MRJ mentions this particular legend in his *Suffolk and Norfolk* (p.102): "A merman was caught at Orford in the thirteenth century, and kept for some time: he could not be induced to take an interest in the services of the church, nor indeed to speak; eventually he escaped. The authority is Ralph of Coggeshall".

Here is part of the official description of *Ness* on the Penguin website:

> Somewhere on a salt-and-shingle island, inside a ruined concrete structure known as The Green Chapel, a figure called The Armourer is leading a ritual with terrible intent.
>
> But something is coming to stop him.

Five more-than-human forms are traversing land, sea and time towards The Green Chapel, moving to the point where they will converge and become Ness. Ness has lichen skin and willow-bones. Ness is made of tidal drift, green moss and deep time. Ness has hagstones for eyes and speaks only in birds. And Ness has come to take this island back.

What happens when land comes to life? What would it take for land to need to come to life?

The five "figures" are *"it, he, she, they, as"*. "It" is formed of "drift" ("it has cuttlefish nails and sea-poppy horns, it breathes in rain & it breathes out rust"). "He" is formed of trees and birds ("his bones are willow & he sings in birds… His head is a raven's, his eyes are wrens' nests"). "She" is formed of fungus and lichen ("She is a rock-breaker, a tree-speaker, a place-shaper, a world-maker"). "They" are formed of stones ("their eyes are hagstones & their words are shingle"). And "As" "…exists only as likeness, moves as mist & also as metal… is the strongest & strangest & youngest and oldest of all the five".

Between the sections describing these figures as they approach the Ness, there are scenes set in "The Green Chapel", where "The Armourer" and his assistants ("The Engineer", "The Physicist", "The Ornithologist", "The Bryologist") explain and recite what they are planning to do. What this is, is not entirely clear, but it's definitely not going to be good: "In the Green Chapel / we simulate all that our / bombs will face when the end times come. / We seek to maximize injuries incompatible with life". And accompanying these sections are the atmospheric, scene-setting (mainly landscape), full-page illustrations of Stanley Donwood.

The Green Chapel is a real place, as Robert Macfarlane explained in an interview conducted by Adam Scovell on the *Granta* website. The Ness, he says, is: "an off-shore desert where British munitions and ballistics, including nuclear weapons, were tested through much of the twentieth century. A place whose past is still shrouded by the Official Secrets Act". And of the Green Chapel itself: "one of the laboratories where the nuclear weapons were stress-tested had cruciform wall-markings in its sunken test-space... Since the abandonment of the site, moss, lichen, bracken and elder have slowly recolonised and reclaimed this chapel, where once the physics of death were worshipped".

Ness is a small book, under a hundred pages, and requires careful, slow reading; almost every line is filled with imagery (not normally the sort of thing I enjoy). And yet it's not in any way a difficult read and there *is* a plot. I got slight echoes of Robert Holdstock's *Mythago Wood* books (especially the third one, *The Hollowing*, with its green cathedral), David Rudkin's *Artemis 81*, and John Wyndham-esque apocalyptic science fiction. But these are only slight echoes. *Ness* is *sui generis*, and it's also impossible to slot into a genre - is it myth or folklore for a modern age; is it supernatural fiction or SF? It's all and none of those.

Robert Macfarlane is an M.R. James fan. In his 2015 *Guardian* article "The Eeriness of the English Countryside", he wrote: "James stays with us [because of] his understanding of landscape - and especially the English landscape - as constituted by uncanny forces, part-buried sufferings and contested ownerships". This could equally well apply to Macfarlane himself. *Ness* is a remarkable creation.

Changing the subject completely, I am second to none in my admiration for the British Library's Crime Classics paperback series, which reprints crime thrillers by mostly long-forgotten authors. Probably my favourites of all their titles are the three by Alan Melville (whom I remember on TV in the '50s and '60s as a regular presenter and contributor to panel shows). The books are *Weekend at Thrackley*, *Death of Anton* and *Quick Curtain*. These are a near-perfect combination of crime thriller/whodunnit and P.G. Wodehouse-style humour (*Quick Curtain* cheekily has no fewer than four plot twists in the final chapter, and I only guessed one of them in advance). But not all of the British Library series is up to this standard, and there are a few books that I've had to give up on. For instance...

In 2017 the BL re-issued Lois Austen-Leigh's *The Incredible Crime: A Cambridge Mystery*, apparently described as "the very essence of mystery" on its first appearance in 1931. The publicity for the new edition emphasised the saleable detail that Ms Austen-Leigh (1883-1968) was Jane Austen's great-great niece. But, more to the point of this column, she and her family were also long-time friends of M.R. James. Ms Austen-Leigh's uncle, Augustus Austen-Leigh, immediately preceded MRJ as Provost of King's College, Cambridge, dying in 1905. *The Incredible Crime* was the first of four crime novels which Lois Austen-Leigh wrote (one of the others having the quaint title, *The Gobblecock Mystery*). But, according to a lengthy 2018 review by Lizzie Hayes on the "Promoting Crime Fiction" blog, MRJ refused to write a review of *The Incredible Crime*. She notes that this fact "came to light quite recently, when some of James' letters were published posthumously". *Ghosts & Scholars* readers excitedly Googling for this 'quite recent' collection of MRJ's letters are doomed to disappointment unless they consider 'quite recently' to include 'over sixty years ago'. That's right, the letters in question are those selected by Gwendolen McBryde for *Letters to a Friend* (1956). The reviewer goes on to say that:

> The reason for this refusal was apparently James' dislike of the description of [the central character] Prudence, the daughter of a bishop... It is easy to dismiss James' objections to Prudence's swearing... as the prejudices of a reactionary. Certainly, James condemned the work of Aldous Huxley and James Joyce and supported the ban on Radcliffe Hall's exploration of lesbian relationships, *The Well of Loneliness* (1928).

Now, I'll admit that MRJ could be reactionary at times, and his pompous condemnation (unread) of *The Well of Loneliness* ("I find it difficult to believe... that its suppression causes any loss to literature") was not his finest hour. But with *The Incredible Crime*, I think his reasons for not reviewing it were more complex and creditable. In Kirsten T. Saxton's gushing introduction to the BL reprint (where she describes MRJ as Lois Austen-Leigh's "close friend and mentor"), she only gives a partial quote from MRJ's "posthumously published letter" to Gwen McBryde. In full (*Letters to a Friend*, p.171), it is more nuanced and reads:

> Lois Austen Leigh has written a novel and sent it me

with the request that I should review it in the Eton Chronicle. I've read it and written to tell her I don't like the heroine at all. The scene is partly at Cambridge which seems very conventionally done and partly in East Anglia which isn't so bad. Anyhow the heroine who's the daughter of a retired Bishop, Master of a College, has a great facility in swearing and on one occasion, lunching at a hotel with an old friend, a gent, takes occasion to swear solidly for two whole minutes: the language isn't reported, but I can't imagine anyone being able to swear for 2 minutes without trespassing a good deal over the limits. (February 18th, 1931)

I don't take from this that MRJ disliked the "heroine" because she could swear like a trooper - surely that's just a little amusing detail he thought Gwen McBryde might enjoy. Rather, he didn't like the character nor the scene-setting because he didn't think they were very well handled. MRJ was an enthusiastic crime fiction reader: there are several mentions of works by other writers such as Agatha Christie and Dorothy L. Sayers in *Letters to a Friend* (in Sayers' *Murder Must Advertise*, MRJ hated the "intolerable" Dian de Momerie, but then, doesn't everyone?). Was he not just comparing *The Incredible Crime* with others in the genre and finding it wanting? I suspect the plot, involving fox hunting (to the best of my knowledge, MRJ never hunted),[1] an obscure poison and drug smuggling, wouldn't have appealed. Anyway, I don't know for certain that MRJ *didn't* review the book for the *Eton Chronicle*. But if he didn't, it wasn't because he was being reactionary on this occasion, but because he didn't want to hurt the feelings of a friend.

For the record, I agree with MRJ. I managed only four or five chapters before I gave up. The style and the central characters were way too arch and brittle for me; not to mention the lacklustre, far from "incredible", plot.

Note:

[1] At one point in her introduction to *Letters to a Friend*, Gwen McBryde says "We sometimes forded the river while hunting...", but I doubt whether that "we" included MRJ.

Lady Wardrop's Notes 2
The Portals of London website

I first encountered the Portals of London website (portalsoflondon.com) back at the start of 2018 after reading an article about it in the *Guardian* (Jan 8th, 2018). The site claims to be the start of a project to catalogue "London's inter-dimensional gateways". From the "About" page we learn:

> It is unclear why London is such a nexus for portals. From doors between worlds to spacetime-crunching wormholes, the city's fabric, dimensionally speaking, seems to be uniquely porous... This blog is an attempt to collect stories of these phenomena - be they historical or contemporary, well-documented or shrouded in myth - in the hope that one day a comprehensive catalogue or encyclopaedia can be put together.

As the site creator/author PoL explained to the *Guardian*:

> A couple of years ago, I worked as a cycle courier, and I got very much into the hidden parts of London... And I have an interest in weird fiction and ghost stories. The blog has influences going back to Victorian ghost stories and MR James - his stories

about the East Anglian marshes and some ancient malevolent terrors out there. I kind of feel a similar thing is in the Thames...

The accounts on the site number a few dozen, on subjects ranging from dimensional timeslips at a telephone exchange ("Whispering Wires: The Holborn Telephone Exchange Crisis") to strange phenomena on the London underground ("Beneath the Overground: The Shepherd's Bush to Willesden Junction Spectre"). From strange Escher-like physics in a house owned by a magician and collector ("A shadow in Georgian London: The House of Hidden Things") to evidence for an overlay of a different London planned out after the Great Fire ("Mist Shrouded Cities: The Newcourt Continuum" - China Miéville would surely approve of that one!). And what of mysterious disappearances associated with a bus garage built on the site of an ancient island in the Thames ("Faraway islands: The Stockwell Bus Garage Manifestation/Simon's Ait"), or the genuinely terrifying haunting of an old summerhouse ("A Hampstead Horror: The Ghost House")?

One piece mentioned in the *Guardian* article, "Wren's Restless Sanctuary: The Church of All-Corners-Within-the-Wall", concerns PoL's fascination with old London churches. The tale is of a lost building's spatial and "temporal untethering", seen for instance as "towers glimpsed down unexpected alleys", but entered at your peril. It was inspired by "the way that even the medieval churches that were burned down in the great fire and weren't rebuilt, some of them kind of still exist as little gardens or courtyards in the City. You can find evidence of even older churches, Roman temples under office blocks, and things like that". There are echoes here of Roger Johnson's classic tale "The Soldier", and I feel sure that PoL has read (or if not, he ought to read!) Michael Harrison's *The London that was Rome* (1971).

From all the above, I think most *G&S* readers will now be aware that Portals of London is a collection of fictional short stories, but with a very carefully built-up façade of fact - some real, some fake but often convincing. London is a strange enough place, as the brilliant Bryant & May novels and short stories of Christopher Fowler attest, so I for one can willingly suspend my disbelief and accept that any of the Portals' tales are true, at least while I'm reading them. As the *Guardian* article says, "It's an example of how websites and social media accounts can be used to create fictional self-contained worlds that are *just on the cusp of believability*" [my italics]. Hookland, Scarfolk, the Black Meadow Project and the Occultaria of Albion spring to mind as others of a similar ilk. I love them all.

When PoL says that some "may feel that the 'fiction' tag is irrelevant. That it is the long, layered history of people and places they touch on that is at the heart of these stories", he could be talking about me. He has, however, been troubled by the reaction of a minority of the Portals' readers. There was a warnings page on the site, "Through the Fourth Wall" (now mysteriously vanished - through a portal maybe), in which he begins: "If you enjoy the mystery of this site, if wondering where the borders between myth, fact and fiction are to be found is part of what you like about the posts, then this [particular] page is not [directed at] you". What worries PoL is that some, including other websites, have apparently been taking everything as factual. In particular, the appearance of the Portals' stories on "a well-known podcast... didn't sit right for me": "The podcast deals with 'Fortean' type stories from around the world. But, unlike the Fortean Times, which - after investigating our blog - described PoL to its readers as 'gently Borgean fiction', the podcast presented the stories pretty much as straight... So here we are... THIS SITE IS FICTION".

And his influences? "MR James, Susan Cooper, Alan Garner, Jorge Luis Borges, Italo Calvino, Hookland, Simon Stalenhag, Scarfolk, Patrick Keiller, Ian Nairn". Again, as in the *Guardian* piece, MRJ comes first: "MR James is key. I call these posts ghost stories. It's true I forgot to put an actual ghost in most of them, but confusing ambiguity is what this site does". It's equally true, and is often remarked upon, that MRJ forgot to put ghosts in most of *his* "ghost stories": demons, elemental spirits and very physical revenants predominate. And while the PoL tales can only occasionally be described as borderline Jamesian, that preference for "confusing ambiguity" is another thing they have in common with the best of James. It's why MRJ's more ambiguous later stories such as "An Evening's Entertainment", "Two Doctors" and "The Experiment" have an on-going fascination for me (and others), while some of his earlier tales don't - not so much anyway. Whether or not MRJ planned that ambiguity, or whether he was just getting woollier and more careless in his later plotting, isn't a question I'm particularly bothered to try to answer. Whatever the explanation, it's what causes me to return to them again and again.

Lady Wardrop's Notes 3 (Part One)
Possible Jamesian aspects of *Detectorists*

In *Ghosts & Scholars Newsletter 33* (2018) I quoted from an email I'd received from Jeremy Greenwood about Mackenzie Crook's BBC TV comedy series, *Detectorists* (not *The*!). "There are," he said, "some clear M.R. James references." As he explained, the second of those references is in episode 1 of series 3. [The scene starts with] "Andy digging up a falconer's whistle. He cleans it and blows it and the landscape warps eerily through a sequence of historical scenes involving the burial of a different treasure." Jeremy is not the only one to see this as a direct reference to "Oh, Whistle, and I'll Come to You, My Lad", but I did note at the time that the scene was apparently inspired by an actual discovery made by Mackenzie Crook while out with his metal detector.

Landscapes of Detectorists, edited by Innes M. Keighren and Joanne Norcup, was published by Uniform Books in 2020. It's a small book of just over a hundred pages, containing four papers by academics in the field of geography and historic geography: *"'When I look at this landscape, I can read it'* - practices of landscape interpretation in *Detectorists*" by Innes M. Keighren; "Hoarding the everyday - the disquieting geographies of the *Detectorists*" by Isla Forsyth; "'*When I get up it all goes to shit*' - unearthing everyday vertical landscapes of *Detectorists*" by Andrew Harris; and "'*That's got to be a first: woman reads map*' - gender, hobbies, & knowledge in *Detectorists*" by Joanne Norcup. By now my readers will, I hope, be well aware of my aversion to academic writing, but I wanted to like these papers, I really did, especially after reading in the Introduction that "Writing this book... has provided, for all its contributors, an escape from the dominant modes of academic production that see value only in certain forms of knowledge making and only in certain types of writing". It's true that all four essays are readable and don't contain much in the way of academic language, but I was left feeling that none of them actually *said* anything or made any points which weren't completely obvious. The best of the four (although what connection it has to geography I don't really get) is the final one, regardless of the fact that I disagree with quite a lot of it.

But getting back to the subject of this column, there are two sections in *Landscapes of Detectorists* that make the whole thing worthwhile: an enlightening "Afterword" by Adam Tandy, the producer of series 1 and 2 as well as the first Christmas Special; and a "Foreword" by Mackenzie Crook himself. In this he tells lyrically of his discovery:

I secured permission to detect on a farm in Suffolk... and dug down four inches to find an exquisite bronze hawking whistle. I... held it to my lips and blew. The note that issued from the whistle was a ghost, a sound unheard for centuries, and the last person to hear that sound, that *exact* sound, was the person who dropped it just yards from where I was standing. And it wasn't a faint, feeble ghost either: it was an urgent, piercing shrill that echoed across the field and back through time.

So, truly an evocative, almost supernatural experience, but one not in any way related to "Oh, Whistle". Unless, that is, an earlier reading of the story had predisposed Crook to perceive the whistle's sound as (figuratively) "a ghost", not unlike the "quality of infinite distance... [that] seemed to have the power... of forming pictures in the brain", sensed by Professor Parkins when he blows the whistle in MRJ's tale.

There remains the question of the 2015 Christmas Special. Following on from the end of series 2, where detectorist Lance digs up a gold Saxon aestel (the head of a bookmarker or pointer, identical to King Alfred's Jewel in the Ashmolean Museum at Oxford), we now see that it is on display in the British Museum. When Lance visits it there, a mysterious cowled figure appears behind him in a photograph, seen only briefly by the detectorists' club meeting before their slide projector spontaneously combusts. Lance feels cursed with bad luck, from an unseasonal wasp sting, to not finding anything but rubbish with his detector and not being able to recognise birdsong. He decides to steal back the aestel to return it to the earth. Soon realising that this isn't going to happen, instead he buries gold coins of the same value (bought with his reward money). Immediately the curse (if it existed) is lifted and he identifies the song of a blackbird. Is this episode, people have wondered, a clear reference to "A Warning to the Curious"? There, of course, Mr Paxton's restoration of the guarded antiquity to the earth doesn't end so happily.

Again, I'm not convinced of a definite MRJ connection. The theme of the cursed object, and what happens when attempts are made to give or put it back where it was found, is not exactly unique to MRJ. Make no mistake, I would love to think that someone as delightful (and a little bit fey!) as Mackenzie Crook so obviously is, could be among our number. One day perhaps we'll get the chance to ask him, and suggest that he might fancy dramatising a suitable MRJ story for TV: "Mr Humphreys and His Inheritance" or "An Evening's Entertainment", for instance. With some reservations, I like Mark Gatiss's Christmas TV MRJ adaptations, but giving the opportunity to someone new one year would be a welcome departure.

Arriving just too late to cover in the original 2021 version of this column was the first issue of *Waiting for You: A Detectorists zine* edited by the admirable Cormac Pentecost, a leader in the very welcome print zine revival. There have been more issues since. The articles included are mostly everything that those in *Landscapes of Detectorists* are not: full of interesting details and insights. Quite often the possible MRJ connection is touched upon. In issue one, for example, David Petts' "Towards a Psychogeography of Danebury" (the fictional Danebury in Essex is the chief setting of *Detectorists*) discusses the events at Seaburgh/Aldeburgh ("A Warning to the Curious") and Burnstow/Felixstowe ("Oh, Whistle"). As befits a paper first delivered at a Hookland conference, they are considered as genuinely having happened. Felixstowe is at the mouth of the River Stour, and Petts theorises that Danebury and Henburystone in *Detectorists* are "somewhere in the lower valley of the Stour". "Does the Stour valley," he asks, "have a genius loci connected with whistles or pipes?" I also chuckled at the quote allegedly from an archaeologist named Michael Shanks: Michael Shanks is the actor who plays the archaeologist Dr Daniel Jackson in TV's *Stargate* (I should know: I named my antiquary's dolls' house "Daniel's House" after him!).

In issue two there is even a *Detectorists*/MRJ collage ("The spirit of M.R. James watches over the seekers") by Chris Whitehead. And in issue three, David Petts turns up again, with "We Three Kings: Early Medieval Burials in Popular Fiction", in which "A Warning to the Curious" features prominently (the article is illustrated with the frontispiece photograph of MRJ from *Eton and King's*).

There's no doubt that other people are seeing the connection between MRJ and *Detectorists* more clearly than I do. I suppose it's because I so badly want it to be true that I'm being very careful not to leap to conclusions at the risk of being proved wrong.

Lady Wardrop's Notes 3 (Part Two)
Did M.R. James read any of Lovecraft's stories?

The idea has been circulating on the Net for a while that M.R. James read and hated H.P. Lovecraft's genre fiction. "13 Things You Didn't Know about M.R. James" on The Spooky Isles website (spookyisles.com) may be partly to blame. Number 6 on the list is headed: "James loved Sheridan Le Fanu but he hated H.P. Lovecraft and Bram Stoker's Dracula". In the entry it says: "... Supernatural writer H.P. Lovecraft was a great James fan, yet the Cambridge Don did not reciprocate the admiration. He disliked the American author's work intensely. James also didn't care much for Bram Stoker's Dracula, feeling it contained to *[sic]* much sex". We can leave aside for an endnote the questionable statement concerning *Dracula*, and also the errors in Number 8 on the list ("MR James' American publisher mistook him as the brother of 'The Turn of the Screw' writer Henry James").[1] The author of the list is Eddie Brazil, a friend whose spooky photography is superb and whose interest in MRJ is genuine: I must emphasise that most of the list is entertaining and accurate.

Whether or not Eddie intended it, many readers seem to have interpreted his statement as meaning that MRJ hated

Lovecraft's fiction writing. In reality, as far as is known, MRJ never referred to HPL's stories anywhere and may never have read any of them. The whole misapprehension seems to have arisen from his comment on HPL's vast essay "Supernatural Horror in Literature", in a letter of January 1928 to Nicholas (Nico) Llewelyn Davies, who had asked for some reading recommendations. "I shall have recourse," MRJ wrote, "to a funny American thing which was sent me the other day. A periodical, apparently, 'The Recluse, issued by W. Paul Cook for His Own Amusement - this being the First Number'. In it is a disquisition of nearly 40 pages of double columns on Supernatural Horror in Literature by one H.P. Lovecraft, whose style is of the most offensive. He uses the word cosmic about 24 times". The editor had sent MRJ the copy of *The Recluse* on publication in 1927 because of the lengthy and enthusiastic section on him in HPL's "disquisition". Other authors covered in the essay, such as Algernon Blackwood, Lord Dunsany and Arthur Machen, were also sent copies (S.T. Joshi, *An H.P. Lovecraft Encyclopedia*, 2001, p.256).

MRJ's letter was first published in *Ghosts & Scholars 8* (1986); it has since appeared elsewhere and it's also on the *G&S* website, so has become fairly well known (and quoted out of context). Incidentally, even if we consider this comment on its own terms, I'm not sure it's entirely fair to say that MRJ "hated" Lovecraft, as, after criticising his style, he went on to praise the scope of the essay: "he has taken pains to search about & treats the subject from its beginnings to MRJ".

Anyway, when it comes to Lovecraft's fiction, and accepting the fact that we have no evidence whatsoever of MRJ's having read any of it, I then started wondering whether he *could* have read any, and if so, where. One possibility is suggested by some lines in MRJ's December 1929 article for *The Bookman*, "Some Remarks on Ghost Stories":

> [E.F. Benson] is however blameless in this aspect as compared with some Americans, who compile volumes called *Not At Night* and the like. These are merely nauseating, and it is very easy to be nauseating... The authors of the stories I have in mind tread, as they believe, in the steps of Edgar Allan Poe and Ambrose Bierce (himself sometimes unpardonable), but they do not possess the force of either.

The *Not at Night* series of books, edited by Christine Campbell Thomson (who wasn't American!) and mainly containing stories taken from *Weird Tales*, was published between 1925 and 1936 - eleven volumes in all, plus an omnibus in 1937.[2] The first five appeared before MRJ's *Bookman* article. Since he is very scathing about the series, it's unlikely that he'd have bothered to read more than one of the books, which gives him a 2-in-5 chance of having come across a Lovecraft tale there. If he did, the first candidate couldn't have been more damaging to any appreciation he might have had for them: it's the despicable and racist "The Horror at Red Hook", which Campbell Thomson reprinted (from *Weird Tales*, Jan 1927) in *You'll Need a Night Light* (*Not at Night* number 3, Sept 1927). The story takes place in the Red Hook area of New York, and features "swarthy, evil-looking" locals who are conducting vile, secret sacrificial rites to Lilith, brought over by them from their middle-eastern countries of origin. MRJ wasn't entirely free of the racial biases of his time (especially in relation to Jews),[3] but the rampant racism of HPL here would surely have appalled him; as would the tale's superficial scholarship on magic and demonology, "copied directly" from the *Encyclopaedia Britannica* (Joshi, *op cit*, p.115).

Much better is "Pickman's Model" (from *Weird Tales*, Oct 1927), reprinted in *By Daylight Only* (*Not at Night* number 5, Oct 1929). This excellent, disturbing tale of an encounter with ghouls, and the consequences for the artist Richard Upton Pickman who paints them (Pickman was a ghoul himself soon afterwards, in HPL's *Dream-Quest of Unknown Ka-*

dath), could have been enjoyed by MRJ. Perhaps he would have noticed the possible influence of "Canon Alberic's Scrap-book". When a photograph taken by the narrator in Pickman's cellar studio unexpectedly shows a ghoul, the reader is told (in typically Lovecraftian italics) that *"it was a photograph from life"* - so very reminiscent of MRJ's "It was drawn from the life", concerning the scrapbook picture of Solomon's demon. "Pickman's Model" was written in late 1926, less than a year after HPL first read "Canon Alberic".

Other contents of *By Daylight Only*, however, would have revolted MRJ. George Fielding Eliot's horrible "The Copper Bowl", for instance, perfectly fits the "nauseating" description. I may be extrapolating way too far from the known facts here, but it is perhaps worth noting that August Derleth also had stories in *You'll Need a Night Light* and *By Daylight Only* ("The Coffin of Lissa" and "The Tenant" respectively). We know that in 1929 Derleth was corresponding with MRJ (see my article "M.R. James and the 'native of Wisconsin'" in *The Black Pilgrimage* Volume 1). Might he have had copies sent to him? It's a flimsy hypothesis, I freely admit, and I'm not making any claims for it beyond demonstrating that MRJ *could* have read at least one HPL tale.

It remains the case, though, that despite what is being said on the Net, there is no evidence at all that M.R. James read anything by Lovecraft apart from "Supernatural Horror in Literature". This is unlikely to change unless something comes to light in a so-far unpublished letter (of which, it's true, there are many).

Notes:

[1] MRJ thought that the novel suffered by excess (not the same as "too much sex"!): "Bram Stoker's Dracula is a book with very good ideas in it, but - to be vulgar - the butter is spread far too thick" ("Ghosts - Treat Them Gently", *Evening News*, April 17th, 1931). It wasn't MRJ's American publisher who made the Henry James mistake. It was a staff member of his British publisher, Edward Arnold, who (as Arnold wrote to MRJ in 1903) "thinks he remembers having once read a very good story by your brother and it occurred to us whether it might be possible to work a joint volume". Michael Cox quotes this in *M.R. James: An Informal Portrait* (p.139), surmising that Henry James is being referred to.

[2] I obtained most of the bibliographical information on the *Not at Night* series from the Internet Speculative Fiction Database (isfdb.org) - an invaluable resource.

[3] MRJ's anti-Semitism is arguably shown in "The Uncommon Prayerbook", and more definitely in a sermon quoted in Patrick J. Murphy's *Medieval Studies and the Ghost Stories of M.R. James* (2017), p.152. On the other hand, in his introductory chapters to *St William of Norwich* (1896), he staunchly defended Jews against the notorious blood libel.

Lady Wardrop's Notes 4
Female Ghosts in M.R. James's Stories and The Recurrence of Characters Named Mary

How many times have we read statements like this one from Darryl Jones's introduction to his *M.R. James: Collected Ghost Stories* (2011): "Women, on close observation, do feature frequently in James's stories, but not necessarily in the ways we might initially expect. They are often the ghosts themselves"? To which I would respond: "Define 'often'". MRJ wrote over thirty tales, and I count just six or seven which include unquestionably female ghosts. Even here, they are sometimes accompanied by male spectres. Yes, there are the ghosts of Theodosia Bryan in "A Neighbour's Landmark", Ann Clark in "Martin's Close", Lady Sadleir in "The Uncommon Prayer-book", and old mother Wilkins in "There Was a Man Dwelt by a Churchyard". There are the three women in "Wailing Well", although they are accompanied by one (eventually two) males; and Phoebe Stanley, the gipsy girl in "Lost Hearts", also accompanied by a male, the hurdy-gurdy playing boy. Slightly grudgingly, I'll add Mrs Mothersole to the list, although the ghosts/demons in "The Ash-tree" are her offspring rather than herself. "The Fenstanton Witch" could be another, but I'm excluding it: while the manifestation does appear on the witch's grave, it is in fact a demon with no suggestion of gender.

Why have I missed out "An Episode of Cathedral History"? Most writers cite this as a prime example because of the final line, *"Ibi cubavit lamia"*, the lamia being a classical female demon who is often described as eating children. Darryl Jones, in his annotations, specifically says: "Thus, importantly, 'Cathedral History' 's demon is *female* (as opposed to its male counterpart in 'Canon Alberic')". But there are two Biblical quotes in the story, both from Isaiah chapter 34 and both describing the (ex-?) resident of the tomb. The other is: "the satyr shall cry to *his* fellow". Then we have its description: "a thing *like a man*, all over hair, and two great eyes to it" [my italics]. Very rarely is this given as an example of a *male* demon in MRJ's tales; except in the theory, which I like very much (despite a well-argued refutation from Peter Bell in *Ghosts & Scholars*), that there are actually two demons in the story - one outside doing the crying, and one initially inside the cathedral. I agree with Patrick Murphy: "...'lamia' appears merely as a scriptural allusion produced by one of the story's characters - Canon Lyall - and is not necessarily to be taken as an authoritative or defining label for what has emerged from the tomb".[1]

Considering MRJ's tales as a whole, and excluding those which feature *only* demons and revenants whose gender is unspecified, there are approximately three times as many male supernatural appearances as female ones. Named examples include Gawdy in "The Mezzotint", Lord Saul in "The Residence at Whitminster", Count Magnus, Sir Everard Charlett in "The Diary of Mr Poynter", Dr Rant in "The Tractate Middoth", Uncle Henry in "The Story of a Disappearance and an Appearance", and of course William Ager in "A Warning to the Curious". I could go on, but I think I've made my point. Why is the preponderance of male 'ghosts' in MRJ's stories not remarked upon? It seems as though people assume the masculine gender is the 'default' position for ghosts and revenants, so that female appearances are singled out as being proof of MRJ's fear of women (a fear of which I've yet to see any convincing evidence). It's no good insisting that the sheer physicality of some of the female revenants is revealing of MRJ's terror of the contact of women's bodies: for every Lady Sadleir ("[she] fell right over on to Mr Potwitch's shoulder, and [her] face hid in his neck... more like a ferret going for a rabbit than anythink else"), I offer you a William Ager ("[Mr Paxton's] ...teeth and jaws were broken to bits. I only glanced once at his face")!

Does it follow, then, that MRJ was repulsed by *all* physical contact? That implication can be found in various essays and articles, especially on the Net. It's nonsense: the writers have clearly not read of MRJ's love of "ragging" - a sort of rough and tumble which could result in the participants ending up "somewhat mixed on the hearthrug", and with MRJ's "long fingers" grasping their "vitals" (Michael Cox, *M.R. James: An Informal Portrait*, p.59). I'd add that most modern commentators interpret "vitals" to mean private parts, and they may be right, but I think it could mean anywhere below the waist.

Returning to the subject of women in MRJ's stories.

It's been noted that E.F. Benson had a propensity for naming his characters Hugh, but I don't remember anyone pointing out a similar tendency in MRJ's tales. He does seem to like giving the name Mary to his more sympathetic female characters. In fact, with the exception of Lady Wardrop in "Mr Humphreys and His Inheritance", whose first name we're not told, pretty much all the best middle-class and upper-class women in his tales are called Mary. I've counted six in total: Lady Mary Hervey (one of the guests at the Hall in "The Ash-tree"), Mrs Mary Anstruther in "The Rose Garden" (I suppose opinions might differ as to whether the bossy Mrs Anstruther is sympathetic or not, but I love her), Miss Mary Simpson in "The Tractate Middoth", Miss Mary Oldys in "The Residence at Whitminster", Mrs

Mary Porter (daughter of Mr Davidson in "The Uncommon Prayer-book"), and Miss Mary Cave in "Speaker Lenthall's Tomb".

Aside from my role model and semi-alter-ego Lady Wardrop, my favourite female in any of the stories is Miss Mary Cave. When David Rowlands wrote his article on "M.R. James's Women" (*G&S 15*, 1993 - also on the *G&S* website), he was remarkably prescient in saying: "Miss Mary Oldys... is perhaps MRJ's most complete attempt at a female character, and an especially delightful one *(though Miss Mary Cave... might have eclipsed her had MRJ persevered with this draft)*" [my italics]. David was judging from just the first few pages of "Speaker Lenthall's Tomb", which was all that had come to light then. Now we have the entire text apart from (seemingly) one page.[2] And how right David was. Mary Cave is a total joy - pretending to be submissive to the male characters' intellect but all the time having the best of any discussion or disagreement (something which MRJ makes blatantly clear to the reader, but which always goes unrecognised by her male family members). In fact, this story is utterly dominated by the two females - young Miss Cave and the aged Elizabeth Lenthall. Both in their different ways represent a force for good and for good taste, and both never fail to outwit and outclass all of the men in the story. Surely no one who has ever read "Speaker Lenthall's Tomb" could continue to claim that MRJ's female characters are all irritating, stupid, evil or practically non-existent.[3] It's such a shame that MRJ never polished up the tale, presumably because he suddenly realised that he had made a huge historical mistake (thinking the tomb in Burford church was that of Speaker William Lenthall, when it is actually that of Sir Lawrence Tanfield), the correcting of which would have entailed a complete rewrite.

The question to ask now, of course, is why Mary? Marys Cave, Oldys and Simpson are portrayed as attractive young ladies of marriageable age: as it turns out, Miss Oldys and Miss Simpson become Mrs Spearman and Mrs Garrett after the events in their respective stories. I half hoped, therefore, that MRJ might have had a bit of a crush on a Mary at some point (I don't think MRJ was gay - he was probably asexual, but possibly bi-). Sadly, I can find nothing specific, although he did have some early crushes on women. But, bearing in mind again that all of the Marys are sympathetic characters, perhaps he was consciously or unconsciously paying tribute to his loving and much-loved mother, Mary Emily James. Is it only a coincidence, I wonder, that Mary Oldys' frequent correspondent in "The Residence at Whitminster" is named Emily? Mary Emily James died in 1898 - probably just before the first of the 'Mary' stories was written.

Notes:

[1] Bill Read, "The Mystery of the Second Satyr", *G&S 31* (2000), pp.46-47. Peter Bell, "The Lamia and the Screech-Owl: Some Thoughts on 'An Episode of Cathedral History'", *G&S Newsletter 16* (2009), pp.27-28. Patrick J. Murphy, "Ex Cathedra", *Medieval Studies and the Ghost Stories of M.R. James* (2017), p.107.

[2] That missing page was seamlessly filled in by John Linwood Grant for the completed version of the story published in *G&S 42* (2022).

[3] S.T. Joshi, for instance, in his introduction to *Count Magnus and Other Stories* (2005), says that "the world of James's fiction is as devoid of significant female characters as H.P. Lovecraft's". Joshi then goes on to describe "Lady Waldrop" *[sic]* as "annoying". How *could* he?

Lady Wardrop's Notes 5
Dogs in M.R. James's Stories

Everyone knows that M.R. James loved cats. His letters often include amusing anecdotes and two-way conversations he had with his own and other people's feline companions. But when I came to add up their appearances in his ghost stories, I was surprised to discover that dogs feature more often than cats. The latter are really only prominent in "The Stalls of Barchester Cathedral" (the "exquisitely modelled [wood carving] of a cat, whose crouching posture suggests with admirable spirit the suppleness, vigilance, and craft of the redoubted adversary of the genus *Mus*", and the infamous "there *is* no kitchen cat" line); "The Ash-tree" (the cruel and gratuitously barbaric fate of the "white tom-cat" in the tree); and *The Five Jars*. Dogs, real and supernatural, on the other hand, can be found in more than half a dozen tales, and they mostly seem to serve one of two purposes.

In a letter to Gwendolen McBryde in August 1922 (*Letters to a Friend*, p.116), written from Angoulême in France, MRJ grumbled that "last night the dogs in the place barked without ceasing". He added, "I got up today with the firm intention of kicking any dog I met that was not too large - but I haven't seen one". Were they trying to tell him something?

Perhaps he should have taken note of the sensitivity of some of the dogs in his own stories, who give warning of supernatural goings-on. In "An Episode of Cathedral History", the verger Mr Worby recounts how, when he was a young lad, his little dog would warn him when the demon from the Cathedral was about in the Close:

> "Night after night," said Worby, "that dog seemed to know it was coming; he'd creep out, he would, and snuggle into the bed and cuddle right up to me shivering, and when the crying come he'd be like a wild thing, shoving his head under my arm, and I was fully near as bad. Six or seven times we'd hear it, not more, and when he'd dror out his 'ed again I'd know it was over for that night."

Another night:

> "I dropped off asleep as sound as a boy does, and all of a sudden the dog woke me up, coming into the bed, and thought I, now we're going to get it sharp, for he seemed more frightened than usual. After about five minutes sure enough came this cry... I slipped out of bed across to my little window giving on the Close - but the dog he bored right down to the bottom of the bed - and I looked out. First go off I couldn't see anything. Then right down in the shad-

ow under a buttress I made out what I shall always say was two spots of red - a dull red it was - nothing like a lamp or a fire, but just so as you could pick 'em out of the black shadow."

When the terror was over for that evening:

"Then come my last fright that night - something come against my bare leg - but that was all right: that was my little dog had come out of bed, and prancing about making a great to-do, only holding his tongue, and me seeing he was quite in spirits again, I took him back to bed and we slept the night out!"

In "The Story of a Disappearance and an Appearance", it's the Toby dog from the Punch and Judy Show which knows something is very wrong. The bagman, a fellow resident at the hotel, tells the epistolary narrator "W.R." that the show has the "best Punch and the best Toby dog... he had ever come across". The narrator writes to his brother, "Toby dogs... are the last new thing in the shows. I have only seen one myself, but before long all the men will have them". When "W.R." sees the show himself:

"The Toby dog was there, as I had been led to expect... The only drawback was the Toby dog's developing a tendency to howl in the wrong place. Something had occurred, I suppose, to upset him, and something considerable: for, I forget exactly at what point, he gave a most lamentable cry, leapt off the footboard, and shot away across the market-place and down a side street. There was a stage-wait, but only a brief one. I suppose the men decided that it was no good going after him, and that he was likely to turn up again at night."

Toby, of course, was aware that Kidman and Gallop had murdered the uncle of "W.R.", and his revenant was about to put in an appearance.

In "Wailing Well", the shepherd tells Stanley Judkins and the other Eton scouts about the clump of trees containing the eponymous well: "All I know is, my old dog wouldn't go through that field, let alone me or anyone else that's got a morsel of brains in their heads". While the dog is busy "making friends all round" with the scouts, the shepherd describes the time when he and the dog got a sight of the undead residents of "Wailin' Well":

"I wasn't for stayin' in that place, and if I had been, I was bound to look to my old dog: he'd gone! Such a thing he never done before as leave me; but gone he had, and when I came up with him in the end, he was in that state he didn't know me, and was fit to fly at my throat. But I kep' talkin' to him, and after a bit he remembered my voice and came creepin' up like a child askin' pardon. I never want to see him like that again, nor yet no other dog."

On the other hand, the gamekeeper's dogs in "The Uncommon Prayer-book" seem to bark "very loudly in unseen places" for no reason. Perhaps they did have a reason, like the little dog in *The Five Jars* who barks "most furiously" at a clothes-line on which only the story-teller, "M", can see a dangling fairy teasing him: "it was the face of an old woman, very cheerful and ruddy... laughing and swinging to and fro". There may be less excuse for the dog in "A Warning to the Curious" that tries to see Mr Paxton off: "he made at me so fiercely that [the cottage owners] had to run out and beat him off, and then naturally begged my pardon, and we got into talk". But we might ask whether it was just being an over-keen guard dog, or did it sense that Paxton was dangerously up to no good?

Then we come to the second category: supernatural dogs. But before that, a word about Mr Denton's "brown spaniel" in "The Diary of Mr Poynter". I don't think we can blame it for the fact that its master at first thought it was the dog who had crawled across the floor to the side of his chair. Reaching down to pat its head, "the feel of it, and still more the fact that instead of a responsive movement, absolute stillness greeted his touch, made him look over the arm. What he had been touching rose to meet him..." Not the dog, but the revenant of Sir Everard Charlett. Presumably the spaniel, like the shepherd's old collie, had thought better of staying around!

In *The Five Jars*, there is an attempt to lure "M", away from the titular jars, which the evil denizens of the hidden kingdom want to steal. He sees this scene enacted:

> Towards the far end of the field, which was a pretty large one, a poor old man was trying to get to a gate in the hedge at a staggering run, and striking now and then with his stick at a great deer-hound which was leaping up at him with hollow barks. It seemed as if nothing but the promptest dash to the spot could save him; it seemed, too, as if he had caught sight of me at the window, for he beckoned.

Luckily, before "M" goes out to rescue the old man, he thinks to look through his field glasses and sees only "a sort of fuzz of dancing vapour". A simulacrum of a dog, then, rather than a supernatural one.

MRJ will have been familiar with the idea of demons manifesting in the form of dogs from his work on such ancient texts as *The Testament of Solomon* (in which a demon named Rabdos or Sceptre takes the shape of a gigantic dog), and the "Twelve Medieval Ghost-Stories" from Byland Abbey in Yorkshire (the second tale features a shape-shifting ghost which appears at a certain point as a dog with a chain around its neck). When the ticket collector in "Casting the Runes" thinks he sees something accompanying Karswell onto the boat to France ("'Ad he got a dog with him, or what? Funny thing: I could 'a' swore 'e wasn't alone"), it's not too much of a stretch to guess that the demon which Karswell had invoked was also a shape-shifter, with the likeness of a dog at that point. This same idea was taken up by Fritz Leiber, to terrifying effect, in his fine story "The Hound" (1942): "Aren't you going to punch in for your dog, too?" "My Dog?" "Well, it was there a second ago. Came in right behind you, looking as if it owned you…"

Another type of supernatural canine, the dog pack that is part of the Wild Hunt, will also have been known to MRJ via his scholarly work. Walter Map's twelfth-century *De Nugis Curialium*, which MRJ knew from his schooldays and translated from the Latin in 1923, includes an account of the Hunt led by King Herla. An interesting twist in this version of the legend has it that Herla is given a "small blood-hound" to carry, with the instruction that on no account should he or any of his companions dismount from their horses until the dog leaps to the ground. Some foolish men ignore this and crumble to dust, but "The dog has not yet alighted". Folklorist W. Sidney Hartland, in his extensive annotations to MRJ's Walter Map translation, has a note on the Wild Hunt at this point, which takes up most of one page, including a list of the various names for the dog pack ("the Wish-hounds, Dando and his Dogs, the Gabriel Hounds, Cwn Annwn...").

I think it's reasonable to assume that the pursuers of Lord Saul in "The Residence at Whitminster" are either dogs from the Wild Hunt (they are certainly hunting Lord Saul) or some sort of hell hound, brought with him from Ireland but that "turned on him at the last". In his scrying glass, Mary Oldys tells her friend Emily that she saw:

> "...a form, at first crouching low among trees or bushes that were being threshed by a violent wind, then running very swiftly, and constantly turning a pale face to look behind him, as if he feared a pursuer: and, indeed, pursuers were following hard after him. Their shapes were but dimly seen, their number - three or four, perhaps - only guessed. I suppose they were on the whole more like dogs than anything else, but dogs such as we have seen they assuredly were not. Could I have closed my eyes to this horror,

I would have done so at once, but I was helpless."
According to the housekeeper, Mrs Maple, "there's the mark still to be seen on the minster door where they run him down". It's very tempting to link this with the 'claw marks' on the door of Blythburgh Church in Suffolk, where, in the sixteenth century, a spectral black dog is said to have invaded the building during a storm. Can it really be true, as the reference books say, that the Blythburgh marks only came to light when the door was cleaned in the 1930s, many years after MRJ wrote "The Residence at Whitminster"?

So did M.R. James much like dogs or did he share fellow ailurophile H.P. Lovecraft's low opinion of them? "The dog," Lovecraft wrote, "is a peasant and the cat is a gentleman"[1] (which may be why I prefer dogs, coming as I do from a long line of peasants with nary a gentleman among them!). The sympathetic (and quite insightful) depictions of the animals in "An Episode of Cathedral History" and "Wailing Well" incline me to think that MRJ did have *some* affection for them, although there is no indication of it in his letters to Gwen McBryde. On the contrary, he particularly seems to have disliked a troublesome dalmatian named Desmond (to be fair, MRJ wasn't the only one). But whether or not he liked dogs, MRJ undoubtedly appreciated their uses in supernatural fiction, both to warn of a threat and to *be* that threat.

One final thought and mystery. About a third of his tales are set in East Anglia, but MRJ never mentions what must be that area's most famous spectre: Black Shuck, the black dog (sometimes headless) that traditionally presages a death.[2] Not in his stories and not (as far as I can tell) in his *Suffolk and Norfolk* guide. There are chapters about something very close to Black Shuck (though called "The Hell Hound" and "The Hateful Thing") in *Bogie Tales of East Anglia*, the little book written by MRJ's cousin, Margaret Helen James (who also compiled the index to *Suffolk and Norfolk*). In "The Hell Hound" chapter, she recounts a legend of the hound from a thinly disguised Aldeburgh - the Seaburgh of "A Warning to the Curious". Although MRJ may have found her book a bit too quirkily-written for his taste, it's hard to believe that he wouldn't have read it on its publication in 1891. It does seem to me, however, that Black Shuck must have been much less generally known in MRJ's day than it is today.

Notes:

[1] Quoted in S.T Joshi, *An H.P. Lovecraft Encyclopedia* (2001), p.35.

[2] A recent book of East Anglian folklore is actually entitled *Shuckland* (Charles Christian, *Shuckland: Weird Tales, Ghosts, Folklore and Legends from East Anglia's Waveney Valley*, 2021).

Lady Wardrop's Notes 6
Geographical Locations in M.R. James's Stories

M.R. James is often thought of as a writer of stories with East Anglian settings, specifically Suffolk where he spent most of his childhood. While it's true that he wrote more stories located in that county than in any other, his settings were actually very much more varied. Making a list proved harder than I'd hoped when I started it, especially as some tales very inconveniently happen to be set in two (or more) locations, but the results are quite enlightening.

I included all the stories and all the unfinished drafts, a total of forty. Of these, six are located wholly or partly in Suffolk: "The Ash-tree", "Oh, Whistle, and I'll Come to You, My Lad" (Felixstowe), "A Warning to the Curious" (Aldeburgh), "Rats", "A Vignette" (Great Livermere) and the later sections of "The Tractate Middoth". If you add in the stories set in East Anglia as a whole it comes to thirteen. That's "The Fenstanton Witch" (Cambridge and Cambridgeshire); "The Experiment" (Norfolk); "The Rose Garden" (Essex - South Weald?), "The Mezzotint" (Essex) and "Count Magnus" (Mr Wraxall's final encounter with the Count and his little friend in the north Essex village of Belchamp St Paul). Plus the Cambridge-set "A Night in

King's College Chapel" and the first scene in "The Stalls of Barchester Cathedral" (a Cambridge college). There are also the Cambridge scenes in "The Tractate Middoth" and "Oh, Whistle", of course, but those tales have already been counted in the thirteen. It's fourteen East Anglian settings if you include "The Haunted Dolls' House" (the house is "not a hundred miles" from the "quiet place on the East Coast" where both Mr Dillet and Mr Chittenden repair for "a bit of a change").

Of the rest, we have five set wholly or partly overseas: "Canon Alberic's Scrap-book" (St Bertrand-de-Comminges, France), "Number 13" (Viborg, Denmark), "Count Magnus" (Vestergothland, Sweden), "The Treasure of Abbot Thomas" (Steinfeld, Germany) and the "Marcilly-le-Hayer" draft (France). And there's the one French scene, the death of Karswell at Abbeville, in "Casting the Runes". Apart from the latter, all the completed Europe-set tales are in *Ghost Stories of an Antiquary* (1904), which may indicate that the "Marcilly" draft also belongs to this earlier period. Two stories have scenes set in Ireland ("A School Story" and "The Residence at Whitminster").

There are four tales where I haven't been able to get more than a rough idea of their main settings: "The Malice of Inanimate Objects", "There was a Man Dwelt by a Churchyard", "The Game of Bear" draft and MRJ's longest story, "The Residence at Whitminster". That one feels like the Midlands to me, but I could be being subconsciously misled by the fact that Mary Oldys' correspondent is in Lichfield (Staffordshire). There is a Whitminster in Gloucestershire, but it can be ruled out: it's a small village, has never had any sort of "minster", and the name is a corruption of Wheatenhurst. Two suggestions I've seen are Southwell Minster in Nottinghamshire, and Wimborne Minster in Dorset. Both are former collegiate churches that MRJ knew and visited. But Dr Oldys is said to have moved "from his Dorsetshire parsonage to the quadrangle of Whitminster", and Mrs Maple the housekeeper complains that "I come out of Dorsetshire to this place", which presumably rules out Wimborne. The setting is so central to the story that it's disappointing we can't know more.

To add to those four unidentifiable tales, there are "The Stalls of Barchester Cathedral" and "An Episode of Cathedral History", based on the cathedrals at Salisbury, Canterbury and Hereford according to MRJ, but with no other solid hints as to the locations for their main events. Several local place names mentioned in the former might offer clues: Sowerby, Pickhill, Candley, Wringham and Barnswood. But all would seem to be fictional. There is a Sowerby in North

Yorkshire, not too far from Pickering (Pickhill?), and this is an area that MRJ knew from a visit in 1885 when, in a local inn, he found a mourning card for the nearby Cropton Lane Farm Murders, as recorded in his *Eton and King's*. If these are not false leads (which they most probably *are*!) then Barchester Cathedral may be Ripon. But why, then, would Archdeacon Haynes's sister Letitia have gone to Brighton for her health, rather than Scarborough? The first time MRJ visited Ripon was in 1929, years after he wrote "The Stalls of Barchester Cathedral".

There are two stories set in areas of outer London: "A School Story" (East Sheen) and "Two Doctors" (Islington - at the time of the story it was "a countrified place"). Four more have major scenes set in London: the trial in "Martin's Close" at the Old Bailey; the famous British Museum encounter in "Casting the Runes" (most of the rest of the story takes place in London too); the sale room and the curtain-making firm in "The Diary of Mr Poynter"; and the denouement of "The Uncommon Prayer-book". Two are in Lincolnshire: "Lost Hearts" (Aswarby) and "Mr Humphreys and His Inheritance" (Wilsthorpe - assuming the named village is its actual setting). One is in Devon: the murder at Sampford Courtenay in "Martin's Close". Two are in Dorset: "An Evening's Entertainment" (in the vicinity of the Cerne Abbas

Giant) and "Wailing Well" (Worbarrow). Three are in Oxford and Oxfordshire: "The Story of a Disappearance and an Appearance" (Bicester), "Speaker Lenthall's Tomb" (Burford) and the framing story (at "another University") in "The Mezzotint".

One tale is set in Buckinghamshire, Eton College to be precise. Given how important Eton was throughout his life, as a pupil and finally as Provost, it's perhaps surprising that MRJ wrote just the one Eton story, "After Dark in the Playing Fields", and then only towards the end of his life. Even his old, and less-loved prep school, Temple Grove, gets a tale ("A School Story"). Whereas there are five with Cambridge scenes. The English settings in "The Treasure of Abbot Thomas" can provisionally be placed in Hertfordshire, the actual location of Ashridge, where MRJ examined the stained glass from Steinfeld Abbey. The "John Humphreys" and "Merfield Hall/House" drafts are set in Cheshire and Bedfordshire/Northants respectively.

Then we get to a very interesting bunch which suggest that MRJ was nearly as keen on the West Midlands and counties adjoining for his settings as he was on Suffolk. In Herefordshire, there is obviously "A View from a Hill", as stated by MRJ himself in his Preface to the *Collected Ghost Stories* ("Herefordshire was the imagined scene of "A View from a Hill"). I would tentatively add "A Neighbour's Landmark", to some extent simply because the setting has a similar feel to "A View from a Hill", and the two stories were written one after the other. But also, as I suggested in *Ghosts & Scholars Newsletter 6*, in my "Notes & Queries" piece "Before someone take and put it right again", one inspiration for "A Neighbour's Landmark" could have been the account of "Old Taylor's Ghost" from Ella Mary Leather's 1912 book *The Folk-lore of Herefordshire*. Old Taylor haunts because he moved a landmark and can't rest until it's put back in its rightful place.

In Worcestershire, not far from the Herefordshire border (or possibly just over it), there's "The Uncommon Prayer-book" (the "valley of the Tent" would seem to be the valley of the Teme River). This is the first tale in the little trio in sequence in the 1925 *A Warning to the Curious* collection (it immediately precedes "A Neighbour's Landmark", with "A View from a Hill" last).[1] Rendcomb Manor in "The Diary of Mr Poynter" is in Warwickshire, as is Mr Karswell's Lufford Abbey, the location in "Casting the Runes" of his terrifying magic lantern show. Simon Loxley, in *A Geography of Horror: The Ghost Stories of M.R. James and the Suffolk Landscape* (2021), devotes an entire chapter to "Casting the Runes", proposing that although MRJ specifically says that

Lufford Abbey is in Warwickshire, he actually based it on Ufford Place in Suffolk. I don't believe there is any evidence for this.

So that makes five altogether in these West Midlands counties - only one fewer than the Suffolk-set tales. As we know, MRJ visited Gwendolen and Jane McBryde in Herefordshire many times, so he knew the area pretty well. Often during his stay he would walk up the very hill of "A View from a Hill", Coles Tump (made famous by Alfred Watkins in his *The Old Straight Track*), and enjoy the view out west towards the Black Mountains. It was "a favourite spot" of MRJ's, according to Gwen McBryde. He describes it so beautifully in the story:

> Across a broad level plain they looked upon ranges of great hills, whose uplands — some green, some furred with woods - caught the light of a sun, westering but not yet low. And all the plain was fertile, though the river which traversed it was nowhere seen. There were copses, green wheat, hedges, and pasture-land: the little compact white moving cloud marked the evening train. Then the eye picked out red farms and grey houses, and nearer home scattered cottages, and then the Hall, nestled under the hill. The smoke of chimneys was very blue and

straight. There was a smell of hay in the air: there were wild roses on bushes hard by. It was the acme of summer.

So what have I proved? Not a lot, I suppose, except that I now have the ammunition to fire at those who say MRJ was chiefly an East Anglian writer. And also that, for MRJ, places he visited all over the country and on the Continent were, in his words, "prolific in suggestion".

Note:

[1] As far as first appearances prior to *A Warning to the Curious* are concerned, it would seem that "The Haunted Dolls' House" (1922) fits in between "The Uncommon Prayer-book" (1921) and the other two (1924/5), although it is the first tale in *Warning*, with the others in second, third and fourth position. I wonder, did MRJ re-order the stories as he wanted the three Herefs/Worcs tales to be read as a group (normally in his collections, he stuck to the chronological order of writing)? Or am I barking up entirely the wrong tree with my sequence/group theory? (The two little stories from Eton ephemerals, "After Dark in the Playing Fields" and "There was a Man Dwelt by a Churchyard", also date originally from 1924 but MRJ clearly didn't consider them worth counting with the rest, until he was - presumably - persuaded to include them in the *Collected Ghost Stories* years later.)

Lady Wardrop's Notes 7
The Supernatural Consequences of HS2

I warn you in advance that my column this time is going to be a bit political (not party political) and maybe controversial. But don't worry, the supernatural will kick in soon enough. So - I want to talk about HS2. For those overseas who have never heard of HS2, let me explain. It's a planned new railway line (with completion many years hence) to link the north of England with London. But don't we already have reasonable rail links, you may well ask (I mean infrastructure, not service!)? Yes, we do, but the new line will remove forty minutes or so from the travel time. For this questionable benefit, the cost will be somewhere in the hundreds of billions of pounds - money the country could scarce afford at the moment, I'd have thought. Businesses in the northwest are supposed to be very keen, and there are claims that many new jobs will be created (don't we have enough trouble now with filling job vacancies?), but no actual *person* I've spoken to (and I *am* in the northwest) wants it.

The monetary cost is great, but there is another which is far worse. Already work is progressing on clearances for the line (not just the line itself but surrounding areas, supposedly to aid access). This has included the wholesale destruction of ancient woodland, trees associated for hundreds of years with local folklore, and more recent ones planted to commemorate a loved one or a fallen hero. New woodland is being created elsewhere, purportedly to balance the environmental damage, but that will take time to grow and I'd ask a question which the powers that be, inevitably, have never taken into consideration. What about the cost to the supernatural denizens?

John Miller's excellent introduction to the otherwise slightly disappointing *Weird Woods: Tales from the Haunted Forests of Britain* (2020), in the British Library's fine "Tales of the Weird" series of anthologies, deals with this subject:

> Biodiversity offsetting has emerged as a controversial mechanism through which the ecological impacts of infrastructure projects *[such as HS2]* can be mitigated: you cut down some trees here, and plant some more over there; kill some weasels in one location, but make a home for some hedgehogs somewhere else. But what about offsetting ghosts?...
>
> [H]istory, folklore and narrative are ways in which woodlands become meaningful to communities and come to form part of the cultural value of specific environments. These are aspects of our experience of

nature that cannot be offset; the history of a place cannot be traded off against the history of another place; you can't erase the history of one location and just put some more history somewhere else. Weird woods are singular places with very specific energies.

Also in his introduction, Miller mentions legends of a grey lady ghost who is said to haunt Oxney Bottom, a wood in Kent near where he grew up. "If Oxney Bottom was bulldozed to make way for a service station," he ponders, "what would happen to the grey lady?" I was reminded of this when I read a letter in the "It Happened to Me" section of *Fortean Times 397* (Oct 2020). "Chris (name on file)" (who presumably didn't want his full name to be given, to avoid ridicule) writes concerning:

>...something I saw about 12 years ago in Crackley Wood, a small piece of very ancient woodland just outside Kenilworth (sadly, it's soon to be trashed by the works for HS2).
>
>I was walking my dog on a cold, bright and slightly breezy day in early January. Suddenly, just a few yards in front of me, a very large, very loose ball of light brown, dead leaves blew from among the trees on my right, across my path towards the trees on my left... In the middle of the ball of

leaves was a little man, dressed from head to foot in the same light brown shade as the leaves. He was about 18in tall and running. As he (and the leaves) reached a tree on the left of the path, they all just vanished, as if they had gone into the tree - but I'm not sure that's what happened. One moment they were there, moving very rapidly, then they were gone...

This is a more benign version, maybe, of the small "men in browny green", who occupy the Fairy Wood in Algernon Blackwood's "Ancient Lights" ("It's not his, it's ours"). Accepting the experience of "Chris" at face value, which as a pagan I'm very willing to do, I wonder what will happen to the elemental/ghost/fairy/sprite or whatever, once his home is bulldozed for HS2? Will he pack his little spotted hanky-on-a-stick and move elsewhere, or will he simply vanish from existence (just another piece of magic lost). Or perhaps he'll take the same approach as the disturbed phantoms in L.T.C. Rolt's "New Corner" and H.R. Wakefield's "The Seventeenth Hole at Duncaster" (to give two Jamesian examples), and those in the countless tales of the dangers of removing ancient stones, and haunt the railway line, putting the wind up the HS2 workmen and eventually the train passengers? I truly hope he does that!

Which brings me to M.R. James's "A Neighbour's Landmark". Not all of the stories in *Weird Woods* are well chosen. Some, such as Arthur Machen's admittedly great "N", don't even seem to relate much to woods at all. But "A Neighbour's Landmark" is definitely one of John Miller's better choices. Lady Theodosia Ivy (Ivie), the "shrieking ghost" of Betton Wood, can never be at peace, even after the wood is scrubbed up, because she moved a neighbour's landmark, illegally appropriating their land for profit. In my previous column I noted that this tale is probably set in Herefordshire and may have been partly inspired by a haunting recorded in Ella Mary Leather's 1912 book *The Folk-lore of Herefordshire*. She tells of "Old Taylor's Ghost" who haunts because he moved a landmark and can't rest until it's put back in its rightful place. Mrs Leather also notes that she has heard of other similar cases. I don't know the technicalities and rules that govern such cursed spectres, but if "Old Taylor" and Lady Ivie can be so troubled beyond the grave by their moving of a landmark, how much greater must be their rage if they find their land and their trees lost to them, dug up through avarice far worse than their own. And are there others of a similar ilk elsewhere in the country? As the *Book of Common Prayer* warns: "Cursed be he that removeth his neighbour's landmark". May we hope that the HS2 people have bitten off more than they can chew? They've taken out injunctions to prevent people protesting on 'their' sites, but (to quote MRJ) "these precautions avail little against the angry dead".

INTRODUCTIONS

Introduction
The Ghosts & Scholars Book of Shadows Volume 1

In 1967, at the age of sixteen, I discovered science fiction fandom and its just-then-blossoming sub-group, horror fandom. Very possibly this was the most important thing that has ever happened to me, as not only would it shape most of my future creative life but it also caused me to meet my late husband, to whom I was married for over fifty years. In 1969, I published my first science fiction fanzine, *Seagull*, and during the following decade I produced numerous other magazines, and co-founded the British Fantasy Society, editing (not very well!) the first four issues of its journal, *Dark Horizons*.

Ten years on from that original duplicated, pink and spelling-mistake-ridden edition of *Seagull*, the first issue of *Ghosts & Scholars* appeared. My primary object was to publish stories in the tradition of M.R. James, but right from the start I featured a certain amount of non-fiction; and for a while that became my main interest. *Ghosts & Scholars* ceased with issue 33 in 2001, and I began *The Ghosts & Scholars M.R. James Newsletter*. Essentially the *G&S Newsletter* was *G&S* without the fiction.[1] This is what it *was*, but I discovered that people still wanted the story content, and that I wasn't quite as tired of it as I'd thought. In 2008 and again in 2009 I ran story competitions, the object being to complete, or to write a new tale inspired by, two of M.R. James's unfinished drafts, "The Game of Bear" and "Merfield Hall/House", respectively. Both competitions were quite successful, producing entries which were relatively small in number but high in quality. The winners were published in the *G&S Newsletter* in 2009, 2010 and 2011. No other unfinished MRJ draft seemed to offer the same potential for completion by a fresh author, but since the inclusion of fiction in the *G&S Newsletter* had gone down so well with my readers, I started thinking what I should do next.

This was the point when Daniel McGachey, my chief TV reviewer and no mean fiction writer himself, came up with the suggestion that a new competition could involve sequels to MRJ's completed stories. This seemed like a good idea to me, but I decided to extend it to include prequels as well as sequels. I hoped that more authors would be interested in participating than in the previous, somewhat specialist competitions, so rather than publish all the winning entries in the *G&S Newsletter* I thought I might print only the one winner in the magazine, and additionally produce an entire book of the best entries. 2012 was the ideal time, it being the 150th anniversary of M.R. James's birth (an event celebrated even by the British Post Office who issued an MRJ stamp in their "Britons of Distinction" series). The first small publisher I approached concerning the project, Sarob Press's Robert Morgan, was every bit as keen as I was, so an announcement appeared in the Spring 2011 issue of the *G&S Newsletter*.

I noted that:

> Of course, there have already been examples of sequels - David Sutton's "Return to the Runes" in the second issue of [the original] *G&S*, for instance - but there are still plenty of possibilities. What happened to the 'satyr' (or 'satyrs') after the end of "An Episode of Cathedral History"? Are the lanes of Islington still frequented by whatever it was that Dr Abell encountered in "Two Doctors". What is left of the residue of the atrocities in "An Evening's Entertainment"; and do Count Magnus and his little friend still lurk at a certain crossroads in Essex? As for prequels, I for one would like to know what sort of treasure Canon Alberic found, how it was guarded, and the details of his death in bed of a sudden seizure. And what exactly was James Wilson's belief system, which prompted him to have his ashes placed in the globe in the centre of Mr Humphreys' maze: what is the significance of the figures on the globe - *was* Wilson

a member of a Gnostic sect? Need I go on? I'm sure you can think of many more mysteries and questions that demand to be solved and answered. I must emphasise that any competition entry which is just a revamp or parody of the plot of the chosen story is unlikely to be placed very highly. I'm looking for something more original than that.

The quantity and quality of entries exceeded my wildest dreams (four times as many as for any of the previous competitions), although they were slow to start arriving and most came within a couple of months of the December 31st, 2011, deadline. I think it was somewhere around the beginning of December that I officially moved from panicking over whether enough good entries would come in for the book, to panicking over the fact that I'd got too many and some worthy ones would have to be excluded (I am a world-class panicker, as those who know me well will attest). Another concern was that everyone would choose the more well-known MRJ stories on which to base their sequels and prequels, but I needn't really have worried: although some tales did inspire more than one entry while others failed to inspire any, the range was quite wide. Most people chose stories from MRJ's first two collections, *Ghost Stories of an Antiquary* and *More Ghost Stories*; disappointingly few picked later ones from *A Thin Ghost* and *A Warning to the Curious*; and a surprisingly large number of brave, nonconformist souls tackled those very late stories which post-dated all of MRJ's four collections: tales which are often, unfairly, considered inferior to what had gone before. My only real regret is that not many of my specific questions, as mentioned in my announcement, had been answered.

The winning story, which was published in the Spring 2012 *G&S Newsletter* first, before appearing here in *The Ghosts & Scholars Book of Shadows*, was hard to choose: I made a shortlist of three or four relatively easily, but which of those to opt for? That was a tough decision as they were all very different, but I think I made the right choice in Christopher Harman's "Quis est Iste?": its sombre, bleak quality was too beguiling for me to resist (dare I say that I find it more frightening and disturbing than MRJ's original?). Doubtless there are readers of this book who will disagree with me and will consider other tales of equal or higher quality, but "Quis est Iste?" is the one that has given me nightmares.

So, in the following pages you'll find prequels to "Canon Alberic's Scrap-book" (Helen Grant), "Wailing Well" (Derek John) and "The Malice of Inanimate Objects" (David A. Sutton); sequels to "The Mezzotint" (John Llewellyn Probert),

"Oh, Whistle, and I'll Come to You, My Lad" (Christopher Harman), "The Treasure of Abbot Thomas" (Jacqueline Simpson), "Casting the Runes" (Louis Marvick), "Two Doctors" (Mark Valentine), "The Experiment" (C.E. Ward) and "A Vignette" (Peter Bell); a combined prequel and sequel to "A School Story" (Reggie Oliver); and one tale (Rick Kennett) which is neither a prequel nor a sequel but offers a new view of events in "The Mezzotint". "The Mezzotint", incidentally, is the story that provoked the greatest number of entries. I'm not sure why this should be: it's true that the central conceit of the moving picture is a great one, but surely the plot leaves few unanswered questions? Or does it?[2] Clearly many of you thought differently. In order not to unbalance the book by including a whole bunch of tales inspired by the same original, I had to be particularly strict with "The Mezzotint" entries, but it is still unique in being represented by two tales here. The same strictness applies to "Casting the Runes" which was - more predictably - a close runner-up to "The Mezzotint" in the popularity stakes.

The competition entries that failed to achieve a place in this volume did so for a variety of reasons; mainly, of course, because they weren't quite good enough. But it was encouraging to discover just how literate and well-written most of them were: back in the '80s and '90s when I was considering fiction for *Ghosts & Scholars*, I'm sure the standard wasn't as high. In some cases, there were promising ideas which were just not well enough executed. Someone extrapolated on the much-discussed possibility of the Dr Watson who treated Mr Dunning's servants in "Casting the Runes" being the same gentleman as Sherlock Holmes' Dr Watson; another managed to link Mrs Mothersole from "The Ash-tree" into events in "The Mezzotint"; and yet another proposed a working relationship between Mr Karswell from "Casting the Runes" and Mr Baxter from "A View from a Hill" (in a tale you'll be seeing elsewhere as it was excellent, but too long for this collection).[3]

Some of the stories which did make the final cut in *The Book of Shadows* are fairly straightforwardly in the M.R. James tradition, others not so much, and a few scarcely at all (it was never a stipulation of the competition rules that they should be). I consider this variety to be very satisfactory, but it does mean that many readers will find not all the tales precisely to their taste. If you're expecting the contents of this book to be indistinguishable from the originals in feel or theme (or, more realistically, to be pale copies - shadows - of them), then you're definitely going to be disappointed. "Worthy of the master himself," might be considered a compliment in most contexts, but not here: the best of the stories clearly show the voices of their authors, sometimes in quite quirky ways, rather than slavishly aping the aforesaid master. But I like to think they haven't made the opposite mistake either: I recently read a collection of tales ostensibly inspired by H.P. Lovecraft, which - with a few rather good exceptions - seemed to have little or no connection to that great American inspirer of pastiches. I felt cheated! Here, however, you'll find that there is always a powerful connection with the MRJ stories in question - just not always the one you expect.

I've chosen to arrange the tales in this book in the same order as the publication dates of the MRJ stories that inspired them. Not only did this seem the most logical way of doing it, but it makes it easier for the reader to refer to the originals in any of the various collected MRJ volumes. Which brings me to a final warning: most if not all of these tales assume that the reader has at least some knowledge of the MRJ stories of which they are the sequels and prequels. Without that, some of them will appear confusing, or even pointless and meaningless. I make no apology for this. If you are not familiar with the fiction of James, then go at once and rectify the situation before venturing forth into the umbral depths of this *Book of Shadows*.

Notes:

[1] In 2018, the *G&S Newsletter* reverted back to the old *G&S* title, continuing the original numbering sequence. It had returned to the format that suited it best and published regular fiction again. Since giving up my editorship in 2019, it has continued under a series of guest editors.

[2] Since this was written, a whole new question has arisen - new to me anyway, as I'd never thought to consider it; and it's not one tackled by any of the *Book of Shadows* entries. Why is the revenant clad in a "strange *black* garment with a white cross on the back"? [my italics] That's hardly a traditional colour for a shroud.

[3] Daniel McGachey's "Ex Libris: Lufford", published in a separate booklet with that title, which rode with *G&S Newsletter 22* in 2012.

Contents of the first *Book of Shadows*

"Alberic de Mauléon" by Helen Grant; "Anningley Hall, Early Morning" by Rick Kennett; "The Mezzotaint" by John Llewellyn Probert; "Quis est Iste" by Christopher Harman; "The Guardian" by Jacqueline Simpson; "Between Four Yews" by Reggie Oliver; "The Mirror of Don Ferrante" by Louis Marvick; "Fire Companions" by Mark Valentine; "Of Three Girls and of Their Talk" by Derek John; "The Gift" by C.E. Ward; "Malice" by David A. Sutton; "Glamour of Madness" by Peter Bell.

Introduction
The Ghosts & Scholars Book of Shadows Volume 2

M.R. James, in the brief Preface to his third and shortest assemblage of supernatural tales, *A Thin Ghost and Others* (1919), had this to say on the risks of follow-up volumes: "...sequels are, not only proverbially but actually, very hazardous things". Some will argue that he was right to pre-empt possible criticisms of what is widely considered to be his weakest collection, but *A Thin Ghost* contains much to enjoy. Stories such as "The Residence at Whitminster", "The Diary of Mr Poynter". "The Story of a Disappearance and an Appearance" and "Two Doctors" can be dismissed as disappointing and - in some cases - confused, slapdash efforts; yet those very flaws can also leave the reader with an elusive feeling that there is a lot more to the tales than meets the eye. This is why the contents of *A Thin Ghost*, while not exactly popular, would seem to be appealing candidates for prequels and sequels.

After the success of *The Ghosts & Scholars Book of Shadows* in 2012, which went out of print very speedily, Robert Morgan proposed a second Sarob Press volume of MRJ prequels and sequels. Although I had a moment of doubt on remembering James's line concerning the hazards involved, I quickly realised that there were plenty of possibilities. The first *Book of Shadows* contained twelve stories inspired by eleven of James's tales. This left something over twenty of his completed stories for authors to choose from: "Lost Hearts", "The Ash-tree", "Number 13", "Count Magnus", "The Rose Garden", "The Tractate Middoth", "The Stalls of Barchester Cathedral", "Martin's Close", "Mr Humphreys and His Inheritance", "The Residence at Whitminster", "The Diary of Mr Poynter", "An Episode of Cathedral History", "The Story of a Disappearance and an Appearance", "The Haunted Dolls' House", "The Uncommon Prayer-book", "A Neighbour's Landmark", "A View from a Hill", "A Warning to the Curious", "An Evening's Entertainment", "There was a Man Dwelt by a Churchyard", "Rats" and "After Dark in the Playing Fields".

Soon after this list was published in *The Ghosts & Scholars M.R. James Newsletter* and on various websites in 2013, the submissions for volume two started to come in and I was quite surprised at the variety. The actual number of submissions was slightly down on those for book one, but the quality was at least as good. I suppose I expected the most popular and well-known MRJ stories, such as "Count Magnus" and "A Warning to the Curious", to be the subject of most entries. In the case of "Count Magnus" this was certainly

INTRODUCTIONS

true, but "A Warning to the Curious" produced no submissions at all, while the supposedly unpopular "The Story of a Disappearance and an Appearance" equalled the score of "Count Magnus". In fact, the contents of *A Thin Ghost* did very well indeed this time around (not counting "Two Doctors", which was already covered in volume one).

This second collection once again contains twelve stories inspired by eleven of James's tales: "After Dark in the Playing Fields", "Count Magnus", "The Diary of Mr Poynter", "The Haunted Dolls' House", "Mr Humphreys and His Inheritance", A Neighbour's Landmark", "Rats", "The Residence at Whitminster" (2), "The Story of a Disappearance and an Appearance", "The Tractate Middoth" and "The Uncommon Prayer-book". I won't say which author picked which story, as I received some complaints when I did so in my introduction for volume one. Some of you considered this an unwanted intrusion of spoilers, when you would have preferred to spot the influences as you read the book. This is fair enough, although spoilers are still provided by the sequence of the following, which - as with book one - appear in the same order as the MRJ tales in the *Collected Ghost Stories* that inspired them.

There are eight sequels and two prequels. Of the remaining two stories, one is (like the same author's contribution in volume one) "neither a prequel nor a sequel but offers a new view on events"; and the other is, to coin a word, a 'midquel' (as Reggie Oliver has pointed out elsewhere, 'prequel' is an ugly Frankenstein's monster of a coinage, so I don't think 'midquel' can be considered any worse!).

The authors include eight who also appeared in the first book and four newcomers, a couple of whom will be familiar names to regular readers of small press supernatural fiction and a couple who may be unfamiliar to you. There was no bias or favouritism in my choices: those writers who have cropped up for a second time have done so purely on the merits of their submissions. One of these and one of the newcomers provide, in my opinion, the two scariest and most chilling scenes in the book, but I'll leave you to come to your own conclusions on which they are. As with volume one, there was no requirement that a submission should, of itself, be in the Jamesian tradition but this time most of them are, at least to some extent. Nevertheless, I think you'll find a nice range of tales. I will just add one question (like M.R. James, I'm not averse to pre-empting criticism!): where are the women? Women are just as good at writing Jamesian fiction as men but, as before, only two of the stories in this book are by those of us of the female persuasion. I'm rather glad that I am myself female, thereby (or maybe not) avoiding accusations of sexism. If and when there is a third volume (we still have eleven MRJ tales to go!), I hope women will be better represented. Let's make Lady Wardrop and Mrs Anstruther, those two powerful and most admirable of women from James's stories ("Mr Humphreys and His Inheritance" and "The Rose Garden" respectively) proud.

Contents of the second *Book of Shadows*
"Lineage" by David Longhorn; "A Tale from Kildonan" by Elsa Wallace; "Touched" by John Howard; "Absalom" by Reggie Oliver; "Slapstick" by Christopher Harman; "The Sands o' Dee" by Peter Bell; "11334" by C.E. Ward; "Dolls for Another Day" by Rick Kennett; "The Desecrator" by Derek John; "The Third Time" by Helen Grant; "Character" by Mark Valentine; "The Partygoers" by John Ward.

Introduction
The Ghosts & Scholars Book of Shadows Volume 3

M.R. James's introduction to his third collection, *A Thin Ghost and Others*, was only a hundred or so words long. I'll try to do a little better here! *The Ghosts & Scholars Book of Shadows* volumes one and two included twenty-four new prequels and sequels inspired by twenty-two of Monty James's tales. That left twelve of his stories for a third volume to complete the sequence. It was always going to be unlikely that I would get excellent submissions for *all* of these twelve, and whilst I may have hoped that the universe would, for once, work in exactly the right way, I didn't really expect it to. I was also worried that the limited choice of remaining stories might put people off. On that count, I didn't need to be concerned: writers seem to have risen to the challenge in a remarkable way and some of the contributions in this third book are among my absolute favourites of the whole series. Here you will find sequels to eight of MRJ's tales: "Lost Hearts" (two), "Number 13", "The Rose Garden", "The Stalls of Barchester Cathedral" (two), "A View from a Hill", "A Warning to the Curious" (two), "An Evening's Entertainment" (two) and "There was a Man Dwelt by a Churchyard". That leaves just four not covered in any of the books.

The most popular tale among submissions this time was "Lost Hearts" - perhaps surprisingly for a story which was not liked by Monty himself, and which most people don't rate amongst his best. In fact, although only two "Lost Hearts" sequels appear here, I actually accepted three: the third (as good as the others but it was simply the last of the three I received) was published in the *Ghosts & Scholars Newsletter* earlier this year. Similarly with "A Warning to the Curious", among the submissions there were three sequels of an equally high quality, so one has gone into the magazine.[1] I like to think that those acted as a kind of taster for the book itself. Looking at the *Book of Shadows* series as a whole, and the charts I've kept of submissions (successful and otherwise), I find that "Casting the Runes" comes top of the popularity list, with "The Mezzotint" and "Lost Hearts" close runners up, followed by "A Warning to the Curious". If there is a moral to this, as MRJ says, "that moral is, I trust, obvious: if it has none, I do not well know how to help it".

Aside from the usual, unfortunate gender imbalance, the contributors to volume three are a good varied bunch: we have three authors who have already appeared in both of the previous books (Peter Bell, Mark Valentine and C.E. Ward); four who have appeared in one of them (John Howard, John

INTRODUCTIONS

Llewellyn Probert, David A. Sutton and John Ward); and five who are new to the series (Katherine Haynes, Peter Holman, Tom Johnstone, Steve Rasnic Tem and D.P. Watt). Of that last group, there are two who I have never published anywhere before.

This time all the stories are sequels, with no prequels at all, and many are set in modern times; there is even one ingenious piece of science fiction which very neatly resolves a source of puzzlement in one of Monty's tales. As usual, they appear here in the same order as the tales in MRJ's *Collected Ghost Stories* which inspired them.

But what of that neglected rump: the stories not featured in any of the *Books of Shadows*? Aside from the posthumously published "The Fenstanton Witch" (which might be considered a special case), these are "Martin's Close", "The Ash-tree" and "An Episode of Cathedral History" (don't be fooled by the title of Peter Holman's story - it's actually a sequel to another tale entirely). There was a sequel to "An Episode of Cathedral History" by Chico Kidd in *Ghosts & Scholars Newsletter 23*, so really it's only "Martin's Close" and "The Ash-tree" that remain.[2] I hope sequels or prequels to those two, and "The Fenstanton Witch", might appear in future issues of *Ghosts & Scholars*, just to round things off nicely.

And have we, I wonder, learned anything about MRJ's own stories from this project? Probably nothing we didn't know already, but it certainly provides proof, if proof were needed, that his themes are not old-fashioned or outdated. The idea of those hidden, ancient and mysterious things (whether physical objects or arcane knowledge), which are best left undisturbed, still fascinates us now and is likely to continue to do so indefinitely. Of course, Monty did not invent the subject - this "digging down to reveal the hidden content of the under-earth" (both literally and metaphorically), as Robert Macfarlane has put it. No one invented it: it's simply part of our make-up as human beings. But it was deeply important to MRJ and he made it his own in a way that perhaps no other author has done. This may be why, in Robert Macfarlane's words: "We do not seem able to leave M.R. James... behind".

Notes:

[1] Jane Jakeman's "The Transmutation of Base Metal" and David Longhorn's "Dug Out" respectively (*G&S Newsletter 29*, 2016).

[2] Chico Kidd's "Quantum of Darkness" (*G&S Newsletter 23*, 2013). A number of other prequels and sequels appeared in the following couple of years in the *G&S Newsletter*. "Martin's Close" was especially well-served, with a prequel, "The Gypsy's Curse" by Carole Tyrrell (issue 30, 2016), and a sequel, "Assizes" by C.E. Ward (issue 31, 2017).

Contents of the third *Book of Shadows*

"Twenty Years Afterwards" by C.E. Ward; "A Gap in Society" by John Howard; "Temus Edax Rerum" by John Llewellyn Probert; "The Man in the Rose Bushes" by Steve Rasnic Tem; "Another Episode of Cathedral History" by Peter Holman; "Holywood" by Tom Johnstone; "Bone Matter" by David A. Sutton; "The Second Crown" by Katherine Haynes; "The Brooch" by John Ward; "We Don't Want for Company" by D.P. Watt; "Blackberry Time" by Peter Bell; "The Mask of the Dead Mamilius" by Mark Valentine.

Introduction (Extended Version)
A Ghosts & Scholars Book of Folk Horror

Folklore is part of our conversation with land. A way of seeing ourselves in the narratives of place. It is our access to the psychic shrapnel of event, embedded around us. This is our line of transmission. It is echo memory, it is fault line. Folklore is narrative constantly cheating death by changing its jacket. Folklore is the liar that tells the truth of soil, of place.
--- David Southwell (creator/rediscoverer of Hookland)

Pinning down exactly what constitutes "Folk Horror" (or what I always used to call "Earth Mysteries Fiction") can seem like an impossible task. As Andy Paciorek says in his introduction to *Folk Horror Revival: Field Studies* (2015): "In a bid to answer 'What is Folk Horror?' one may as well attempt to build a box the exact shape of mist; for like the mist, Folk Horror is atmospheric and sinuous. It can creep from and into different territories yet leave no universal defining mark of its exact form". The best succinct, if too narrow geographically, definition I have been able to find is the one provided by Stephen Gray on his Folk Horror website (www.folkhorror.com):

Folk horror is a sub-genre of horror fiction... characterised by reference to European, pagan traditions. Stories typically involve standing stone circles, earthworks, elaborate rituals or nature deities. While the genre is not overtly concerned with Christian ideology, frequently used terms such as 'demon' and 'devil' appear to associate folk horror with Christian demonology.

And yet, as Andy Paciorek also notes, "...there appears to be a 'Folk' ambience and aesthetic that more often can be felt intuitively rather than defined logically".

That being the case, opinions are bound to differ on exactly which of M.R. James's stories fit within the Folk Horror category. Surely no one will disagree that *some* do. Adam Scovell, in *Folk Horror: Hours Dreadful and Things Strange* (2017), goes so far as to assert that "James and the ideals he represents create the topographical backbone for Folk Horror". As Jim Moon writes, in his article on MRJ in *Folk Horror Revival: Field Studies*: "that view of James' tales being cosily enclosed in the study rooms and libraries of old universities is actually... fallacious... more often than not the main action of the stories occurs far from the groves of academia, and indeed far from the safety of towns or cities". This is not to say that a supernatural tale set in the countryside must by definition be Folk Horror. In his 2015 *Guardi-*

an article, "The Eeriness of the English Countryside", Robert Macfarlane explains:

> James stays with us [because of] his understanding of landscape... as constituted by uncanny forces, part-buried sufferings and contested ownerships. Landscape, in James, is... a realm that snags, bites and troubles. He repeatedly invokes the pastoral - the green dream of natural tranquility and social order - only to traumatise it.

But is "Casting the Runes", for instance, a Folk Horror tale? Stephen Gray lists it as such, along with "The Residence at Whitminster". The latter probably is, for the central character of Lord Saul apparently acquires his secret knowledge while frequenting the ancient raths in Ireland. But "Casting the Runes" doesn't get onto my list - I don't think the fact that Mr Karswell wrote a dubious book on the *History of Witchcraft* and "invented a new religion for himself" is enough (some scenes in *Night of the Demon*, the 1957 film version of "Casting the Runes", *are* Folk Horror, however). On the other hand, Kai Roberts has James's "The Ash-tree" in his thought-provoking "Twenty Classic British Folk Horor Stories" web page (kairoberts.wordpress.com/2015/07/08/twenty-classic-british-folk-horror-stories/). "This tale of witchcraft, familiar spirits and an ancestral curse," he writes, "is steeped in atmosphere and culminates in a truly unnerving manifestation; which, whilst having no root in folkloric witchcraft, invokes a unique maleficium that feels entirely consistent with tradition." I would certainly agree with that, but others will rule it out because, as he says, it (arguably) has "no root in folkloric witchcraft".

In 2015 I compiled a list of the MRJ stories which I personally would define as Folk Horror, and then put it into my contribution for The Everlasting Club ghost story APA. Thanks to the input of a number of the members there (and some animated arguments!), I added several more titles. Here, then, is our list of James's Folk Horror tales (some definite, some with scenes or touches which might or might not qualify them). It's a long one, containing nearly two-thirds of his ghost story output:

"After Dark in the Playing Fields"
"The Ash-tree"
"Count Magnus"
"An Evening's Entertainment"
"The Fenstanton Witch"
"Martin's Close"
"The Mezzotint"
"Mr Humphreys and His Inheritance"
"A Neighbour's Landmark"

INTRODUCTIONS

"Oh, Whistle, and I'll Come to You, My Lad"
"Rats"
"The Residence at Whitminster"
"The Rose Garden"
"The Stalls of Barchester Cathedral"
"Two Doctors"
"A View from a Hill"
"A Vignette"
"Wailing Well"
"A Warning to the Curious"
"John Humphreys" (unfinished draft)

Ghosts & Scholars and its successor the *Ghosts & Scholars Newsletter* were created to cover the writings of James himself and Jamesian fiction in general, both old and new. It's hardly a surprise, therefore, that many of the stories published in the magazines over the past four decades have also been Folk Horror. I've been able to come up with a list of over fifty tales, and these are just from new fiction in the two magazines, and not in any of my other Haunted Library booklets or the three *Ghosts & Scholars Books of Shadows* from Sarob Press.

From this list I've chosen ten of my favourites, which I think are representative, but which are also among the lesser known, for many *Ghosts & Scholars* stories have been reprinted more than once (this explains the exclusion of some tales that might have been expected to feature). Here you'll find Folk Horror in a variety of expected and unexpected settings, from ancient burial mounds in Wiltshire and East Anglia to a park in Liverpool, by way of ruins in Ireland, and the countryside/villages of the Lake District, Dorset, Derbyshire and an unspecified southern county. In fact, Derbyshire seems to be a particularly popular setting for Folk Horror in *G&S*: no fewer than three of the stories are set in that county ("The Walls", "The Spinney" and - although not stated in the tale - "The Lane"). In date, the stories range from 1980 (the second issue of *G&S*) to 2013 (*G&S Newsletter 23*). It might seem surprising that two of them are inspired by one of MRJ's least, and least-loved tales, "After Dark in the Playing Fields", but we shouldn't underrate the more sinister aspects of that late and under-appreciated story.

For the second section of this volume I invited submissions of new Jamesian Folk Horror. To the difficulty of defining Folk Horror was therefore added the problem of defining once more what constitutes "Jamesian". Having published Jamesian fiction for nearly forty years, I'm still not sure I can say what it is,[1] but I console myself with the thought (right or wrong) that by now I can surely spot it instinctively. That's a good enough excuse for *not* defining it here, other than to say that at the core of the Jamesian story (and others, I acknowledge) is the idea of 'hidden things best left hidden'. I had to reject a few new stories which were good Folk Horror but had no Jamesian aspects as far as I could detect, but the seven I accepted all seem to me to fulfill the criteria, at least to some degree. In this section, the settings range further afield and include Scotland and Greece. In one case, while the setting is Scotland, the Folk Horror comes terrifyingly from pre-war Germany.

A final quote from Hookland's David Southwell, I think, sums up what I'm aiming for in this book: "...folklore - that dark sediment of decomposing memory, disturbed by ritual, disturbed by our being in a place".

Note:

[1] Now, a few years further on, I still wouldn't want to try to define "Jamesian". I doubt whether I ever will with any degree of certainty.

Contents of the *Book of Folk Horror*

"Meeting Mr Ketchum" by Michael Chislett; "Figures in a Landscape" by Chico Kidd; "The Burning" by Ramsey Campbell; "Where are the Bones ...?" by Jacqueline Simpson; "The Spinney" by C.E. Ward; "Beatrix Paints a Landscape (1884)" by Philip Thompson; "The Walls" by Terry Lamsley; "The Peewold Amphisbaena" by Kay Fletcher; "The Lane" by

Geoffrey Warburton; "Lorelei" by Carole Tyrrell; "Variant Versions" by Gail-Nina Anderson; "The Valley of Achor" by Helen Grant; "The Cutty Wren" by Tom Johnstone; "Sisters Rise" by Christopher Harman; "The Discontent of Familiars" by John Llewellyn Probert; "The Dew-Shadows" by David A. Sutton; "Out of the Water, Out of the Ground" by S.A. Rennie.

Introduction
The Ghosts & Scholars Book of Mazes

The history of mazes and labyrinths is a long one, dating back at least to classical times if not earlier. In Great Britain, the first walkable mazes appeared in the medieval period, and mostly consisted of unicursal examples (i.e. with only one path) marked out in turf or stones, or as mosaics in churches. These seem to have been used as aids to prayer and meditation. The first hedge puzzle mazes were built in the Tudor era and grew in popularity until the eighteenth century; in their heyday examples could be found not only in the grounds of stately homes, but in Victorian municipal parks and gardens. Other mazes have been built in a variety of mediums such mirrors, and in recent years temporary crop (or maize) mazes have become very popular. Examples of all types of maze can be found in short fantasy and supernatural fiction, and some are even located on other planets (H.P. Lovecraft's nightmarish 1939 tale "In the Walls of Eryx" is set on Venus). The Internet Speculative Fiction Database lists over two hundred stories and novels with the word maze in their title, of which over thirty are called "Maze", "The Maze" or "In the Maze". While some of these won't concern mazes in their true sense, many must - and then there are all the stories about mazes which don't have that word in their title...

M.R. James's "Mr Humphreys and His Inheritance" is one of the most famous maze short stories, if not *the* most famous. In it, Mr Humphreys inherits from his uncle an estate at Wilsthorpe (Lincolnshire?) containing a yew hedge maze. It was erected by his uncle's grandfather in the late eighteenth century. When Mr Humphreys enters it, through an archway over which is inscribed *Secretum meum mihi et filiis domus meae* ("My secret is for me and the sons of my house"), he discovers a pedestal at the centre topped by a copper globe on which are etched mysterious figures from the Old Testament, ancient history and mythology. All have in common that they embody evil or dark magic in some way ("The scheme of the whole, indeed, seemed to be an assemblage of the patriarchs of evil, perhaps not uninfluenced by a study of Dante"). Mr Humphreys has several increasingly disturbing experiences until finally discovering, with the aid of the maze expert Lady Wardrop, what it is in that brass globe.

The story has had an influence on other writers, notably Edmund Crispin, whose Gervase Fen detective novel *Frequent Hearses* (1950) contains a dramatic scene in a maze: it's a maze which, as with MRJ's, has the remains of its maker at its centre. Crispin, who wrote a couple of fine Jamesian tales himself, quotes extensively from the "Parable of this Unhappy Condition" in "Mr Humphreys": "...he begun to be sensible of some Creature keeping Pace with him and, as he thought, *peering and looking upon him* from the next alley to that he was in...", etc.

Michael Cox, in his notes on "Mr Humphreys and His Inheritance" (*Casting the Runes and Other Ghost Stories*, 1987) suggests that an inspiration for the tale might have been the mid-nineteenth-century maze at Somerleyton Hall in Suffolk. It *is* a yew maze like Mr Humphreys', so it may have been - I'm sure MRJ would have known about it. But there is little other resemblance between the two: the Somerleyton maze has a small artificial knoll with a pagoda at the centre. I have long thought that the maze on the village green at Hilton, a few miles from Cambridge, is a better candidate. Although the Hilton labyrinth is a unicursal turf example (originally marked out with pebbles), as opposed to Mr Humphreys' puzzle hedge maze, both have a central column on top of which is a globe. Admittedly in the Hilton case it's made of stone rather than copper, but it *is* incised - not with Biblical and mythological figures but with the markings for a sundial (compare this with Mr Humphreys initial thought when he first explores his maze that "the central ornament was a sundial").

The Hilton maze itself was either cut or possibly recut by the nineteen-year-old William Sparrow in 1660, to commemorate the Restoration of Charles II (the Sparrow family were keen Royalists), but the pedestal and globe in the middle, comprising "Sparrow's Monument", were erected in 1729, the year of William Sparrow's death. The pedestal is inscribed with his coat of arms and: *"Sic Transit Gloria Mundi. Guilielmus Sparrow, Gen., natus ano. 1641. Aetatis sui 88 quando obit, hos gyros formavit anno 1660"* ("...William Sparrow, Gentleman, born 1641, died at the age of 88, formed these circuits in 1660").

According to Nigel Pennick's authoritative *Mazes and Labyrinths* (1990), the globe and sundial gnomon from the pedestal were removed in 1899 and placed on an entrance pillar to a nearby farm. So when "Mr Humphreys" was written *circa* 1911, the globe would no longer have been in position. But by 1899 MRJ had been at Cambridge for around seventeen years, so it's very likely that he will have visited and known about such a rare local antiquity before the loss of the globe. The site was restored in 1891 after a period of neglect when "the grass was allowed to overgrow the maze, and cattle grazed upon it, using Sparrow's Monument as a rubbing post". But the missing globe wasn't put back until later, probably in the 1920s. It was either restored or replaced in the 1960s (the gnomon is long gone). The maze is well looked after today.

The globe and pedestal in the middle of the Hilton labyrinth are a *memorial* to William Sparrow rather than his actual resting place, so not exactly the same as that of Mr Humphrey's uncle's grandfather James Wilson, but to have a commemoration of a maze-builder at the centre of his maze seems unusual enough that it may have impressed itself on MRJ.

Given that so many weird tales have been written about mazes, it is surprising that until now there doesn't seem to have an anthology entirely devoted to them. For *The Ghosts & Scholars Book of Mazes* I have picked eight maze stories to reprint, all of them taken from small press journals and books, and some of them never previously reprinted. The mazes range from unicursal turf through puzzle hedge to modern crop examples; one tale is a prequel to "Mr Humphreys and His Inheritance". The second part of the book consists of brand new stories which range even more widely, from a Roman mosaic maze to a mirror maze at the top of a high-rise office block! All of the stories have a folklore, folk custom and/or antiquarian background, but in most other ways, they are very different. I leave it up to you to decide whether all in their various ways are (to quote the lettering incised into the underneath of the stones from Mr Humphreys' maze):

> PENETRANS AD INTERIORA MORTIS...

Contents of the *Book of Mazes*

"As Blank as the Days Yet to Be" by Mark Valentine; "The Maze" by Michael Chislett; "My Dancing Days are Over" by Paul StJohn Mackintosh; "The Outsider" by Rick Kennett; "The Rustling of Tiny Paws" by Carole Tyrrell; "The Maze" by Geoffrey Warburton; "The Faerie Ring" by John Reppion; "The Maze at Huntsmere" by Reggie Oliver; "The Lost Maze" by Helen Grant; "Mr Rhodes and the Crawshay Inheritance" by Katherine Haynes; "Real Estate" by C.E. Ward; "The Air of Glory" by John Howard; "Mouselode Maze" by Christopher Harman; "The Mosaic Maze" by Victoria Day.

Introduction
The Ghosts & Scholars Book of Follies and Grottoes

What is a folly? No two books on the subject seem to agree exactly; in fact, sometimes two books by the same author disagree! I first became fascinated by the subject when I read Barbara Jones's *Follies and Grottoes* in the 1970s (the second edition was published in 1974). I still think it's the most inspirational volume on the topic, so it's disappointing to see that her definition is rather too narrow for me: "A folly might be defined as a useless building erected for ornament on a gentleman's estate". I prefer one of the descriptions given on the "Folly" Wikipedia page. After noting that some "have no purpose other than as an ornament", it adds: "Often they have some of the appearance of a building constructed for a particular purpose, such as a castle or tower, but this appearance is a sham. Equally, if they have a purpose, it may be disguised". You will find edifices fitting into this category several times in the stories I've gathered together here.

Follies may be fake temples, belvederes, pyramids, obelisks and towers, sham castles and ruins, eye-catchers, faux druid circles and hermitages (with or without a fake hermit!), and many other things besides. Folly grottoes are often cut out of rock and decorated, frequently with shells (such as the one at Margate in Kent, which is famously often claimed to be genuinely pre-Christian). Sometimes a folly on a Georgian or Victorian gentleman's estate will reflect his experiences on the Grand Tour of Europe. An example of this is the copy of the Temple of the Sibyl at Tivoli, which seems to have made such an impression on M.R. James that it turns up in two of his stories (I don't think he ever visited the original building in person). In the gardens of Castringham Hall in "The Ash-tree", "...a reproduction of the Sibyl's temple at Tivoli was erected on the opposite bank of the mere". It plays no part in the plot, but the same type of folly has a more important role in "Mr Humphreys and His Inheritance". It is a subsidiary role to that played by the maze, but it is still significant.

"What is that white building on the mound at the end of the grass ride?" asks Mr Humphreys, during his first tour of the garden of his newly inherited estate at Wilsthorpe. The gardener, Mr Cooper, replies: "...the Temple of Friendship. Constructed of marble brought out of Italy for the purpose, by your late uncle's grandfather. Would it interest you perhaps to take a turn there?" Mr Humphreys sees that:

> The general lines of the temple were those of the Sibyl's Temple at Tivoli, helped out by a dome, only

> the whole was a good deal smaller. Some ancient sepulchral reliefs were built into the wall, and about it all was a pleasant flavour of the grand tour. Cooper produced the key, and with some difficulty opened the heavy door. Inside there was a handsome ceiling, but little furniture. Most of the floor was occupied by a pile of thick circular blocks of stone, each of which had a single letter deeply cut on its slightly convex upper surface.

Those blocks of stone are from the floor of the maze and later, when put in order, reveal a clue as to what is contained in the globe at its centre.

In Steve Duffy's excellent "The Last of the Scarisfields" (1998), the "peculiarly ugly and prominent species of belvedere", likened to a "suburban-size" version of the Acropolis, was also built ("it is conjectured") after a scion of the family returned from the Grand Tour. But his delving into the Black Arts, later taken up by a nephew, sees that building put to demonic use of a Judaeo-Christian rather than a classical kind, resulting in two terrible deaths there.[1]

Considering the atmospheric eccentricity of many real follies and grottoes, surprisingly few are reputed to be haunted. Of course, the follies and artificial tunnels at West Wycombe (Bucks), the eighteenth-century home of the Hell Fire Club's

Sir Francis Dashwood, are supposed to be beset by unexplained manifestations, but this may be a modern phenomenon having more to do with lucrative ghost tours and TV investigations. More interesting is Dinton Castle (also Bucks), long a ruin but now converted into a luxury home. This mock castle was built in 1769 by Sir John Vanhatten to house his collection of fossils, which are incorporated into its walls. The supposed ghost isn't as old as the fossils (nor as old as the Saxon burial ground on which the tower was built), but it pre-dates the tower by more than half a century. John Bigg, the "Dinton Hermit", was clerk to Simon Mayne who was executed for his involvement with the trial of Charles I. One rumour has it that Bigg was the King's executioner. After the accession of Charles II and the death of Mayne, Bigg lived the life of a hermit in a cave or tunnel at Dinton (possibly the tunnel discovered to lead from the folly to the main Hall) until his death in 1696. As with West Wycombe, it's difficult to say how old the legends of his ghost are, but they may have arisen at the same time as twentieth-century claims about UFOs in the area (and the tower is said to be on a ley!).

The rarity of actual haunted follies is echoed in the relatively few examples of weird or supernatural tales making use of the possibilities of such settings. Can the Italian "Tower of Sacrifice" with its infinite stairs, in Marghanita

Laski's classic "The Tower" (1955), be considered a folly? Probably not, as the tower is dated to the first half of the sixteenth century, making it far too early, although in many other ways the story would certainly qualify. Don Tumasonis's splendid "What Goes Down" (2001) has something of the same feel as "The Tower"; but the ancient Danish building in it is even older. Whatever it is, it's not a folly.

Two of the best short stories unquestionably involving follies are, in fact, by crime writers, and feature their most famous detectives. In both, the deaths have rational explanations, and yet I would argue that they also come within the supernatural fiction genre. Dorothy L. Sayers' short story "Striding Folly" (1939) is ostensibly a Lord Peter Wimsey murder mystery, in which the body of the victim is found in the "ridiculous stone tower known as the Folly" of the title. However, the supernatural aspects of the story can't be ignored. The plot centres around Mr Mellilow's strange dream, where the folly also appears. In a much distorted, surreal fashion, his dream predicts the future. The tower moves, crossing rivers and leaping woods, and seems to be pursuing him. Then another tower, the mirror image of the first, also appears and the two pin him between them, while "about their feet went a monstrous stir, like the quiver of a crouching cat". Later, the dream is echoed in his chess game with a sinister stranger.

The murder in Agatha Christie's 1928 tale "The Idol House of Astarte" is solved neatly by Miss Marple. The "Idol House" is a folly built by the new owner of an estate on Dartmoor. The folly is in the middle of a grove in which, supposedly, in ancient times the locals worshipped Astarte/Ishtar. The building, a sort of stone summerhouse, contains a small statue of "a woman with crescent horns, seated on a lion". A socialite member of a house party seems briefly to be possessed by the goddess, during which episode the estate owner falls dead, stabbed by a blade that is not to be found. While the explanation is straightforward (and obvious, once it is explained by Miss Marple), the reader is left in no doubt that the folly and the grove have an evil atmosphere: "There were a dozen soft sounds all round us, whisperings and sighings". One character talks of places "imbued and saturated with good or evil influences".

As with my previous Sarob collection *The Ghosts & Scholars Book of Mazes*, I've included here (five) reprints selected from small press books and journals, some of them never previously reprinted. The eight brand new stories similarly range widely, from mysterious towers and classical temples to hidden grottoes; from revivals of the worship of ancient gods to unexpected distortions of space and time. All of the authors have provided their own take on the subject, and I hope you will agree that they have definitely recognised the eerie potential of such strange, eccentric and wonderful creations.

Note:

1 If this story is so excellent why, you may well ask, did I not include it in the book? The answer is simply that I forgot about it until some time after the contents had been finalised.

Contents of the *Book of Follies and Grottoes*

"Baines' Folly" by Christopher Harman; "Lady Elphinstone's Folly" by John Ward; "The Ptolomaic System" by David Longhorn; "The Crooked Rook" by Rick Kennett; "Sweet Folly" by Gail-Nina Anderson; "Branks's Folly" by C.E. Ward; "Folly" by Sam Dawson; "Minter's Folly" by Chico Kidd; "Mothrot Hall" by Katherine Haynes; "'Father' O'Flynn and the Fressingfold Friezes" by Tina Rath; "Mad Lutanist" by Mark Valentine; "When I Heard My Days Before Me" by John Howard; "And Music Shall Untune the Sky" by S.A. Rennie.

Introduction
The Angry Dead (2021 edition)

But these precautions avail little against
the angry dead
from M.R. James's
"The Malice of Inanimate Objects"

I can remember exactly where I was when I got the idea for the first of the twelve stories which were eventually collected together in *The Angry Dead*, published by Richard Fawcett in 2000. I was at Euston Station about to get on a train to go home from London to Liverpool, and suddenly an ending came into my head, which I thought was pretty original. I still do - it's the climax of "The Sheelagh-na-gig". I then wrote the story (including some opinions on the nature of sheelagh-na-gigs which I've long since abandoned). I was not happy with it, and put it away, showing it only to David Rowlands, then assistant editor (fiction) on *Ghosts & Scholars*. Unlike all the tales which followed, it was written in the third rather than the first person. Eventually I threw the manuscript away (this was before I got a computer and became quite OCD on backing up). Next came several stories in a rush and I can't remember in which order I wrote them. All I do recall is that I seemed to produce one every few weeks for a period of months in the 1980s. If I'd kept up this schedule I could be today's Lionel Fanthorpe (who wrote a total of 381 tales for *Supernatural Stories* in the '50s and '60s). But no, the urge to write fiction left me as suddenly as it had arrived, and it has never really returned.

From 1983 to 1985, stories appeared in small press zines: Jeff Dempsey and David Cowperthwaite's *Dark Dreams* ("Hold Fast"), Jessica Amanda Salmonson's *Fantasy & Terror* ("The Blue Boar of Totenhoe", "The Hatchment") and *Fantasy Macabre* ("The Wandlebury Eyecatcher"); and in Jessica's two *Tales by Moonlight* books ("Joan", "The Gravedigger and Death"). It's less the case now, but back then I was a little wary of editors including their own stories in collections, which is why I was unsure about putting any of mine in *Ghosts & Scholars* until David Rowlands jokingly gave me an ultimatum: either I put "The Gravedigger and Death" in *G&S*, or he wouldn't let me publish his Father O'Connor tale "Conkers". So both went into *G&S 5* (1983), to be followed by two stories in the 1985 Haunted Library booklet *A Graven Image* ("Ne Resurgat" and "Margaret and Catherine", with two more by David and two by Roger Johnson). The Haunted Library was my imprint for single-author and single-topic booklets, and in this case all of the contents had Essex settings. I decided I would slightly disguise my identity with the Mary Ann Allen pseudonym (part of my two forenames plus my maternal surname), but it was never anything other than an open secret. It wasn't fooling anyone.

In 1986, Jeff Dempsey and David Cowperthwaite's Crimson Altar Press published *The Angry Dead*, a booklet containing ten of Mary Ann Allen's stories along with an introduction by me under my own name, explaining that Mary Ann was something of a "mysterious, reclusive figure", and couldn't be persuaded to compose her own foreword. The two missing tales were "The Sheelagh-na-gig", and the night-climbing story "The Cambridge Beast" (both, incidentally, displaying my cheerful obsession with apocalypses). All of the stories apart from "The Cambridge Beast" featured the church restorer Jane Bradshawe,[1] who seemed to encounter the supernatural not just in ecclesiastical buildings but all over the place. Several of Jane's experiences were inspired by my interest in such things as inn signs and follies ("The Blue Boar of Totenhoe", "The Wandlebury Eyecatcher"); others by places I'd visited (Cotehele House in Cornwall is the thinly disguised setting for "The Chauffeur", which is based on a genuine haunting); and one or two on my particular knowledge of certain types of church furnishings. As I explained in the booklet introduction, concerning Mary Ann (i.e. me!):

Outside the supernatural genre her only writings have been on the rather esoteric subject of Royal Coats of Arms in Churches... Royal Arms (and the related, but even more esoteric subject of Commonwealth Arms) feature prominently in one story, "Hold Fast", and peripherally in another, "Joan". The former was inspired by the discovery of a Commonwealth Arms - every bit as rare as described - in Ramsey, Essex, and its subsequent restoration. I'm told, though, that in real life nothing untoward has resulted from the arms being re-erected in the church. The letter quoted in the story is based on an authentic one sent to Hertfordshire churches.

"The Gravedigger and Death" was inspired by a fragmentary wall-painting at Yaxley church in Huntingdonshire. The Reverend Sir Adam Gordon, mentioned in the story, really did exist and was rector of West Tilbury (alias West Tilford) at the beginning of the nineteenth century, although his local history book is entirely fictional. For further information on him, see my article, "A Hertfordshire Church's Memorial for a 'Mad' King", *Hertfordshire Countryside,* November 1975.

In "Margaret and Catherine", Crossley Abbey is Waltham Abbey in Essex, and the Bisham Tomb is based on the Denny Tomb there. My description in the story is fairly close to the real thing: "a large Tudor tomb with reclining life-size figures of a lady and gentleman". On a panel along the front is:

> ...a row of praying offspring... Of the five daughters shown, three were kneeling modestly in their Elizabethan caps and ruffs, but the fourth had half-turned to look at the fifth and smallest who was tugging at her sleeve and obviously trying to draw her away from her devotions.

What was the mystery of that fifth figure? The story explains it as far as the fictional Bisham Tomb is concerned, but the panel on the real Denny Tomb is much as described except that there are six boys on one side as well as the (four) figures on the distaff side, and the smallest of the latter is actually a boy and not a girl. The littlest girl and the boy were apparently twins, which accounts for their being together, but there is surely more to it than that. *Is* the boy pulling on his sister's arm, causing her to turn slightly, or is she leading him? What the full story behind the unusual pose is, I've yet to discover (the twins didn't die young).

The later, out-rider of my stories, "The Cambridge Beast", was written a couple of years after the booklet and was published by Jeff and David in *Dark Dreams 6* (1988). In 1991, "The Chauffeur" was reprinted by Richard Dalby in *The Virago Book of Ghost Stories, Volume II*.

After this, every so often, someone would try to encourage me to write a new Jane Bradshawe tale. It wasn't going to happen! But then Barbara and Christopher Roden asked if I'd do something for their 1997 Ash-Tree Press anthology, *Midnight Never Comes*. Ruefully, I remembered "The Sheelagh-na-gig", thinking that it was a shame I'd disposed of my copy - it might have deserved rescuing, if only for that original climax. I mentioned this to David Rowlands, and miraculously it turned out that he'd kept the hard copy I'd sent him. So, with some revision, it appeared in the Ash-Tree book (and was, incidentally, reprinted by Mark Valentine in *The Black Veil* in 2008). The first Mary Ann Allen story to be written was thus the last to see print. At some point before publication, I altered it from third to first person and also toned down the dubious fertility goddess explanation for the sheelagh-na-gig - I've done more of that in the latest revision, without, I hope, lessening the impact of the ending (described by Glen Hirshberg in a review as "subtle, sensual and unnerving" - wow!).

Richard Fawcett and Jessica Amanda Salmonson started a short-lived publishing project around the turn of the century - most notably, perhaps, they reprinted all of Augustus Jessopp's supernatural short stories in *The Phantom Coach and Other Ghost Stories of an Antiquary* (1999). I never did really understand why Jessica liked my stories so much, but she was a huge supporter of them, and finally the result in 2000 was a nice little book from Richard Fawcett, reprinting all twelve of them together for the first time, and illustrated by Wendy Wees. Meanwhile, Jane Bradshawe had been turning up elsewhere. In David Rowlands' above-mentioned "Conkers", she quite literally trips over Fr O'Connor. As the good Father tells it:

> I... entered the cool interior of the church... I fear I am getting rather deaf, and received ample confirmation of the fact. In stopping to make arthritic obeisance to the altar, I had not heard the young lady following close on my heels; with the result that she shot headlong over my sprawled feet, making a clatter with a galvanised bucket and uttering some exclamation that also evaded me. I helped her up, with due apologies... She told me, speaking clearly, that she was an artist specialising in church restoration work, and had been summoned hither by the Diocesan authority to inspect the condition of the wall-painting over the chancel arch.

In Jessica Amanda Salmonson's own tales concerning paranormal investigator Penelope Pettiweather (first published in her 1990 Haunted Library booklet *Harmless Ghosts*), it was revealed that Penelope was a regular correspondent of Jane's, and several of the stories take the form of letters to her.[2] And the young female restorer working on a series of hatchments in a church on the Wirral, in Peter Bell's 2012 tale "Conservation", is that author's "tribute" to Jane.

So there the history of the not-very mysterious Mary Ann Allen might have ended but now, thanks to the powers-that-be at *Occult Detective Magazine*, her stories have a fresh lease of life. For this new 2021 edition of *The Angry Dead*, I've completely revised all twelve of the stories, making substantial changes and also retitling one, because I thought that the original title gave part of the plot away (never a good thing). I'm afraid there's still no hope of any new stories though!

Notes:

[1] I chose Oundle in Northamptonshire as the location of Jane Bradshawe's home and workshop in the stories, purely (as I thought) because it's a nice town that I'd visited during the peregrinations for my booklet *Royal Arms in the Churches of Northamptonshire and Rutland* (1976). I've since discovered that at least one of my ancestors, on the Allen side of the family, came from Oundle. Just a coincidence? You decide!

[2] In 2016, Peter Coleborn's Alchemy Press published *The Complete Weird Epistles of Penelope Pettiweather, Ghost Hunter*, reprinting twelve Penelope tales and adding two new ones.

INTRODUCTIONS

Contents of *The Angry Dead*

"The Gravedigger and Death"; "Hold Fast"; "Joan"; "Annie's Ghost" (retitling of "Annie and the Anchorite"); "Margaret and Catherine"; "Ne Resurgat"; "The Blue Boar of Totenhoe"; "The Chauffeur"; "The Hatchment"; "The Wandlebury Eyecatcher"; "The Sheelagh-na-gig; "The Cambridge Beast".

BOOKLETS

The Cropton Lane Farm Murders

*...a bleak rustic tragedy that would
not be out of place
in a Thomas Hardy novel*
--- from Mark Valentine's review on the
Wormwoodiana blog

- *1* -

In his 1926 memoir, *Eton and King's*, M.R. James tells of a trip to Yorkshire in the Easter vacation of 1885, when he was aged 22. With his four companions, he stayed at the Tancred Arms in Hawnby on the North York Moors, about six miles north-west of Helmsley and sixteen miles west of Pickering. After quoting some verses from a couple of songs heard in the Tancred Arms bar, which James claims to remember verbatim, he then recalls that "I also retain in memory a quatrain printed on a mourning-card in one of the bedrooms. I have no other knowledge of the incident it records:

'No one to help them, no one to save,
No one but Heaven to point out their grave!
The poor man and his son, who had done him no harm,
Were murdered by Charters at Cropton Lane Farm.'"[1]

The mourning-card itself can be found on the Net in the JTR

Forums,[2] and a comparison of the text shows that James had the rhyme largely correct, although he did add an 's' to the name of the culprit (it's doubtful that he had really memorised it so accurately for so long - I suspect he'd written it down in one of his many notebooks), but he omitted the important details at the top of the card:

In Memory of
JOSEPH WOOD,
AGED 58 YEARS,
AND HIS SON
JOSEPH THOMPSON,
AGED 9 YEARS,
Who were brutally Murdered by Robert Charter,
at Cropton-lane Farm, near Pickering, May 17th, 1872.
No one to help them - no one to save,
No one but Heaven to point out their grave,
The poor man and boy who had done him no harm,
Were murdered by Charter, at Cropton-lane Farm.

The murders were something of a local *cause célébre*, partly because of the apparently horrid nature of the crime and partly because a mystery remained as to what exactly happened. But the case has been largely forgotten: I have not found any substantial modern references to it in any 'true crime' books or even on the Internet, and only a couple in local history publications.3   Possibly this is because of the ultimate verdict of the jury when the case came to trial.

Joseph Wood was a yeoman farmer of 80 acres near Cropton, about four miles north-west of Pickering. At the time of his death, aged 57, in May 1872 he was struggling. His "late housekeeper", Catherine Thompson, the mother of his children, had died several months previously, aged only 43; and his fourteen-year-old daughter Charlotte Ann had recently left home to move in with her grandparents, saying that looking after the farm was too much for her alone and that "Mr Wood would not get anyone to help her"4 (a servant, Jane Dring, is listed in the 1871 census but had also left by this time). Joseph Wood was living at the farm with his two sons, the elder being Joseph Thompson, aged 8; the younger Thomas, aged 4 (the lads took their surnames from their mother). On Monday, May 13th, a few days before the two Josephs were apparently killed, Robert Charter, a cousin aged 53, who farmed about 20 acres at nearby Lastingham, came to do some work on the Wood farm, bringing with him "a pair of horses drawing a cart full of barley" to plant, and intending to stay all week.

When Joseph Wood and his elder son disappeared during the night of May 17th/18th (they were last seen by anyone other than Charter at 7.30pm, "sitting at the fire in the kitchen"),⁵ the younger son Thomas remained safely in bed at the farm.⁶ Charter claimed that the missing pair had gone away suddenly in the early hours of May 18th. John Wood, Joseph's younger brother who farmed on the neighbouring property, recounted how Charter told him that "some time in the morning, [Joseph] shouted to him 'Robert, we're going away for two or three days. You must stop till we come back'". (Or "you must stay at Cropton-lane and settle up my affairs".) Charter, who was in bed (he thought the time was about 3am or slightly later), said that he got up soon afterwards and "went into the lane, looking both ways, but he could see nothing of them". Enquiries were made in some of the nearby towns and villages. It was initially thought that Joseph Wood and his son might have gone to see Charlotte Ann Thompson at the home of her grandparents in the village of Nawton, a few miles to the west, to try to get her to return to the house, but there was no sign of the pair there or anywhere else. Charter reassured John Wood, telling him: "You needn't be uneasy about anybody going away for two or three days".

Then, on May 23rd, Robert received a letter, addressed to "Robert Charter, with Joseph Wood, Cropton", and postmarked for the previous day, from Liverpool. It was supposedly from Joseph Wood (but not in his handwriting), written prior to his embarking on a ship to an undisclosed destination:

> Liverpool, May 20, 1872
>
> To Robert Charter
>
> Dear Cousen, -- i write these few lines to let you know that I am going to take the water, foreign, you must stay at Cropton-lane, and get my affairs settled up as soon as you can, we are going either to-day or to-morrow. I will let you know in my next what i have done and where i am going. Excuse my bad writing, a bad pen and in haste
>
> JOSEPH WOOD

This missive Charter showed around the family and neighbours to prove his story, saying to one of them, "it is a very short letter, but it has a deal of meaning in it". Joseph was known to be rather "odd and queer in his ways", and prone to doing unexpected things, especially since the death of Catherine, so the family were even more concerned. His brother John telegraphed the shipping office at Liverpool, but no trace of Joseph and his son could be found among the booking and travel records. Eventually John Wood called in the Superintendent of the County Constabulary from Pickering, John Jonas.

East Anglian former shoemaker John Jonas joined the Essex Constabulary in 1842. His most notable case while in Essex occurred in June 1851, when he was one of three policemen involved in the apprehension of three thieves, who were attempting to burgle a farmhouse at Twinstead, near the Essex/Suffolk border, south of Sudbury. The constables had had the building under observation for a month since a previous failed burglary. The thieves violently resisted arrest and several of the participants were injured, including an employee of the farm owner, who lost an arm as a result of being shot by one of the robbers with a gun he had grabbed from the farmer. John Jonas was hit on the head with a chisel, but continued to fight "single-handed in a most gallant manner" until the other officers appeared on the scene to support him. One of the miscreants later died of head injuries and the building was reported to have been left "in a state resembling a slaughterhouse, from the desperate nature of the attack and defence". Promoted to Inspector in 1853, just under four years later Jonas resigned in order to join the North Riding Constabulary as Police Superintendent at Pickering.[7]

-2-

Searches of Joseph Wood's farmhouse were undertaken but nothing of significance found. As the months went by, Robert Charter made desperate efforts to pass the farm back to the Wood family, saying that he needed to get back to his own farm and that his wife Hannah (whom he had brought to live with him) did not like being away from home for so long. In mid-September, the Charters left the Cropton Lane farm in the hands of another of Joseph Wood's brothers, William, a grocer and draper, who made an inventory of the contents. It was noted that both of Joseph Wood's silver watches were still in the house.

In early November, more intensive searches were instigated after Joseph Wood's boots were discovered in the corn store at the Cropton farm. When a pond was investigated by John Wood and his son, armed with a long pole, they found "part of a pair of trousers, such as his brother used to wear... part of a coat and part of a shirt like his brother's. There was a knife in one of the trousers pockets, which had belonged to the boy". The next day, the pond was pumped out under the supervision of Superintendent Jonas, and a "human left hand" was found along with some more clothing. On November 7th, in the orchard, other remains were dug out from under a stick heap: "a right hand, clenched, two feet, and a stocking. The feet and stocking were so placed as to lead to the conjecture that the body might have been buried there on its back". Some hair was clutched in the clenched hand.

The hunt then moved to Robert Charter's farm at Lastingham, where Superintendent Jonas and Inspector Thomas Nicholson first searched the house and discovered an envelope and half-sheet of paper which, judging from the watermark, was the other half of the sheet on which the Liverpool letter had been written. The envelope was also of the same kind. Moving outside, on November 12th, at the bottom of one of Charter's fields by an old watercourse, Jonas and Nicholson spotted some apparently disturbed soil on the bank:

> They consulted, and decided to dig into this place. They did so, and found two feet down a quantity of stones, which appeared to have been recently placed there. They removed part, and dug one and a half feet down. A sack was found, and when more soil was cleared, a leg bone was found, shown by a cut in the sack... [They] took hold of the sack, which they at last extracted. Laying it on the grass, they opened the end, and found the remains of a human body. It had been put in feet downwards. A rope was round the neck of the body, and a black silk handkerchief tied tightly in a double knot.

Robert Charter had meanwhile been arrested, as were his son-in-law William Hardwick (husband of Robert's daughter Sarah) and Robert's son John (John was soon released without charge).[8] The inquest was held at the Horse Shoe Inn,

Pickering, in mid-November, and the body identified as that of Joseph Wood by his brother John, who recognised his whiskers and "peculiarly placed" lower teeth, with one tooth "crossways in the jaw"; and by Charlotte Ann Thompson, who identified his clothing, including stockings which she had darned. Charlotte was praised by the coroner for giving her evidence "with great intelligence".[9]

While in custody, Robert made two statements. The first, on November 14th, implied that he hadn't even touched Joseph Wood, and that Wood's death was perhaps the result of some sort of accident:

> A little before three o'clock on Saturday, the 18th of May, I heard a noise, and got up and came out. I found Joseph Wood leaning against the gatestead leading from the front garden to the stick heap in the orchard. He was dead. There was some blood about his head and on the ground. I took him into the barn, and placed him amongst the straw in the barn, thinking I should be blamed for murdering him. I went and foddered the horses and cows. I let him lie there about a week. I then took and laid him in the orchard, near the stick heap. About three weeks after, I found three bones of the boy in the fold yard. It appeared as if he had been devoured by the pigs.

They were leg bones. I buried the bones against his father. I let them remain there till about a week before I was coming away. I tried to pull him out. His clothes slipped off. I took his clothes and threw them into the pond. I took the remains and put them into a bag, and took them to one of my fields near Lastingham, and placed them in a hole in the corner of a field next Lastingham. No one had any concern in it but myself. After that I began to feel concerned about it. On Sunday, the 19th of May, I thought I should be blamed for murdering him, and I wrote a letter, and I saw a young man coming from Rosedale, and asked him if he was leaving Rosedale, and he said that he was going to Liverpool, and going to leave this country for America. I asked him to go into the house with me, and wait a few minutes whilst I wrote a letter. He went in, and I gave him something to eat. I then wrote the letter, and gave it to him, and told him to post it at Liverpool. I thought it would save so much trouble searching and rummaging about till things got settled. I received the letter back again in a day or two afterwards from the postman. John has nothing to do with it; he knows nothing about it. I have never seen him since the Sunday before Kirbymoorside Steeplechase.

(Signed) "ROBERT CHARTER"

The second statement, made the next day, offered additional details which seemed to get closer to the truth of the matter:

[In the night of May 17th/18th, Joseph Wood] called to me to get up and take my barley back again. I said I would take back what was spared. He insisted on me getting up and going back then and there. I told him I did not want to get up. He came up stairs, and he said I was to get up; so I got up and went down stairs, and he said I was to go and take my barley back. I begged on him to let me be till daylight, and then I would see. He then ran into the house and got the gun. I missed my click. I then ran behind the wall corner. He followed me with the gun. I took an iron off the wall and struck him on the head, and knocked him down, and took the gun from him. I then went into the house and fastened myself in, and when I came out again I found he was dead. I then took him into the barn. I fastened myself in the bedroom for most of an hour. I did not think I gave Joseph such a blow. I had no thoughts of killing him. I never saw the boy at all.

(Signed) "ROBERT CHARTER"

After this second confession, acting Police-Sergeant Thomas Silversides noted that "Charter seemed to be very depressed... cried a good deal, frequently said, 'Lord, have mercy upon me,' and wanted to get the matter off his mind".

In the light of Charter's claims concerning his finding of a few bones belonging to young Joseph Thompson, the search was meanwhile renewed and, sure enough, on November 16th:

> ... the right femur, the left tibia, and scapula, such as would answer to the bones of the missing boy, were found among the spread manure in the field. There were two fold-yards, the contents of one having been led out and ploughed in for wheat and sown; the contents of the other being spread upon the land for use for spring corn, and it was among this manure that the bones were found. They have not been boiled, as was supposed, but the cartilages are gnawed, which, together with a pig's bone being found, suggests the horrible idea that the boy was really eaten by the pigs...[10] The lad, it was generally believed now, saw the murder, and was murdered in consequence.

In December some more small bones - a vertebra and two ribs - were picked out from the manure.

-3-

The inquest jury found a verdict of wilful murder. It was also clear that Charter, in inventing the mysterious stranger from Rosedale who had taken the letter to post in Liverpool, was only trying to protect his son-in-law, William Hardwick, who had actually made the trip. Later (when the first of Joseph's Wood's remains were found), Hardwick tried to persuade Charter's other son-in-law, George Kirby, to give him an alibi for the relevant days. Hardwick was charged as an accessory after the fact, both for this and for possibly assisting Charter to hide the crime in other ways. It is a notable feature of the evidence given by Robert throughout that he was always keen to protect his family members from any implication of involvement.

By this time he was in a terrible state. "Much reduced in strength, and evidently suffering keen mental agony", he could not leave his cell, and the inquest jury had been forced to go and see him as he lay on his pallet there. The *York Herald*, not prone to exaggeration, reported: "Serious fears are entertained that by long confinement in a solitary cell, with the dreadful remembrance of the past, and the awful prospect afforded by the future ever present to his mind, the prisoner's reason may give way. The dizziness of which he complained... is regarded as an ominous indication of what may happen... many do not hesitate to say that it is highly probable he may die before he is tried".

Charter's mood can hardly have been improved by the four-day Magistrates' hearing in Pickering, when the streets were thronged with people:

> The Court, which was held in a small building known as the Savings Bank, sat at ten o'clock. Fully an hour before that, however, it was a work of difficulty to approach it, so eager were the crowds of people... to obtain a sight of the prisoners. The statute hirings[11] were held in Pickering that day, and the streets were consequently unusually busy at an early hour. The itinerant showmen, whose stalls were ranged up the sides of the principal street, were completely deserted between nine and ten o'clock, when Charter and his son-in-law were brought to Court, and at night when they were removed in a cab under a strong escort of police. Charter... appeared to be in a state of absolute terror, as, amid the groans and yells of some hundreds of people, he was hustled out of the cab and hurried up the narrow stairs to the Police-station... [M]any and loud were the threats and expressions of disapprobation which were heard against him... The cab had been brought up for [the

prisoners'] use; but its windows were smashed, and as the vehicle seemed likely to be destroyed, it was sent away.

On the fourth day, the situation on the streets was, if anything, even worse: "a very large crowd, mostly farm servants, now at liberty for Martinmas, assembled before the police station, and when the prisoners came out to enter the cab they set up a yell, and ran after the cab to the court, hooting and jeering. At the court a large crowd had already assembled, who did likewise". Given this potential market, it's no surprise to read that "the ballad-mongers crowded the town, and vended thousands of copies of 'authentic histories' of the awful tragedy, and even old copies of newspapers containing the least scrap of information about the murder were readily disposed of". A broadside published at this time was representative of the current opinion of the "Cropton Tragedy":

Horrible Murder
AND MUTILATION OF THE BODIES OF
JOSEPH WOOD AND HIS SON,
At Pickering, in the North Riding of Yorkshire, on or about the 17th or 18th of May 1872.

In the quiet village of Pickering,
Among the Yorkshire farming grounds,

A cruel murder, sad and startling,
Has aroused the country round.
One Joseph Wood a well known farmer,
In seclusion there did dwell.
His son and him they lived together,
Their sad fate we now must tell.

CHORUS

No one pities the cruel monster,
For the deed that he has done,
Altho he killed the poor farmer,
Why didn't he spare the helpless son.

These two poor victims have been missing,
Since nearly six long months ago,
Their cruel relation, Robert Charter,
A Liverpool letter he did show
The letter said, the poor old farmer
And his son had gone away
From Liverpool to cross the ocean,
And would return some other day.

There was many had their own suspicions,
That some foul play had been done,
But nothing could be found to prove it,

THE CROPTON LANE FARM MURDERS

Or bring it home to the guilty one;
At last some old shoes were discovered,
Belonging to the missing man,
The Police were quickly made acquainted,
And the search once more began.

They searched the fields in all directions,
With pick and spade turned up the land,
At last beneath some muddy water,
They saw the murder'd farmer's hand;
They found the feet and parts of clothing,
A sad and sick'ning sight to see,
The remainder of the decaying body
Was buried beneath an old oak tree.

They tried to find the poor boy's body,
They search'd around both night and day,
Human bones they have discovered,
That ravenous pigs had gnawed away;
The cruel monster perhaps did murder,
The helpless unoffending boy,
And threw his body in the pigsty,
There all traces to destroy.

> But God's all-seeing eye was watching,
> To bring to light this fearful crime,
> And now the murderer pale and trembling,
> Awaits for trial the appointed time.
> If the jury find him guilty,
> To eternity he'll soon be hurled,
> To meet his mutilated victims,
> Face to face in another world.[12]

In fact, it was already evident that Charter was no psychotic maniac, cutting up the bodies of his victims. The partial dismemberment of Wood's body was due entirely to the removal and reburial of the decaying and disintegrating remains. But was Robert a murderer? That was what the Crown Court jury had to decide. He was charged with "feloniously, wilfully, and of malice aforethought killing and murdering Joseph Wood, at Cropton-lane Farm, on the 17th of May"; Hardwick was charged with having "feloniously received, harboured, and maintained" Charter, "well knowing him to have committed the said murder". When they were brought into court, Charter was described by the *York Herald* as having "all the appearance of being, as he was, a poor farmer"; "somewhat tall and slender, with what may be called iron-grey hair, and whiskers of a darker colour". Hardwick, aged 37, was "less in stature, rather stouter, better dressed, and look[ed] more intelligent".

-4-

A fair proportion of the evidence at both the Magistrates' hearing and the two-day Crown Court trial which followed at the Spring Assizes in York Castle on March 25th/26th, 1873, revolved around two remaining questions (just before the Crown Court trial, the Grand Jury threw out the charge of murder respecting young Joseph Thompson, because, with so little physical evidence, it was impossible to come to any conclusions as to his fate). The first question was how many of the multiple injuries to Joseph Wood's remains were perimortem and how many might have been caused postmortem by the burying and reburying of the body. If there was evidence of many blows, then Robert Charter's assertion that he "only struck him once, gentlemen", in self-defence, and "oh, gentlemen, I did not strike Joseph with intent to kill him", could not be believed.

The second question concerned exactly how much William Hardwick was involved. A procession of witnesses of variable reliability came forward, who maintained that they had seen Charter and Hardwick together at the end of October or the beginning of November, digging and working in the field near the beck where Joseph Wood's body was found soon afterwards. But Charter remained adamant that Hardwick was not involved except in taking the letter to Liverpool: "No one in the world," he said, "knew anything of it but myself. I want to clear Hardwick. I positively swear to that. I never said anything about it to any one". It seems surprising, anyway, that the body should have been reburied this late: it was in September that Charter returned to his own farm, removing the remains from Cropton and burying them at Lastingham. John Wood, who took over the general caretaking of the Cropton farm after Charter left, confirmed the timing of this removal, saying that the initial burial place of the body, near or under the stick heap in the orchard, was not disturbed again once Charter had returned to his home.

There is no reason to think that Charter moved or reburied the remains again after September. Indeed, this was acknowledged by the judge, Lord Chief Justice William Bovill, in his summing up where he went so far as to advise the jury "not for an instant to believe a single syllable of the statements" of some of the witnesses who claimed to have seen suspicious activity in the field in October. The testimony of others suggests that nothing more sinister than ploughing and (as Charter maintained) straightening work on the beck was going on there. Nevertheless, it was certainly bad timing. Was Charter perhaps concerned that the spot he had chosen for the burial in September was too close to the beck and that if the water level should rise due to heavy Autumnal rains, it might wash the body out?

Returning to the medical evidence, the magistrates and the jury could be excused for feeling confused by it. Mr John Harrison Walker, a Pickering surgeon, noted that the hair grasped in the clenched hand found in the orchard at Cropton, "resembled that of the prisoner Charter", but the main part of his evidence concerned Joseph Wood's head injuries:

> He considered that death had been caused by a blow with a blunt instrument on the left side of the head, which had produced a fracture of the skull. He thought that the blow had been given by some person standing behind the deceased. Other blows had been given, and there were numerous fractures... *(evidence given at the Magistrates' hearing).*
>
> He thought it was unlikely that the upper group of fractures could have been produced by one blow. It was possible, but it must have been a tremendous blow. He did not include in this the blow at the back of the head and the blows on the cheekbones. The injuries at the top of the skull could not have been caused by a fall, as they were too high up, and a fall would not have been attended with sufficient violence to have caused these injuries... [his] reasons

for saying that he believed the wounds he had indicated were caused before death were because of the marks of extravasation of blood and the extraordinary violence at the base of the skull... It was next to impossible to fracture the base of the skull after death *(evidence at the Crown Court trial).*

Dr Thomas Procter of York agreed that more than one blow must have been struck before death, and that "a blow on the top of the head had been given during life, because, as a matter of fact, it was extremely difficult to fracture the base of the skull after death, and the fracture at the extreme part of the base of the skull was what would be likely to be produced by a blow at the back part of the top of the head". Mr William Bird, a surgeon of York, considered that "four blows must have been given to produce the fractures on the top of the head and the temple. Two blows must have been given before death, viz. - that on the top of the head and that on the left temple".

On the other hand, Mr William S. Schofield, another Pickering surgeon, when questioned at the Crown Court trial, thought that the fracture at the base of the skull "connected with the triangular fracture on the left temporal bone". He opined that:

...all the appearances he observed in the skull might

have been produced by one blow... He considered the fracture on the right temporal bone and the one on the left temporal bone to be all one fracture, and produced probably by one blow on the left temple... [this] blow at the side of the head certainly was sufficient [to cause death]... He could form no opinion whether the blow on the back of the head was given before or after death; but he had formed an opinion that the blow on the side was given before death.

Schofield suggested that "the fracture at the back of the base of the skull might have been caused by a waggon coming into contact with the head, by the ironshoe of a heavy farm horse, or by the spade of a labourer... He thought it probable that the cheek bones were driven in after death". Under quite severe cross-examination from the judge, Schofield admitted that the fracture at the base of the skull was more likely caused before than after death.

-5-

No doubt the "throng... gathered round the entrance to the Castle", which required considerable effort by the police to keep under control, were looking forward to a guilty verdict and consequent death sentence. They must have been both shocked and disappointed. William Hardwick was acquitted of all charges and Robert Charter was found guilty only of manslaughter. When asked whether he had any words to add before sentence was passed, Charter ("touching his forehead with his right hand") stated: "I have done innocently what I did".

One feels that Hardwick had a lucky escape.[13] Although he probably had nothing to do with the disposal of Joseph Wood's body, it's impossible to believe that he didn't have any suspicions at all of foul play when he was asked by his father-in-law to take the fake letter to post in Liverpool. But the verdict on Charter was probably correct: the case for a murder conviction had not been proven beyond reasonable doubt. The judge, in sentencing Charter, concluded that the death of Wood was "caused by two blows upon the head, which have smashed the skull from side to side in one direction, and which have fractured the skull in another direction. These blows must have been separate blows, and of great violence in each instance". He considered that, even in self-defence, there was an unnecessary use of a "fearful" weapon: the iron bar ("A bar of iron about a foot and a half long… used for extracting the linch-pin of a waggon",[14] which searchers had discovered, hidden on a beam in the carthouse at Cropton). For this reason, and because of his subsequent attempts to cover up his actions, Charter was sentenced to twenty years in jail. He spent his incarceration in Parkhurst

Prison. His wife, Hannah, went to live with her daughter Martha and the rest of the Kirby family at Ryton, south of Pickering.

The Wood farm seems to have remained unoccupied for a while. When Joseph's funeral procession passed by in November, just after the Inquest, the *York Herald* noted that "The blinds were not drawn, the gates were open, but the absence of anything living, the disordered orchard, the smokeless chimneys, and the heaps of mould in the garden all told the story of the terrible crime". It then went on to (slightly mis-) quote from Thomas Hood's poem, "The Haunted House":

> A sense of mystery and fear
> The spirit daunted,
> And said, as plain as whisper in the ear,
> The place is haunted!

Haunted or not, the surrounding area may have acquired a bad reputation. The same newspaper, on September 20th, 1873, reported:

> SERIOUS ACCIDENT. - On Friday afternoon, a serious accident happened at Cropton, near Pickering, which nearly proved fatal to a man and a boy. A waggon drawn by three horses, belonging to Mr. Thos. Stephenson, of Cawthorn, and driven by a boy

named Thos. Pennock, was proceeding down Cropton Lane, and when near the farm of the late Mr. Joseph Wood, who was killed by Robert Charter, the lad lost all control over the animals, which started off at a furious rate. The lane here is very narrow. A young man named Frank Fairchild, who was in the lane, being on his way to Rosedale in search of work,[15] shouted at the horses to try and stop them. He got up into the hedge to get out of their way, but was struck by one of the horses and thrown over the hedge into a field. A little further down the lane the leading horse fell, and was run over by the shaft horses, and Pennock was thrown out of the waggon, but, strange to say, he was only slightly stunned, and escaped with a few trifling bruises. The horse that fell was found to have broken one of its fore and one of its hind legs, and was at once shot. Fairchild was conveyed to Pickering Workhouse, and was at once attended to by Dr. Schoefield, when it was found he had received a compound fracture of the left collar bone. He is progressing as favourably as can be expected.[16]

Robert Charter was released on 'ticket of leave' before the end of his sentence and returned to Yorkshire, where he is said to have become a Methodist preacher.[17] There was nothing left for him in Lastingham: a sale of his property had been held in 1876, and there is a local story that the villagers demolished his farmhouse stone by stone. Certainly a nineteenth-century photograph is extant which shows a building very like an 1872 *Illustrated Police News* picture of Charter's house, in the process of being pulled down.[18] Robert was at Norton near Malton, south of Pickering, in 1891, "living on [his] own means" according to the census. His wife was with him, but tragically she died later in that same year. In the 1901 census he was registered at Scagglethorpe (close to Norton), but by 1907 he was seriously ill in the Malton Workhouse infirmary.

Then came the final twist to the story. Apparently, Charter confessed on his deathbed to knowledge of what had happened to young Joseph Thompson. Some 1907 newspapers announced gleefully that the confession was to murder, but it seems more likely that he admitted only to having disposed of the body. The *Manchester Courier* of Monday, March 4th, 1907, gives what may be the most reliable account: "Charter declares [in his new confession, that]... the boy had fallen downstairs and broken his neck, and that he kept the body for some time before giving it to the pigs". This could tie in with the testimony of a day-worker on the

Cropton farm, Thomas Stead, who saw the pigs in the fold-yard there, eating some suspicious-looking flesh three or four weeks after the disappearances.[19] It might even explain an unpleasant smell which Stead noticed earlier coming from some decaying meat in the cellar, although the court seems to have accepted that this was putrid beef. Stead threw it to the pigs but seemed unsure as to the date and doubtful whether it could have been the same meat he later saw in the fold-yard.

-6-

Robert Charter died at Malton Workhouse in July 1907, aged 88. Was he finally telling the whole truth on his deathbed? Was his crime only to defend himself (with one or more blows from the iron bar, a "chance weapon") against an attack by the armed Joseph Wood; an attack heard by Joseph's son who then perhaps came rushing down from his bedroom so quickly that he fell and broke his neck on the stairs? In these circumstances, Charter's panicked disposal of the bodies is understandable, if not excusable. Throughout the case, he comes over as a very ordinary man, keen to protect his family, and driven almost to the point of mental collapse by events largely beyond his control. Whereas the "odd and queer" Joseph Wood had a history of unpredictable behaviour. His family were concerned that he "was going wrong in his head. Other members of his family had gone wrong, and had to be taken to the asylum" (this apparently referred to a sister). On one occasion, Wood reportedly threatened "a man named Ford without cause". On another, he terrified "a boy named Pennock" (possibly the same lad as the one who later had the accident in Cropton Lane), frightening him with a gun. He had also "threatened to give Thos. Coulson [a waggoner] a bit of lead". Some thought "it was dangerous that the deceased should have a gun; people did not like it when he went out to shoot birds".

Ten years before his death, Joseph Wood was involved in events which showed him in a far from favourable light. At the Pickering Petty Sessions on September 29th, 1862, a young man named William Porteus, described as Wood's servant, was charged with indecent assault on another of Wood's employees, sixteen-year-old Jane Ann Rooks, "whilst in the harvest field". Joseph Wood was also summoned because, when Rooks made her accusation against Porteus, Wood apparently immediately discharged her and refused to pay the wages which were due to her. In his absence, Wood was ordered to pay Rooks £4, with 9 shillings in costs (as opposed to Porteus who was fined only 5 shillings with 13s 6d costs).[20]

If Robert Charter *did* deliberately murder Joseph Wood,

what could his motive have been? At the time, the London *Telegraph* (in claims worthy of a modern tabloid) suggested that it could have been that old perennial explanation: money. Wood, it claimed, "was believed to be possessed of a considerable sum of ready money" and had "latterly got into the habit of paying the tradesmen of Pickering double the amount they asked for their goods"; little Thomas Thompson was even said to have seen Joseph counting his money in the kitchen on the night of his death! The *Sun* of New York maintained that "one of [Wood's] peculiarities was to keep a large quantity of gold and silver in the house".[21] But, in reality, it was clearly shown at the trial that Wood was in danger of losing the farm: his brother John said that Joseph told him he "was pressed for taxes, and some of his sheep were taken in a distress" to pay his debts. Only through the intervention of another brother, Thomas Wood, were the animals released. Joseph was obviously struggling and the trial produced little evidence of his having any money to speak of; in the judge's words, he was "unfortunate and not prosperous in his occupation".

No other likely motives spring to mind, or were put forward at the trial, apart from spur-of-the-moment rage - something which is far more typical of Wood than Charter. No, unlikely as Charter's version of events might seem, I'm inclined to believe him, and to think that the jury got it right. If so then, while neither Joseph Wood nor his innocuous son deserved their fate, a fair conclusion has to be that poor Robert Charter also had a *very bad day indeed*, back in May 1872.

Notes:

[1] M.R. James, *Eton and King's: Recollections, Mostly Trivial: 1875-1925* (1926), p.191 (Ash-Tree Press reprint, 2005, p.125). It's a shame that James did not follow up the Cropton case himself. He enjoyed reading about true crime, especially when an interesting trial was involved. For instance, in April 1932 he wrote a letter from Aldeburgh to his friend Gwendolen McBryde, in which he told her: "Several jobs of work I've brought with me, but so far have been absorbed in the trials of Crippen, Lawson [sic], Monson and Rouse..." (*Letters to a Friend*, 1956, p.180). Hawley Harvey Crippen, George Henry Lamson, Alfred John Monson and Alfred Arthur Rouse all stood trial for murder (between 1882 and 1931), and all but Monson were found guilty and executed.

[2] www.jtrforums.com/showthread.php?t=8510.

[3] Colin Wilkinson, "The Cropton Murders", *Cleveland Family History Society Journal,* Vol.12, no.2 (April 2013), pp.43-44; Tom Scott Burns, "Robert Charter - The Cropton Murderer" in *Round and About the North Yorkshire Moors, Volume 2: A Further Glimpse of the Past*, 1988, pp.37-39 (also p.105, "Robert Charter's House"). Since the publication of my investigation in 2018, a write-up of the case has appeared on the Lastingham Village website (www.lastinghamvillage.org), which is less sympathetic to Robert Charter than I was (and continue to be). It ignores Joseph Wood's tendency to violence and (against the evidence) maintains

that he was well off. I believe my booklet *may* be an uncredited source for some of it, but there is also some valuable local information on farm names, locations, etc.

4 All quotes unattributed in the text are from the inquest, Magistrates' hearing and Crown Court trial reports in the *York Herald* (November 23rd, 1872; November 30th, 1872; and March 29th, 1873, respectively).

5 Seen by Joseph's brother John Wood, who "went up to see if they had done with a barrow he had lent him". John added that Joseph had said nothing about going away, and that his horse was lame.

6 Young Thomas William Thompson seems to have been adopted (formally or informally) almost immediately by the local Dobson family: he is listed as a "boarder" with them in the 1881 census. John Dobson was a farmer who knew the Wood family well, and sometimes did work for Joseph. Thomas appears in the 1891 census living in York and working as a draper's assistant; ten years later, aged 33, he was married, a "shopkeeper on own account", and still in York. He died, aged 38, in York in late Spring 1905, leaving a wife, Jane Ann.

7 *The Times*, June 17th, 1851. John Jonas retired in 1878, aged 60. His work on the Cropton case was greatly appreciated by the Wood family. In May 1873, John Wood "and friends" presented Jonas with a gold watch inscribed "as a mark of esteem for his indefatigable exertions in the Cropton Murders". According to the Cropton Village web site, this watch is still in the possession of the Jonas family (www.gocropton.co.uk/history/).

8 John Charter left the area soon afterwards and by the 1881 census he was working as a coalminer in County Durham.

9 Charlotte Ann Thompson married William Burnett, a local blacksmith near Malton, in 1879. She died very young in 1885, aged 27, leaving two children, Joseph (born in 1880, and surely named after her late brother

rather than her father) and Hannah (born in 1881).

[10] *The Times* on November 25th showed a touching concern for the pigs, or possibly for those who might inadvertently have acquired porkers with a taste for human flesh: "... it is the opinion of many that [Joseph Thompson's skull] will not be [found], as the pigs would eat it up in order to reach the brains. The bones, however, already found show very conclusively that they have all been gnawed, doubtless by the pigs. 'What became of the pigs?' is a general question in Pickering, and it is stated they were sold at the sale, and went nobody seems to know where".

[11] "Statute hirings" or "hiring fairs" were held annually, frequently at the end of the farming year around Martinmas (November 11th). This was when "Prospective employees, often with some sort of badge or tool to denote their speciality, would gather in the street or square... and employers would look them over and, if all was well, strike a bargain for the coming year..." The event featured sideshows, music, foodstalls and "all the other trappings and attractions of a real fair... and also attracted condemnation for the drunkenness and immorality involved" (Jacqueline Simpson and Steve Roud, *Oxford Dictionary of English Folklore*, 2000, pp.177-178).

[12] This broadside is reproduced, with the aforementioned mourning-card, on the JTR Forums: www.jtrforums.com/showthread.php?t=8510. It is also on the Lastingham Village website - see note 3.

[13] The 1871 census lists William Hardwick as a farmer of sixty acres, but by 1881 he is described as an "agricultural labourer" of Wrelton, just south of Cropton. He and Robert Charter's daughter Sarah had a long life together. They married in 1866, and both were still living in Wrelton (with various children and grandchildren) in 1911, with William working as a "jobbing gardener". In 1914 Wrelton village was in the unusual position of having thirty residents aged over 70 among a population of 150.

A photograph was taken to commemorate this, and William Hardwick, aged 80, was one of those featured (Sarah Hardwick was ten years younger than her husband so didn't qualify). The photograph is reproduced in *Ryedale from Old Photographs* by Gordon Clitheroe (2010). Hardwick died, aged 87, in April 1922, three years after his wife.

14 Quote from *The Times*, March 26th, 1873.

15 High quality iron ore was discovered at Rosedale in the 1850s and over the following seven decades it became a magnet for men seeking work as miners in that industry. Doubtless this was why Frank Fairchild was heading to the village. It also explains why Robert Charter thought Rosedale was a suitable place of origin for his fictional traveller to Liverpool and America.

16 Could there be a connection here with another local murder? Notice that the boy driving the waggon was a Thomas Pennock (if I have identified him correctly in the censuses, he was only eight or nine at the time). In November 1888 one James Pennock, a gatekeeper and railway worker at Black Bull Crossing near Pickering, slaughtered his wife Hannah with a hatchet and then committed suicide by drowning in the local river. His body was not found for some months and meanwhile an innocent man had been briefly arrested and questioned on arrival in North America, on suspicion of being either James Pennock or Jack the Ripper! Admittedly, Pennock seems to be a fairly common local name in Pickering and its surrounds, but I do wonder if James and young Thomas could have been related (evidently not brothers, but perhaps cousins or uncle/nephew - both of them were born in Cropton).

17 Tom Scott Burns, "Robert Charter - The Cropton Murderer", in *Round and About the North Yorkshire Moors, Volume 2: A Further Glimpse of the Past* (1988), p.39.

18 Tom Scott Burns, "Robert Charter's House", in *Round and About the*

North Yorkshire Moors, Volume 2: A Further Glimpse of the Past (1988), p.105. *Baker's Chronology of Local Events in Malton, Norton and District* says that the sale of Charter's property took place on March 6th, 1876, at the Bay Horse Inn, Pickering. In its November 23rd, 1872, edition, the *Illustrated Police News* covered the case with an illustrated write-up (I reproduced all of the illustrations in my booklet).

[19] During the Magistrates' hearing, Thomas Stead stated that "three weeks to a month" after the fateful night, he observed "three pigs pulling at something like a piece of flesh... I can't say the size of the flesh I saw with the pigs. It was like pig's flesh". Robert Charter responded that "It is not much use talking to him; he has told a parcel of lies". Was Charter protesting too much? The *York Herald* thought so: "During the period of Stead's examination, [Charter] paid very marked attention to the evidence... It is generally believed that Stead feels convinced that the flesh he saw was part of the body of the boy: but he is a particularly nervous and timid witness, and seemed afraid of being committed to anything that might tend to criminate himself".

[20] *Yorkshire Gazette,* October 4th, 1862.

[21] The *Telegraph* as reported in *The Newfoundlander*, December 20th, 1872. Another dubious assertion of the New York *Sun*'s report (December 6th) was that, although Thomas, "who was in the house at the time of the murder", "can remember nothing with certainty. He fancies there was a great light after he had gone to bed..." It's hard to see what is implied by this.

Acknowledgments:

My thanks to Stewart Evans for his considerable help in tracking down the *York Herald* and other early sources, and to Colin Wilkinson for his assistance with more recent sources. An earlier, shorter version of this booklet originally appeared as an article in *The Ripperologist 142* (February 2015).

"The Old Man on the Hill"
English Hill Figures in Supernatural Fiction

Re-enchantment is Resistance
--- David Southwell (Hookland)

- 1 -

Rise up! Rise up, Cormoran. Woden. Jack-of-Green. Jack-in-Irons. Thunderdell. Búri, Blunderbore, Gog and Magog, Galligantus, Vili and Vé, Yggdrasil, Brutus of Albion. Come, you drunken spirits. Come, you battalions. You fields of ghosts who walk these green plains still. Come, you giants!
--- from the final scene of Jez Butterworth's *Jerusalem* (2009)

The giant figures cut into the hillsides of England are cloaked in mystery. Apart from some of the more recent examples, no one knows why they were made and in many cases *when* they were made. Modern scientific methods have dated the earliest figures but sometimes this just adds to the questions they raise. We now know that the oldest by a long way is the Uffington White Horse (Berkshire, now Oxfordshire), which was cut around 1000 BCE, on the cusp of the Bronze and Iron Ages. Was it a tribal symbol? A god? Theories concerning the Cerne Abbas Giant in Dorset have ranged from its being a Celtic god, through to a seventeenth-century satire on Oliver Cromwell. But soil analysis has now shown that it is neither: a date of between 700 and 1100 CE makes it either late Saxon (there are old accounts of the local worship of a god named Helith) or Christian - perhaps a saint? Similarly, the earliest outline of the Wilmington Long Man in East Sussex has been scientifically dated to the Tudor period. The Whiteleaf and Bledlow Crosses in the Chilterns are old, but evidence for a phallic pre-Christian form is tenuous.

Of the lost figures, the Red Horse of Tysoe (Warwickshire) may have been Saxon. Written records of Plymouth's Gogmagog Giant(s) in Devon and the Giant on the Gogmagog Hills at Wandlebury near Cambridge prove that, at the latest, they were cut in the fifteenth and early seventeenth century respectively. The original Westbury White Horse (Wiltshire) may have been ancient, although the present example is much more recent. Of the many other existing White Horses proliferating on the hills of (mainly) southern England, none pre-date the eighteenth century. The twentieth century saw the addition to the landscape of military badges such as a dragon and a kiwi; and the huge chalk lion marking the approach to Whipsnade Zoo (Bedfordshire) has signalled the start of a delightful day out for countless southern children (including me!).

Who knows how many other hill figures have disappeared and have been irretrievably lost to human memory over the centuries? It's remarkable that so many have survived, for they need regular scouring, often with associated festivities as recounted amusingly in Thomas Hughes' *The Scouring of the White Horse* (1859). Aerial and infrared photography might reveal some of the vanished examples, but are the likes of the landscape markings that could be the remains of the Firle Beacon Giant (legendary opponent of the Wilmington Long Man) and the two gods (one horned, the other wielding a spear) at Upper Wanborough (Wilts) really there, or just wishful thinking? Perhaps time will tell.

A practice which has endured for three thousand years (or more: the 'discoverer' of the Wanborough Giants believes one is Neolithic!) surely requires some sort of explanation from deep within the English psyche or its countryside, as well as a consideration of each case individually. This is especially true as, although other countries, especially in South America, have their own figures or geoglyphs marked out in the landscape, there is nothing anywhere in the world resembling the English hill figure tradition (extending into Scotland with a couple of late outliers). They are even more distinctively British than the wild bluebell. Little wonder then that Jez Butterworth, who has a deep-seated, instinctual knowledge of the "Matter of England", included the cutting of a new hill figure, and scenes set at the Uffington White Horse, in series three of his superb TV drama *Britannia*.

Legend: The Cerne Abbas Giant
Women who want to get pregnant are supposed to have sex on the Giant, although the relevant organ was not originally as large as it is now. Aside from the obvious fertility aspects, legend has it that he was an actual giant or ogre, who rampaged through the countryside, devouring maidens, until some farmers tied him to the ground as he slept, killed him and cut the figure around the body.

- *2* -

Since so many mysteries abound concerning these figures, it is surprising that that they have been the subject of comparatively little supernatural fiction, even with the growth of the folk horror genre which is teeming with stone circles, barrows, etc. Sometimes, as in Jessie Kerruish's 1922 werewolf novel *The Undying Monster*, the figures are used purely as a scene-setting device; and they also appear in the SF and fantasy works of such authors as Terry Pratchett, Neil Gaiman,

Alan Garner, Robert Holdstock (see "English Hill Figures: Addenda" below), Keith Roberts, William Horwood, Susan Cooper and John Whitbourn, but in none of these examples are they central to the plot.

I have ancestors who were born in the Vale of the (Uffington) White Horse, so perhaps my fascination with hill figures is in my blood. I have long harboured a wish to edit a collection of supernatural short stories featuring them, but my hunt for suitable examples to reprint has only come up with a few. There *are* also some full-length genre novels that centre on them: Marcus Sedgwick's disappointing pre-teen book *Witch Hill* (2001) is a fairly recent one. Unusually, the figure, outside a West Country village named Crownhill, seems to be a crown, supposedly carved at the restoration of Charles II in 1660 (there *is* a chalk crown, cut near Wye in Kent, but that's a mere 120 years old). I say "seems" because, when it is freshly scoured, it turns out to be something else; a naked, crouching, female figure that more resembles the goddess Magog from T.C. Lethbridge's dubious excavation at Wandlebury in the 1950s. Given the title of the book, Jamie the young protagonist's dream of a "horrible, scary old woman" right at the start, and flashbacks to a witch trial interspersed throughout, plus the village's long history of unexplained deaths, there is little mystery as to what the word

Crownhill is a corruption of. The girl put on trial as a witch may have been an innocent who suffered an awful fate, but there *is* evil in the hill. It takes a while for the characters to catch up with the readers (even, surely, the young target audience): only close to the end does Jamie realise that "Crownhill used to be called Cronhill, and before that it used to be... Just add an 'e'".

Much better is John Gordon's outstanding early novel *The Giant Under the Snow* (1968), intended for an only slightly older readership. In this, Gordon invented a very believable legend about a Wiltshire chalk figure of a giant, which was reputed to have disappeared from its hill in times long past and strode across the country to East Anglia. What happens to the three teenagers who follow up the mystery of the buried giant, the "Green Man", is as satisfyingly unpredictable (if a little farfetched!) as *Witch Hill* is predictable. It helps that they are up against amongst the most sinister of Gordon's inventions, the very Jamesian Leather Men ("Brown and wrinkled, a thin shape of a man covered entirely in leather skin. Even his head. But the skin had shrunk to a skull and was smooth, so smooth that the head was faceless without eye sockets or mouth. Yet the head saw him and it snarled"). They are the soldiers of an ancient invading warlord who had used the risen Giant to gain power many centuries before. He wants to do so again, but he is finally frustrated and destroyed thanks to the teenagers and a local guardian spirit.

When I first heard of *The White Dragon* by Richard Garnett (1963), I was a little worried, as I understood that it featured ice-skating in the Fens and a dragon or serpent. This sounded very much like another book by John Gordon, *Fen Runners* (2009). Surely Gordon couldn't have copied the idea from the earlier book? I needn't have worried - the two are very different. I also wondered how there could possibly be a hill figure in the very flat Fens. I was fully expecting it to turn out to be marked out in the landscape like Somerset's Girt Dog of Langport (if that exists!), rather than on a hill. But the white dragon in question is cut on the side of a small man-made hill, the significantly-named Wormell, near the village of Fen Burton (the real Bluntisham-cum-Earith) in the Cambridgeshire Fens. The "worme" can only be seen in certain weather conditions, and links to a dragon, Old Snap, which has a part in a local, moribund Plough Monday Mummers' Play. The teenaged protagonist of *The White Dragon* helps to revive the old custom and mans the front of the fire-breathing dragon. Legend has it that after being killed by St George, Old Snap, the "Great White Worme", is chained up on Wormell until the coldest day of the year snaps his chains and he is revived for St George to fight again. In fact, the figure appears only once in a blue moon towards the end of winter, when the snow is thawing. The mystery of the hidden dragon runs throughout the book, but it's mostly a sort of "boys' own" adventure involving skating and "ice yacht" competitions. The one interesting female character is an aunt who is some sort of folklore writer (busily working on her next book, *The Horned God*), but she hardly appears at all after the first chapter

In Juliet E. McKenna's *The Green Man's Challenge* (2021), the fourth in her very enjoyable Green Man series, Dan and his girlfriend Fin are faced with a giant. It is just a shadow but gaining strength, and needs to devour humans to do so. It seems that the chalk (and other) horses cut into the southern English hillsides are landscape guardians. They have been guarding the countryside from threats like the giant since time immemorial - the present figures are all replacements of the ones which have gone before. Dan and Fin have to find the lost hill figure of the giant, so that they can secure it in place with a yew wood stake before it does any more harm. The book has a good sense of place (mainly Wiltshire), likeable central characters, and the description of the awakened white horses galloping through the air is lovely:

The silver radiance swelled and shifted... High in the air above that distant hillside, the great horse... was on the move again. It shone as bright as a full moon. Brighter than the actual moon above us... As [it] grew closer, I realised I wasn't only hearing one set of hooves. There wasn't only one horse racing through the night sky, though I could only catch glimpses of the others. I saw white forelegs pawing the air, and an elegant head tossing a silver mane...

Legend: The Long Man of Wilmington
Legend has it that the figure is cut around a giant who died upon the hill, but there are various stories about the manner of his death, the most amusing being that he tripped over his own feet, fell and broke his neck; or that a local shepherd threw a cheese sandwich at him which was so hard it killed him. Alternatively, and more romantically, he died in a rock-hurling fight with another giant on the nearby Firle Beacon.

- 3 -

Of short supernatural fiction for my proposed anthology, I've so far found ten significant stories (some, but not all, worth reprinting). I'll start with the Giants, and an M.R. James tale which deserves to be better known than it is.

"An Evening's Entertainment"
by M.R. James (1925)

Written in 1925 for the fourth of MRJ's collections *A Warning to the Curious,* published in that year, "An Evening's Entertainment" appears to have been composed in a hurry to replace another story which he was trying to write to fill up the volume, but which "would not come out" (as he told Gwendolen McBryde).

The account is narrated by a grandmother to her two grandchildren, Charles and Fanny, to warn them off from going blackberrying in one particular lane. It concerns a certain Mr Davis, a man of unknown means, who lives in a cottage somewhere in the south of England (this would be around the beginning of the eighteenth century). One day he brings an unnamed "young man" back from market, who moves in with him. The two of them are seen "late and early" going about the countryside together, especially in the vicinity of the barrows on the downs, and the ancient figure, "the old man on the hill", cut into the hillside. Sometimes they camp out overnight. One morning in September, at the equinox, their bodies are both found in terrible circumstances: the young man is discovered hanging from an oak tree in the wood, "dressed in a sort of white gown" and with a bloody hatchet at his feet; and Mr Davis himself is lying on a table in his cottage, tied up with linen bands, his chest bare and "the bone of it... split through from the top downwards with an axe". For years afterwards, strange, black, poisonous flies of a possibly supernatural nature seem to haunt the lane outside the site of Mr Davis's demolished cottage.

MRJ was definitely thinking of the Cerne Abbas Giant in Dorset when he set the story in the shadow of "the old man on the hill". In the months before he wrote "An Evening's Entertainment", he was completing and proofreading his book *Abbeys* (1925), where he writes of the abbey at Cerne (of which little remains):

> That [it] is really old I have little doubt; I have always supposed that it was set up here as a counterblast to the worship of the wicked old giant who is portrayed on the side of Trendle Hill just behind the Abbey. He is surely of very great antiquity, and is perhaps the most striking monument of the early paganism of the country. Whether he is British or Saxon, who shall say? Some have thought that he represents what Caesar describes - a wicker figure in which troops of victims were enclosed and then

burnt to death. On this hypothesis the figure would have been marked out by a palisade of wattles on the ground, and the victims, bound, crowded into the enclosure.

We now know, thanks to the new scientific dating methods, that the Cerne Giant is roughly contemporary with the founding of the abbey, which rules out MRJ's bizarre 'Wicker Man' theory (it isn't original to him, having been first suggested in 1872). But taking the theory as MRJ's belief in relation to the events in "An Evening's Entertainment", we have a good explanation for the deaths of Mr Davis and his young man (are they magician and scryer, as also depicted in MRJ's "The Residence at Whitminster"?). They died as sacrifices to the "old man on the hill", an ancient Celtic god, possibly Taranis. But were they alone? The young man reveals more than he should when he speaks of "not wanting for company" while they are out among the barrows. The two of them seem to know a lot about the residents of the barrows; more perhaps than if they had simply been doing some secretive excavations. Who or what have they awakened? Or is the "company" a group of fellow pagan worshippers of the "old religion"? MRJ is known to have credited the theories of Margaret Murray on that subject, and he owned a copy of her *The Witch-Cult in Western Europe* (1921). Were the deaths of Mr Davis and the young man murder/suicide? I think not as, if that had been the case, the "white gown", "like a mockery of the church surplice", which the young man was wearing, would have been covered with Mr Davis's blood. An outside agency must have been involved, but was it human or supernatural (or both)?

These unresolved questions make "An Evening's Entertainment" one of MRJ's most intriguing stories, and one which repays multiple rereadings.

"The Madness of a Chalk Giant"
by Colin Insole (2013)

Colin Insole's "The Madness of a Chalk Giant" is a superb short story, told partly from the viewpoint of the Giant, who is clearly based on the Cerne hill figure. He laments the disappearance of his worshippers, who used to bring offerings, light beacons and hold festivals in his honour:

> Fear had created him. The Celtic tribes, staring out into the vastness and void of the heath, had carved him into the hillside with iron and flint. His nakedness protected them from the ghosts and spirits of their imagination and his massive club threatened their neighbours' advance from across the valley.

Now, many of the nearby residents live on "new estates,

which straddled and impinged upon the heath, like a creeping decay... with their glass and steel". One of the newcomers, Trevor Fernsby, has been driven to arson by:

> ... the emptiness, under those grey lowering skies. I saw the ridges of the barrows, gathered on the far hills and felt the cold shadow of centuries - the brief fitful lives of the flint people and their descendants... And my own house seemed more transient and impermanent than the remnants of iron tools, carved bone and the spent musket ball I found one afternoon.

Echoes, maybe, of the discoveries of Mr Davis and his young man among "the barrows on the down" in "An Evening's Entertainment"? Fernsby's hatred centres on the husk of an old oak, once a gallows tree, known as "The Naked Man", which he attempts to burn down, along with the surrounding heathland. A psychiatrist sent to assess him, a woman lacking in poetry and imagination, fails to see that "The houses were merely facades of modernity - temporary scene changes, propped up in an ancient hostile landscape".

The local priest delights in his new, soulless church ("a plain modern building that might have been a warehouse or office facility... empty of religious imagery and symbolism"), and longs for the day when the old, now ruined, chapel, known locally as "The Chapel of Fools", can be demolished. It's a building which had syncretised Christianity with the earlier religion, a medieval monk having made the stained glass: "The 'spirit that stands by the naked man' was fixed on that benighted tree and the painted devils of the windows gave shape and reassurance to the nightmares of the congregation". Back then, the local people had continued to scour and commemorate the figure of the Giant, if only out of superstition and a belief that it was warding off devils and evil spirits. Almost within human memory, they had still lit beacons for him, "And they had gathered together, clasping the fire and hugging themselves to drive away the darkness within them". Not now, for no one believes in him any more; he is just an object to be mocked and joked about. In the end, the Giant sees a bonfire, but it's not in celebration of him; it's one built by the priest to burn down the chapel. The madness in this story isn't the Giant's, but the priest's and the arsonist's... and perhaps, as the final paragraph suggests, all the local residents' ("The flames would bring them no comfort but draw them out into the wilderness").

"The Madness of a Chalk Giant" is a poetic threnody to the loss of the spirit of the English landscape. There is no hope in it, only a threat of the dangers that might be a consequence. A remarkable and, I'd have thought, important tale, which also gives a believable explanation for why the old abbot would have approved the continued scouring of the Giant in medieval times. It's a shame that the story wasn't picked up for any of the *Year's Best* volumes, and has never been reprinted.

"Figures on a Hillside"
by Steve Duffy (1998)

Mr Fielding, protagonist of Steve Duffy's marvellous "Figures on a Hillside", is "a scholar of the Celtic tradition in its later period", with a particular interest in the Druids and in hill figures. He has developed a theory that all of the chalk giants are images of Gogmagog, who (he believes) later became Lucifer/Lugh. There is an intriguing link here with "An Evening's Entertainment", in which a local equates the Cerne Giant with Beelzebub, "Lord of Flies"; a connection also made independently, via Mummers' Plays, by Stuart Piggott in an article in a 1929 issue of the Folklore Society's Journal. In "Figures on a Hillside", as well as the giants at Cerne Abbas, Wandlebury and Wilmington (and closely resembling the latter), there is the "Long Man of Cheney Barrow" in Dorset:

> ...an imposing, featureless giant measuring some hundred and seventy feet from head to toe, with his

legs akimbo and his arms flung wide, holding in each hand a spear or rod as tall as himself... It is conjectured that he was first cut in pre-Roman times, in the days of the Druids who peopled old England with gods long since forgotten, and offered those gods blood sacrifice in their strange stone circles.

During his researches, Mr Fielding encounters a seventeenth-century Book of Wonders, which states that, while the Long Man represents a god of light, there was at that time a second figure. A traditional rhyme given in the book identifies them: "Gog-magog and Shuttle-go/Lord above and Lord below". That the rhyme goes on to warn of "Terror there and sore Affright/Till the coming of the Light" would deter anyone but an antiquary in the M.R. James tradition! Of course, Mr Fielding can't resist attempting to find this second figure, and he, and a fellow guest at the local inn, set out to discover it using the same suspect methods as T.C. Lethbridge used on the Gogmagog Hills at Wandlebury (the earlier mention in the story of Wandlebury is a clue that this was likely to happen).

What is revealed, when marked out with tape, is a hideous figure, perhaps cut at an earlier period than the Long Man who may have been added as a protection against it:

Imagine a profile view of a man, or perhaps one of

the higher apes, thin-limbed and crouching on all fours; endow this figure with an unusually large and shapeless head set deep into the torso with no suggestion of neck... with a peculiar hunched awkwardness suggestive of both indifferent artistry and (at the risk of appearing over-dramatic) a formless kind of malignity, a disfigurement going beyond mere shoddiness of execution.

Needless to say, once revealed, Shuttle-Go proceeds to haunt the night. The incessant barking of the local dogs is the first hint of something amiss. Then "a strange sort of deep bellowing noise" is heard and seems to be coming nearer. The mangled body of a sheep is found on the newly excavated figure, and further investigation comes up with the buried bones of many animals, the remains of sacrifices made until only a few hundred years before. When Mr Fielding, his friend and the innkeeper finally see Shuttle-Go, it is attacking the innkeeper's dog, and is every bit as awful as the reader might expect: "...In those subhuman eyes lay all the impurity in the world - all the malevolence, all that was foul and unwholesome".

Only one safe course of action is open to Mr Fielding and his friend - they remove the tape and all evidence of the figure. Although at the end of the story "it was permissible to hope that... peace and normality had returned to the downs", a doubt surely remains. Can it *really* be that easy?

"The Pharisees' Glass"
by R.B. Russell (1992)

"The Pharisees' Glass" by Ray Russell was published five years after the Great Storm of 1987, which did so much damage to the southern counties of England. It is that which forms the backdrop to the story's main events. The narrator is a man formerly from Sussex, who is on an errand in a northern town. Visiting a local pub, The Bull, he is introduced by the landlord to another ex-resident of that county. We discover that this gentleman, Mr Graham Goring, used to live in a cottage near Wilmington, and his experience, as told to the narrator, is what this tale is about. He begins by explaining his feelings concerning the area:

> There is something almost mystical about the South Downs. It's something that can be seen and felt. It's a retention of the memory of their ancient past... They're beyond all doubt the nearest point on earth to the heavens, and the wooded valleys hide secrets that stem from the very bowels of the earth.

After the Great Storm, Mr Goring had been sent to check on an old man, Daniel Pettit, who was injured in the mayhem.

Pettit is decidedly eccentric and believes in "the strangest things and ideas, phenomena that I [Goring] have guessed at only in the wildest flights of fancy". In particular he talks of "fairies or 'Pharisees' as Sussex folk called them". Mankind cannot understand the nature of fairies and how insignificant humanity is to them. Terms like good and evil mean nothing to them. Goring finds it hard to believe in their existence without solid, physical proof.

So Pettit takes Goring up to the hill figure of the Long Man of Wilmington. A few theories on its origin are discussed, and also how the figure might have changed over the years (one old drawing depicts it holding farming implements instead of staves, for instance). Then Pettit unwraps the "Pharisees' Glass", a piece of dark glass in a wooden frame. He was, he says, knocked out during the Storm and, while unconscious, the fairies had come to him and told him where to find the Glass, under a stone torn up by the uprooting of an ancient oak tree. But they also warned him that he should only look through it from one side, not the reverse. He hands the glass to Goring who does as he is instructed and sees "a supernal light over everything that I had once known, and a beauty and complexity in everyday things that the most colourful of imaginations could never hope to dream of".

But the inevitable happens. In giving it back to Pettit, Goring's hand shakes and the Glass falls out of its wooden frame onto the ground. When Pettit picks it up, he peers at it and "his expression was one of profound realisation and horror". He has looked through the Glass, even ever so briefly, from the wrong side. Goring is sure that (in a Machensesque phrase) Pettit had "'seen Pan'; he had seen nature as it really is, in all its awful and terrible wonder". Pettit hurls the glass down in shock and in pushing it away Goring has a quick inadvertent glance through the forbidden side. He sees:

> ...something far worse than that mythological creature. I have seen the Long Man of Wilmington for what it really is. Through the Pharisees' Glass I saw him as he was originally depicted in the chalk upon the venerable South Downs. He wasn't holding staves as he does today - he was standing in an open doorway, guarding what is beyond.

At this point Goring quickly gets up and leaves The Bull, saying only that he would never tell the narrator what he had seen through that doorway.

Although "The Pharisees' Glass" is one of Ray Russell's early tales, it's well-written and has much to commend it, not least the potentially terrifying ending. The idea that the

Long Man is actually standing in a doorway is not completely original, but it's the most enticing theory to explain the figure's pose. Here it's both enticing *and* chilling.

"Chalk"
by Katherine Haynes (2018)

Pansy Williams, the central character in Katherine Haynes's "Chalk", has been brought up to believe that her prettiness gives her the right to have everything she wants. But the one thing she doesn't have is a relationship - in fact she is still a virgin. So she joins an on-line dating agency, hoping for "a man who would marry her and declare that no wife of his was ever going to have to work, so she could stay at home all day in a big, comfortable house, and afford to have staff do the cooking and cleaning". She finds a man she likes the look of, Rufus Fisher, and they agree to meet for a weekend at the White Horse Hotel, somewhere in Wiltshire. We might therefore expect the hill figure in this story to be a White Horse, but it isn't. In her room at the hotel there is: "A somewhat indifferent mezzotint, it showed a hillside with a figure marked out on it, presumably in chalk. The gigantic man was drawn in outline only, but was anatomically correct and clearly in a state of arousal" (notice the direct quote, "indifferent mezzotint", from M.R. James's story "The Mezzotint").

Of course, when Pansy meets Rufus, who apparently lives in the hotel and has for many years, he is nothing like his photograph: "She could just about recognise him from the picture he had emailed, but he was much skinnier and weaker than she had expected. She knew he had been ill, but he looked as if he'd been at death's door…" The difference between the picture and the actual person proves to be significant: "I'm older than I look", Rufus tells her. Why are the locals so keen that the two of them should get along, and solicitous of Pansy's welfare? That night she has a disturbing dream. She sees the Giant on the hill and then:

> [She was] gazing down into a cavern, its walls appearing to be made of chalk. An arm emerged; stick thin and white as bone. Fingers grasped the edge of the chasm and something pulled itself up and rolled out onto the grass. Another slender figure followed, and then another and another. A company of women, all of them very pretty, rose to their feet and tripped towards the maypole.

The women's clothing seems to come from various different times: "There were a few in modern day costume, some twentieth century girls, and ones from the eighteenth century and earlier, much earlier".

Next day Rufus takes her on a picnic to the Cerne-esque chalk figure, known as the "Standing Man". Pansy fears that Rufus will want to have sex with her, or even drug her and force himself on her. But that is not what he has planned. Virgins are required to nourish the land and to renew the Standing Man, who is personified in Rufus. As Pansy slowly fades and is absorbed into the chalk, Rufus becomes strong and healthy again. Pansy is the latest, but not the last, of many. The villagers will celebrate with a festival and Rufus will go seeking for the next sacrifice. Pansy is so unlikeable that the reader feels she deserves her fate; at least in death she had a use!

"Chalk" is a nice take on the folk horror cliché of the ignorant townie who gets swept up in a pagan country tradition that results in their death. It doesn't lead exactly where one expects it to lead. I also like the hint of some sort of connection between Rufus Fisher and the Fisher King, as well as to King William II, William Rufus, who was killed, accidentally or deliberately, in the New Forest and (according to Margaret Murray!) may himself have been a sacrifice.

"The Rude Woman of Cerne"
by H.E. Bulstrode (2016)

Beatrice Clemens, the title character of this novella, is a

"crusader": H.E. Bulstrode doesn't use the pejorative phrase "social justice warrior" in the story, but you know that's what he means (he *does* use that phrase about her on his website). Beatrice runs a B&B, the Briars, near Cerne Abbas. Chloe and Ben have booked a stay to celebrate their anniversary but, when they arrive, Beatrice only reluctantly provides her guests with cows' milk; and she serves them cakes that are vegan and gluten-free. The guesthouse has a "meat-free Monday". Horrors! She espouses many good causes and is a woman of strong leftwing opinions, "absorbed wholesale from *The Guardian*'s opinion pages". True, sometimes she tries too strenuously to force her "sanctimonious" opinions on others, which makes her nothing more than an unpleasant caricature - the way people like Bulstrode see people like me, I guess. On the other hand, he indicates that Beatrice's mother is on the side of the angels in her interminable and deeply troubling defence of the British in Africa (and I noticed a couple of snide references to the great Billy Bragg). I confess I did wonder whether there was going to be much of a plot at all, let alone anything concerning the Cerne Giant.

On their first night, Chloe has a disturbing dream of "a figure running through the darkness towards the house... His eyes were blank, like those of a statue". She recognizes it as the hedger she had seen earlier, as they arrived at the B&B.

Strangely, he seemed to be wielding a sickle; hardly a hedger's tool. At the same time Ben, who can't sleep, hears the sound of someone outside sharpening a blade on a whetstone. Later on in their stay, a local tells how a friend was illicitly metal detecting on the Trendle, the Iron Age earthwork above the Giant, and found some silver coins. But he dropped them and fled when a glowing figure came running up the hill towards him carrying a curved blade - the hedger again. The figure then took the coins and ran back "in the direction of the Rude Man".

When "The Rude Woman of Cerne" was first published in 2016, the most popular theory for the Cerne Giant's identity was that it was a caricature of Oliver Cromwell. So Bulstrode says in his blog: "if we take him to be a representation of the humourless, self-righteous spirit of seventeenth-century puritan religiosity, he has now been provided with a spiritual heir in the form of Beatrice Clemens". In the story, however, the various theories about the Giant are mentioned, and I think the favoured one seems to be that he is a *genius loci*, originally "the local headman" of the Celtic Durotriges, "a great warrior". Beatrice doesn't approve: she believes he is "a symbol of phallocentric power and male violence".

Clearly such an uppity woman needs to be put in her place. The *genius loci*, in the form of the hedger with the sickle, who is presumably the Giant personified, is the author's chosen instrument. The hedger pays Beatrice a visit and: "He lifted his cloak to reveal what he held beneath, and with a flash of gold, he deftly sliced". Beatrice's head, mounted on a spear, is later found on the Trendle. The hedger is no longer seen in the county but some say he is still occasionally heard: a warning to "have a care to pay your respect to the old ways, and seek not to upset the old gods; it is their land, and they wish to be left in peace". That's telling us!

I'm very glad that most members of the folklore community interpret respect for the old gods and the land in a different way. "The Rude Woman of Cerne" claims to be a satirical comedy - it's neither satirical nor amusing.

Legend: The Uffington White Horse

A wish made upon the eye of the Horse is supposed to come true. The figure is said to be "creeping up the hill", and to be shod at the nearby Wayland's Smithy (a chambered long barrow). Legend has it that it is not a horse at all but a dragon: the very dragon killed by St George on nearby Dragon Hill. Even now, no grass grows there, supposedly because the ground is tainted with the dragon's blood.

- 4 -

He picked up the stone. The cut horse stretched along the whole length. The line of the body, tail and legs was made up of five curves; the head square, the eye a dot, the ears two spikes, the muzzle an open beak.

  --- from Alan Garner's *Treacle Walker* (2021)

Taint what a horse looks like, it's what a horse be.

  --- from Terry Pratchett's *A Hat Full of Sky* (2004)

The Uffington White Horse is the inspiration and setting for the final four stories. I haven't included an early piece of juvenilia by Richard Jefferies: "A Strange Story", published in the *North Wiltshire Herald* in 1866. Although the first scene takes place on Dragon Hill overlooking the Uffington Horse, with two companions sitting there and one telling the other a tale of death foreshadowings, the events don't relate to the White Horse itself.

"All I Ever See"
by Mike Chinn (2021)

According to the accompanying note to its publication in *The Mammoth Book of Folk Horror*, Mike Chinn's fine "All I Ever See" was inspired by the author's reading about the odd, animated black stick figures that people have reportedly been seeing, especially (but not solely) in recent years.

Bryan is on the way to recovery from a debilitating illness, and has long wished to visit the Uffington White Horse, the oldest of all the existing hill figures (but not, as the story claims, "one of Britain's oldest Neolithic monuments" - out by over a thousand years!). His wife, Jen, still thinks he's too weak to get there from the car by his own steam and, against his will, pushes him in his wheelchair. As he gets up from the chair and begins to walk around the figure, he hears a buzzing and faints. Back at the local inn where they are staying overnight, there is the first inkling of something seriously odd going on: "Something moved under the wooden bench running under the window. A black cat, he thought. He waited, but it stayed in shadow, refusing to show itself". The wife of the innkeeper doesn't see it. When it does come further into the light (still seen only by Bryan), its shape is revealed: "It was a crude outline, a two-dimensional stick figure. Identical to the Uffington Horse. Except it was completely black, and less than two feet long". The picture this conjures is in danger of being risible, or even cute, but in the light of later happenings, it's neither.

The next day Bryan and Jen return to walk the White

Horse and again Bryan hears a buzzing, while Jen complains that she can't get a good photograph on her mobile phone - the pictures are coming out too shadowy. Driving home after their trip, the country roads seem filled with odd shapes, and then Bryan sees: "something black and spiky [which was] keeping pace with the car. It looked like the bottom half of a black stick figure, just the legs, moving with odd, ponderous leaps. There was no way it could be moving fast enough to keep up". Later there is another (or the same) figure: "Tall, impossibly thin, and moving with a peculiar grace that didn't prevent it from loping across the ground at speed... It loped closer, bending so low it could have been running on all four limbs".

Jen sees nothing until the shape finally appears in front of the car and causes her to crash. We never learn exactly what she saw ("What the hell!" is her reaction), as she remains unconscious (or possibly dead), while Bryan leaves to try to get a signal for his mobile and call for help. Despite the fact that they had driven for miles, he finds himself back on the White Horse, and is surrounded: "Right on the limits of visibility, little stick men pulled themselves upright and pranced about the chalk outline, their movements slow and unnatural. Or were they so small?" Looking back towards the car, he sees: "Something even blacker, elongated, moving in a slow, peculiar manner... It was another black outline, with no more depth than a charcoal sketch. Man-shaped? Or horse? With each bizarre step it changed outline, bending into itself, flowing like ink". It seems to pass right over him and he stumbles back to the car, but there is no safety there!

It is never quite clear why the stick figures are linked to the White Horse, except that the carving itself is a kind of stick figure of a horse. And it's never clear why Bryan alone sees them. Alone, that is, until the end when Jen also sees *something*. Are they hallucinations connected with his suspected chronic fatigue syndrome? Is it to do with the atmosphere of antagonism between Bryan and Jen as their marriage breaks up? If they are hallucinations, what did Jen see that caused her to crash the car? Could this figure be a tulpa created by Bryan's anger and made real?

These are unanswered questions, but ones which make the story even more effective and disturbing.

"Vale of the White Horse"
by Scott Thomas (2001)

Scott Thomas is an American writer who has long had a "fascination with the British Isles", according to his introduction to *Vale of the White Horse* (2021), in which this story is reprinted. He also reveals that his "favourite supernatural fiction author" is M.R. James. Another tale in the book, "The Cathedral at Humberfield", is his "ode" to MRJ (it's not very good though!).

The protagonist of "Vale of the White Horse", Alfred Tymms, first encountered a hill figure at the age of ten when he attended a family wedding at Cerne Abbas and learned all about the Cerne Giant. His interest in "Britain's colossal white oddities" grew so that, some years later when a student at Cambridge, and being from a wealthy family, he decides to hire a balloonist to take him above "his beloved chalk figures" to photograph them from the air (this is in 1875). Along with the balloonist Wilson, Alfred takes a college friend. All goes well for the three of them to begin with ("England from a bird's eye view is a wonder of prehistoric landmarks, the wide and sprawling land dotted with megaliths and plump barrows, puckered with earthworks..." and so on). On the first day at Cerne, and on the second at the Long Man of Wilmington, Alfred gets the photographs he wants. On the third day the weather forces them to stay on land, but the next day they reach Uffington and the White Horse.

In a rather laboured info-dump, they discuss the nature of the "gracefully thin, stylized image of some type of animal": is it actually a horse, perhaps symbolising the Celtic horse goddess Epona; or a dragon as some legends have it; or even a cat? Suddenly, as Alfred starts to take photographs ("he ducked down under the black cloth... and peered down at his skeletal prey, which appeared to be prancing across the Berkshire Downs"), a wind gets up and the balloon seems to be dragged to the ground by a mysterious force. When the trio recover themselves, they find that they are in some sort of nightmare landscape version of the countryside. Everything is moonlit dark and everything distorted. A black field contains only shoes and boots; another contains many scarecrows (but why does a field need that many?). In the nearby village, there are horses but they are all dead, propped up by poles. Worst of all, in a final field are shapes like "writhing oversized maggots", that "might have been bodies wrapped in damp grey shrouds" (an image Thomas seems unhealthily fond of - it also appears in his "Dream of Dead Eyes"). Wilson strikes one with his knife, separating the shroud, only to have it revealed as "a man-sized quantity of powdered chalk".

The trio are in the broken-up, segmented world of the White Horse, either *containing* the Horse or perhaps formed *from* it. Nothing is as it should be - and they are being pursued by those shrouded figures. In their panic they come to the conclusion that, since it was the White Horse that caused them to crash-land and brought them to this version of reality, it must also return them home. They are wrong! As they step onto the hill:

> ...the chalk horse rose from its bed of dark grass, not as a spindly horse or dragon, but as a broken thing of many white shapes like featureless men. A chorus of horrible voices flew up and the earth shook beneath a storm of feet. [Then] ...the horse was gone, and a ghostly moon-white army roared down upon them.

After a flatly-written beginning, "Vale of the White Horse" comes to life in its unsettlingly surreal second half. It's nothing like as good a story as Mike Chinn's, but it is interesting that both have an original (but different) take on the peculiar representational form of the Uffington White Horse, involving its division into separate humanoid figures.

> *... the potent image of the [Uffington] chalk horse can act as a trigger or master key, unlocking pent-up dream worlds, wild psychic landscapes and spiritual cravings, while retaining its essential enigma.*
> --- from Paul Newman's *Lost Gods of Albion* (1997)

Paul Finch's admirable *Terror Tales...* series of anthologies, each of them covering a particular geographical area, has featured two hill figure stories. One is "The Pale Man" by Andy Briggs: see "English Hill Figures: Addenda" below. The other is in *Terror Tales of the Cotswolds*:

"The Scouring"
by Thana Niveau (2012)

Thana Niveau's "The Scouring" is a subtly poignant tale with a kick. After just six years of happy marriage to Michael, Natalie is widowed, with a young son who shares his father's artistic leanings. A year later, Natalie and six-year-old Charlie are on holiday, visiting various sites in the Cotswolds: "...the original plan had been to show him Oxford, with detours to Stonehenge and Avebury on the way back. But Charlie had spotted the numerous 'White Horse' references in the road atlas and insisted that they investigate".

The little boy is fascinated by the White Horse, even after an elderly walker tells him, disappointingly, that it's much more recent than the dinosaurs. The man also explains that the periodic scouring of the figure was necessary because: "...The horse would get hungry, you see, and its guardians had to release it from the hillside so it could feed. They would make offerings, chant songs, that sort of thing. All sadly lost to time now".

Charlie draws the Horse, first as it appears in reality and then a different version:

> He had connected its two floating legs to its body and lengthened them. Now the horse appeared to be rearing up. He had turned the beaked square into a long thin head with a proper mouth. ...Instead of widening the thin line of its body to make it more realistic, Charlie had drawn a row of jagged ribs.

Settled in for a meal and overnight stay at a local inn, Charlie tells Natalie that he has been hearing his dead father, who says that he goes for rides on the White Horse, and that "she" likes the boy. ("How do you know it's a she?" "Daddy told me.") When their food is brought, the waitress looks at his drawing of the Horse and is horrified. She won't explain why, and leaves quickly. The young waiter who replaces her supposes that Charlie had reminded her of her own son, who "wandered off one night and was never found".

I think from this point we know exactly what is going to happen. That night, Natalie wakes up to the sounds of scratching: Charlie is sitting up in bed, gouging the lines of his drawing of the White Horse - or "scouring" it. Later, she awakens again to find him gone. Knowing where he must be, she drives out to the White Horse. The Horse is on the move:

> She watched in horror as it peeled itself up from the grass like a fossil come to life... Then it heaved its

torso up and she gasped to see her son's depiction before her. A row of spiky ribs stuck out where its belly should be and she remembered something else the old man had told Charlie. He'd said that the pagan ritual was meant to free the horse when it got hungry. So it could eat.

Natalie spots Charlie climbing the hillside but she is too late to save him. The Horse knocks her to the ground. Charlie, lured there by the conversations he believes he has had with his father, goes up to the beast, "a smile playing at the corners of his mouth". The Horse brings its "razor sharp hooves" down upon the unsuspecting boy. Lying at the bottom of the hill with a broken leg, Natalie looks up at the Horse, and sees it "grazing placidly and occasionally pawing at the ground with one slender leg. After a while it lifted its head and snorted. Its muzzle was stained with blood". Little Charlie is never seen again and we leave Natalie in hospital, scraping and scouring a photograph of him and his father.

"The Scouring" is touchingly sad, and the reader feels for Natalie, her mourning for her husband and love of their child. But it works well too because it is also quite brutal in its final depiction of the nature of the White Horse.

"'A View from a Hill': A Christmas Ghost Story"
by Stewart Lee (2012)

The title of Stewart Lee's "A View from a Hill" is taken from the story by M.R. James (which has no hill figures, but there might be a ley!), and this isn't the only connection with that author. Lee's first-person tale is topped and tailed by part of a report on his arrest on "multiple charges of arson, assault and grievous bodily harm" by "Detective Inspector M.R. James". Comedian Lee writes as though this is a true account of events which happened to him. One Winter Solstice, back in 1988, he and an Oxford college friend, Julian Fullsome-Swathe, had paid a visit to the Uffington White Horse, after partaking of magic mushrooms supplied by "an old didgeridoo player who lived in the public car park on Port Meadow". Lee told his friend: "They say that if England is threatened, the horse will rise up from the hill and take revenge". To which Julian had replied: "The White Horse is rising, Stewart... Can't you see it?"

Moving forward to 2012, Lee isn't having a good lead-up to Christmas, with two sick children to take care of while trying to meet two writing deadlines (one being this present story for the *New Statesman*!). Asked to write a piece for *ShortList*, a "men's lifestyle" magazine, on the ten things he most hated about the year, one that he picks is Paddy

Power's addition of a jockey to the Uffington White Horse to promote betting on the racing at the Cheltenham Festival, "driving pegs into its prehistoric surface": "Paddy Power desecrated what is either a religious site, a work of art, or both, in the name of grubby commerce, and then treated anyone who objected as if they were a humourless curmudgeon". Lee writes in graphic terms that he hopes all who work for Paddy Power get their just deserts. After submitting this and his other listed diatribes to *Shortlist*, he is told by the magazine that only some of the milder, more personal entries will be printed. Motivated by "That night on the White Horse with Julian..." a quarter of a century earlier, when he "genuinely believed the hill figure to be an expression of the triumph of the human spirit and imagination", Lee withdraws the entire article (this actually took place: the withdrawn article is published in full in Lee's *Content Provider: Selected Short Prose Pieces, 2011-2016*, just before the reprint of "A View from a Hill").

In Malvern, on the way to a pre-Christmas visit with his stepfather, Lee encounters Julian again - a broken and destitute man, still obsessed with the hill figure. The meeting reminds Lee of their experience on White Horse Hill. Julian had claimed that the Horse had genuinely risen (Lee didn't see this): "...slowly the equine figure shook itself free of the turf, and stood and stamped its feet. Then it turned, snorted and leapt through the snow and out into the stars". Julian had then told Lee that if he ever wanted "anyone eliminated, and without a paper trail", he could arrange it for him.

So starts a sequence of atrocities in 2012, with all the people and organisations Lee berated in his unpublished article suffering such things as waking up with the severed heads of white horses in their beds, eighty-eight branches of Debenhams finding dead horses on their doorsteps, and comedian Jack Whitehall's hamster being eviscerated (poor thing!). It was Julian, right? But why is it that Stewart Lee has been arrested? Because Detective Inspector M.R. James could find no record of Julian's existence, as if Lee had "fabricated the character in his *New Statesman* Christmas story for some reason".

I like Lee's "A View from a Hill" very much. It's a justifiably angry polemic hidden inside a mildly comedic piece of metafiction. The Paddy Power outrage did happen and I thoroughly agree with Lee's disgust. It's true that the jockey figure was only temporary and removed within a few hours, once they'd had their publicity, but to use that as justification (as they did) only goes to show that Paddy Power were entirely insensitive to the harm they'd done. This is not the only time a hill figure has suffered such vandalism, sometimes by those who should know better (although I can't find it in my heart to condemn the mischievous people who briefly added a disposable horn to the Westbury White Horse in the 1980s: I love unicorns!).

> *Those that think folklore does not exert gravity on us, those that think it is dead, these are the people who know not themselves or the landscape they live in.*
>
> --- C.L. Nolan (Hookland)

Sources:
Short Stories:

H.E. Bulstrode, "The Rude Woman of Cerne" (self-published 2016; reprinted in *Uncanny Tales from the English Shires*, self-published 2018)

Mike Chinn, "All I Ever See" (*The Mammoth Book of Folk Horror*, Skyhorse Publishing 2021)

Steve Duffy, "Figures on a Hillside" (*The Night Comes On*, Ash-Tree Press 1998*)*

Katherine Haynes, "Chalk" (*Waiting in the Shadows*, Sarob Press 2018)

Colin Insole, "The Madness of a Chalk Giant" (*Elegies & Requiems*, Side Real Press 2013)

M.R. James, "An Evening's Entertainment" (*A Warning to

the Curious, Edward Arnold 1925; etc.)

Stewart Lee, "'A View from a Hill': A Christmas Ghost Story" *(New Statesman,* December 2012; reprinted in *Content Provider: Selected Short Prose Pieces, 2011-2016,* Faber & Faber 2016)

Thana Niveau, "The Scouring" (*Terror Tales of the Cotswolds,* Gray Friar Press 2012)

R.B. Russell, "The Pharisees' Glass" (*Aklo 5,* 1992)

Scott Thomas, "Vale of the White Horse" (*Vale of the White Horse and Other Strange British Tales,* Weird House Press 2021; reprinted from *Cobwebs and Whispers,* Delirium Books 2001)

Novels:

Richard Garnett, *The White Dragon* (Rupert Hart-Davis 1963)

John Gordon, *The Giant Under the Snow* (Orion Books 1968)

Juliet E. McKenna, *The Green Man's Challenge* (Wizard's Tower Press 2021)

Marcus Sedgwick, *Witch Hill* (Orion Books 2001)

Background:

Rodney Castleden, *Ancient British Hill Figures* (S.B. Publications 2000)

--- *The Cerne Giant* (Dorset Publishing Company 1996)

--- *The Wilmington Giant: The Quest for a Lost Myth* (Turnstone Press 1983)

Timothy Darvill et al, *The Cerne Giant: An antiquity on trial* (Oxbow Books 1999)

M.R. James, *Abbeys* (Great Western Railway 1925)

T.C. Lethbridge, *Gogmagog: The Buried Gods* (Routledge and Kegan Paul 1957)

Paul Newman, *Lost Gods of Albion: The Chalk Hill-Figures of Britain* (1987, Sutton Publishing 1997)

Rosemary Pardoe, "The God(s) of 'An Evening's Entertainment'" (*The Ghosts & Scholars M.R. James Newsletter 19*, 2011; retitled "'The Heathens and their Sacrifices': The God(s) of 'An Evening's Entertainment'" in *The Black Pilgrimage & Other Explorations*, Shadow Publishing 2018)

--- "'The Old Man on the Hill': Beelzebub in 'An Evening's Entertainment'" (*The Ghosts & Scholars M.R. James Newsletter 7*, 2005; *The Black Pilgrimage & Other Explorations*, Shadow Publishing 2018)

Stuart Piggott, "The character of Beelzebub in the Mummers' Play" (*Folk-Lore 40*, 1929)

--- "The Name of the Giant of Cerne" (*Antiquity 6*, 1932)

Various Authors, *Folklore, Myths and Legends of Britain* (Reader's Digest 1973)

Jennifer Westwood and Jacqueline Simpson, *The Lore of the*

Land: A Guide to England's Legends (Penguin 2005)

S.G. Wildman, *The Black Horsemen: English Inns and King Arthur* (John Baker 1971)

Websites: Wikipedia pages for "Hill Figure", etc. "Cerne Abbas Giant age revealed by scientists", BBC website, May 12th, 2021

"The hills have eyes... and a spear", *Swindon Advertiser* website, August 6th, 2013 (Wanborough 'giants')

English Hill Figures: Addenda

A few items were omitted from my booklet *"The Old Man on the Hill": English Hill Figures in Supernatural Fiction*, some because they didn't quite fit, and some because they appeared just too late for coverage. I'll start with a story I mentioned in passing there, but which was published soon afterwards in *Terror Tales of the West Country*.

"The Pale Man"
by Andy Briggs (2022)

Escaping from an abusive relationship with Michael, the unnamed narrator/protagonist and her friend Sarah are on a road trip from the north down to the West Country. They are somewhere in Somerset when the fog sets in and their GPS and phone reception start playing up (they never would have had the ensuing trouble if they'd used *proper* maps!). Out of the mist looms a tearoom, The Pale Man, where they are disconcerted by the fact that the old woman who comes out to wait on them is blind. The only meal she can offer them is a ploughman's, and while they wait for that, the narrator thinks she sees a shadow in the fog outside the window, moving with an "awkward, disjointed motion". Shortly afterwards, the mist clears briefly and, on an opposite hill, "a huge chalk figure of a stooped man wielding a cudgel" can be seen. The narrator is reminded of the shadow that had just passed by the window.

The hill figure is the "Pale Man", which was, according to the blind waitress, cut into the chalk "long ago. Before the Romans, Before most things. It was a time when we needed a guardian. An earth spirit to look after the land. And us... He's always watching". Seemingly, the guardian is still needed. The fog clears briefly again and this time the giant is no longer "stooped"; it's upright with "the cudgel angled over its shoulder in an almost jaunty manner". When the hill becomes visible for a third time, there is no figure on it.

The waitress reappears holding an eight-inch carving knife and says quietly, "Not the best time to be venturin'... I mean midsummer". Oh-oh! Sarah goes outside to get some cash from the car and doesn't return. When the narrator follows her, she sees that the front of the vehicle is a crumpled wreck. And there are others, many others. As she retreats to the tearoom, a shadow looms up out of the fog, "A distinctly human shape some forty feet tall... It was stooped, pulled to one side as it dragged something behind it".

And noises are coming from the boot of their car...

Now the story takes an unexpected turn. It's revealed that

we are in unreliable narrator territory here. There was an abusive relationship, that's true, but the abuser wasn't Michael. He was despised and beaten for being "A meek man. A waste of time and my life". Finally he'd started to fight back, which "wasn't something I could encourage". The narrator had murdered him in horrific fashion, and she and Sarah had put the body in the boot with the plan to dump it somewhere far away from home. Now Michael is back as a revenant with revenge on what passes for its mind; a mind animated, presumably, by the spirit of the Pale Man. Not so much a guardian, after all, as a judge.

The narrator is killed by the waitress, but continues her narration as her corpse watches Michael attack Sarah, who re-enters the tearoom at that moment. The narrator finds herself surrounded by "thousands of other restless souls", their vehicles their only tombstones. Whether or not she deserved her fate, and whether Sarah did so for aiding and abetting, it's hard to believe that all of these thousands received fair justice from the giant.

I do not like this story at all. Admittedly it's well-written enough, and the twist is unexpected, removing all risk of its becoming the cliché 'townie gets sacrificed in pagan ritual' plot. But it's viciously cold in its portrayal of the two female characters and I may be wrong but I get a distinct anti-woman vibe from it. More to the point when I've been considering the other hill figure tales from a folkloric, landscape-evoking viewpoint, "The Pale Man" fails because it is completely free of any authentic-feeling sense of place. It's just a horror story.

The Hollowing
by Robert Holdstock (1993)
No other author has so successfully captured the magic of the wildwood.

--- Michael Moorock

I have read and reread Robert Holdstock's sequence of Mythago/Ryhope Wood novels more often than just about anything else. That's to say, I've repeatedly reread the first three and the last one: a couple in the middle aren't so good. The series begins with *Mythago Wood* (1984), continues with *Lavondyss* (the best of the lot, 1988) and ends with *Avilion* (2009), published just a few months before Rob's tragically premature and sudden death. Despite being generally downbeat, they seem to be my go-to reading when I'm feeling sad (I couldn't stop reading them over and over for several months after my husband's death). The premise of the series is that some ancient woodland has created "mythagos" from the fears, myths and legends of humanity since prehistoric times (so some are tantalisingly familiar, others buried more deeply in our psyches). Among the author's most original creations are the Green Jacks, his version of the Green Man. These are the forbidding but not usually dangerous Daurog in summer, but become the terrifying Scarag in winter when they "stalk the snow wastes and the bare forest for prey". Tallis, the central character in *Lavondyss*, briefly becomes a "Holly-jack" during her transformative later years.

For obvious reasons, woodland isn't the best place to find hill figures, but one personified is lurking in Ryhope Wood and plays a part in the third book, *The Hollowing*. As is explained there: "a Long Man... the living reflection of the chalk figures that could be found on the English downlands, and whose origins and identities and functions remain a mystery". The Long Man, "an absolute image now of the Long Man of Wilmington, in Sussex", is the opener of portals (or "hollowings"). Walk between his two tall poles and he can transport you out of danger or to another place, though it seems that he has no precise control over where the portals might lead to.

The first of the two times he appears, "the figure... of a man, a tall, lean man of huge height, carrying two staffs", he speaks - "Helpen", he asks. The central character, Richard, is looking for his lost son, being aided by a team of scientists exploring Ryhope Wood. But they don't realise what help it is that the Long Man is offering. The second time, Richard is in a desperate situation and is initially terrified when "the Long Man barred his way". Then the figure beckons, shouting "words that could have been 'Come on!'" Richard grabs the Long Man's shoulders and both go through the hollowing, ending up at the edge of the Wood, close to Richard's home. The Long Man is none too happy with this and offers to take Richard back in, but he refuses and the Long Man "grinned, touched a finger to his right eye, then turned and stepped between his poles. The air popped, sending a gust of wind around the small clearing that had once been a garden, and the giant had gone". Never to reappear. In the hands of a lesser writer, he could have become an easy 'with one bound they were free' escape from any danger, but not in *The Hollowing*. He is not at anyone's beck and call.

The Long Man seems to be one of the more benevolent occupants of Ryhope Wood, a "myth imago" from an unknown time in England's past. There have been a number of suggestions for what the *actual* Long Man of Wilmington is holding, including a theory that the staffs do indeed form a gateway of some sort, with the figure being a guardian of the way. I like the fact that Rob Holdstock had picked up on this, the most romantic of the theories. Others are that the poles are measuring rods for surveying and positioning leys, or a rake and a scythe, with the top details lost over time (a 1776 sketch of the Long Man does show him holding these farming implements, but the artist may have had an overactive imagination!). Recent scientific dating methods seem to indicate that the Long Man isn't as old as many had thought - perhaps only going back five centuries or so - but instinctively one feels that he must be older, and I'm sure Rob Holdstock would have agreed with me on this.[1]

Note:

[1] I can't precisely put this into words, but I think I'm talking about the difference between *actual* reality and *poetic* reality, which may be just as real. I'm afraid I read Robert Graves' *The White Goddess* at a dangerously formative age!

Hoebury Hill
by Richard Daniels (2022)

Hopefully many readers here are fans of *The Occultaria of Albion*. The first time I saw Facebook ads for their booklets, I thought they were about real hauntings in various areas and actual buildings. But they're nothing so mundane; instead each booklet or "volume" or "research paper" contains items of fiction and fakelore dressed up and illustrated convincingly to look like the real thing. They're in the tradition of the likes of the Portals of London website (see "Lady Wardrop's Notes 2" above) and Hookland. Titles have included *Melwerther Hall, Spanton Industrial Estate, Wittley Holt Station* and *Thornley Mill Shopping Precinct*. When I first decided to give the booklets a try, and realised just how very strange they are, I naturally asked their creator Richard Daniels whether hill figures had appeared anywhere so far. He said they hadn't, but that he'd add them to his list of ideas for future booklets. Little could I have guessed how quickly he'd act on my suggestion.

Booklet 14, which was published in August 2022, is about *Hoebury Hill*, in West Sussex: "Hoebury Hill is considered by some to be one of the most abstruse and arcane sites in southern England. Many have heard of the Uffington White Horse, the Chanctonbury Ring and the Cerne Abbas Giant, but virtually no one will be familiar with the unusual chalk figure known colloquially as UFO Mo". The hill is the site of an Iron Age camp and possibly a Romano-British temple. The figure was discovered by a 1960s sexploitation starlet Maureen Munsen/Monroe, who fell in with a Hollywood cult called The Temple of Xubix. As a result of a series of weird dreams, she came to England, rented a cottage at Hoebury and began clearing the dense "grass and scrub" from the eastern side of the hill. What she found was a relatively small hill figure like no other: "a sort of sheela na gig but with what looks to be a UFO or flying saucer where its vulva would be" (a restrained "artist's impression" appears in the booklet). "It immediately attracted the attention of historians, archaeologists and ufologists alike", some of whom believed it to be as old as the Uffington White Horse, or Saxon, or dating back no more than a hundred years. One academic paper suggested that it was from the 1940s and "some sort of lewd gesture to the Luftwaffe". Another section of the *Hoebury Hill* booklet would appear to support an older date than this. It recounts the experience of Spencer Sheehan while hang gliding off the hill in 1982. After coming out of a cloud, he seemed to have been transported into the past, to around 1000-1300 CE, and he saw the figure clearly back then.

Or perhaps his vision of the past was just a drug-induced hallucination, and the figure was nothing more than a modern publicity stunt, since the latest film of Maureen Monroe's friend and sexploitation director, Roscoe Kroger, had been *Fallen Angels* about "provocative females arriving on Earth in flying saucers". In 1971, the year after the excavation was completed, and while Maureen and her husband were holidaying in Scotland, a huge thunderstorm scattered debris over the figure and blew down the tents of ufologists camped nearby. Enthusiasm for its restoration and upkeep waned so that already by the mid-70s it was "covered by dirt and undergrowth"; and now "the chalk figure is once again almost completely obscured by grass and vegetation and is mostly forgotten as a site of interest".

Maybe it's time for another excavation on Hoebury Hill, but we have to find it first!

AND FINALLY

The Wormwood Interview: Rosemary Pardoe

Rosemary Pardoe is the Founding Editor of the long-running M.R. James journal *Ghosts & Scholars* which continues under her guidance with guest editors. She has compiled *A Bibliography of the Writings of M.R. James* and a checklist of stories in the James tradition, *The James Gang*. She has also edited several volumes of stories under the Ghosts & Scholars banner with Sarob Press. Her essays on supernatural fiction were collected as *The Black Pilgrimage & Other Explorations* (Shadow Publishing 2018) and a new edition of her own excellent antiquarian ghost stories, *The Angry Dead*, appeared from Cathaven Press as an 'Occult Detective Magazine special edition' in 2021. We're most grateful to Rosemary for agreeing to tell us about some of the books important to her.

The first book I remember...
For my sins, I collected Enid Blyton's Noddy books from an early age! But more important for forming my later tastes was a book we had in reading classes at my primary school in a village near Oxford. I suppose I would have been six or seven. One story in it was the famous County Durham folk

tale of the Lambton Worm. It both terrified and fascinated me: a small worm that grew into a monstrous serpent! I almost believed it was a true account and was relieved that the serpent was eventually killed.

The first book I bought for myself...
I think it would have been TV astronomer Patrick Moore's non-fiction *Science and Fiction*. I definitely had the original 1957 edition as I recognise the dust-jacket artwork, but I was only six then so it must have stayed in the shops (I bought it in W.H. Smith's, if I remember rightly) for at least four or five more years. It was a revelation, and opened so many doors for me; only much later did I realise just how narrow Moore's definition of good science fiction was (it had to be *scientific*, you see!). Around the same time I was spending my pocket money on the Red Planet series by Angus MacVicar, and Patrick Moore's own series of SF books featuring Maurice Gray. The latter were filled with nice young men (no women!) who visited Mars, and I was at the age when I quickly had crushes on several of them (I suspect Moore probably had crushes on them too!).

The book I thought was my discovery...
It might have been E.G. Swain's *Stoneground Ghost Tales*

(1912). I first found this in the 'local interest' section of Huntingdon Library some time in the 1970s, a few years before I started *Ghosts & Scholars* and was introduced to the range of writers in the M.R. James tradition, including Swain. But Swain is only featured among the 'James Gang' because he was a friend of Monty's. His stories, with the exception of "The Rockery", don't contain the malign ghosts that James thought essential for good supernatural fiction. I didn't like the book - I thought the stories were dull and insipid! But soon after editing the first issue of *Ghosts & Scholars*, I was persuaded by David Rowlands (himself a writer of some superb ghost stories) to give Swain another try. I did and, with different expectations this time, I found the stories absolutely delightful.

The book that changed me...
It has to be *The Collected Ghost Stories of M.R. James* of course! When I first met my late husband Darroll (I was eighteen), he came to our relationship with three books which he convinced me I had to read: *The Collected MRJ*, George R. Stewart's *Earth Abides* and Philip K. Dick's *The Man in the High Castle*. I could never get into the third of those and while I enjoyed the second I didn't love it enough to ever reread it. But *The Collected MRJ*: well, the rest is

history... nine years later the first issue of *Ghosts & Scholars* appeared. As it turned out, I realised that I had read one story by Monty in a ghost story anthology long before. It was "An Episode of Cathedral History". I'd really enjoyed it, and hoped to find more antiquarian tales like it, but the name of the author didn't stick with me at the time.

The book a friend told me about...
Assuming Darroll counts as a friend as well as a husband, it would be *The Collected MRJ* again; but I have David Rowlands to thank for turning me on to many other Jamesian collections such as A.N.L. Munby's *The Alabaster Hand* (1949) and R.H. Malden's *Nine Ghosts* (1943). It was my sister Jane who first recommended John Gordon's *The House on the Brink* (1970) to me, and I still think it's one of the best two Jamesian novels ever written.

The wildest weirdest book I ever read...
It might be Robert Anton Wilson and Richard Shea's *Illuminatus!* trilogy (1975). It's a wild ride though conspiracy theories, with a tremendous climax at Lake Ingolstadt where a whole army of Nazi zombies are waiting to be revived! I read it first on publication, and still reread it every few years.

Or perhaps it's S.G. Wildman's *The Black Horsemen:*

English Inns and King Arthur (1971), which theorises that inns named The Black Horse mark the travels and battles of King Arthur. Not content with that, Wildman goes on to rediscover the Red Horse of Tysoe (Warwickshire) and associated hill figures. Unfortunately, he used the same methods as those used by T.C. Lethbridge on the Gogmagog Hills; methods which are dubious to say the least. Some of my ancestors lived in the Vale of the White Horse, in the shadow of the Uffington White Horse, so my life-long fascination with hill figures may be in my blood.

Then again, surpassing them both in weirdness is Michael Harrison's *The London that was Rome* (1971). Harrison was a prolific writer, whose most well-known (or notorious) book may be *Clarence*, his biography of Eddie, the Duke of Clarence (in which he theorises that J.K. Stephen was Jack the Ripper). He also wrote a strange and quite disturbing story, "Some Very Odd Happenings at Kibblesham Manor House", which revolves around a cursed object from Roman Britain (*Fantasy & Science Fiction* 1969). *The London that was Rome* centres on Harrison's proposition that it's possible to identify the locations of many London buildings from the Roman era, via the names of more recent and current edifices on their sites. Thus the church of St Magnus Martyr was, he claims, built on top of a temple to Magna Mater, Cybele the Great Mother; Hadrian's "deified catamite" Antonous is remembered in St Antholin, Watling Street; and I'll leave you to work out whose temple is underneath St Dionis Backchurch. There are pages and pages of these!

The book I treasure most...
How can I answer that? There would never be just one book I could pick if I had to pack a case for that mythical desert island. But narrowing the question down to books I treasure because they're now hard to find, I think I'd pick M.R. James's translation of Walter Map's twelfth-century *De Nugis Curialium* in the original edition (1923), with vast numbers of notes by folklorist E. Sidney Hartland. There have been several more recent editions of James's translation but, as far as I've been able to discover, none of them include the notes. It's those which I treasure, with their descriptions of fairy abductions, vampires, ghosts, the Wild Hunt, etc. On some pages the notes completely overwhelm the actual text: definitely my sort of book! I see my copy is priced in pencil at £40. Can I really have paid that much when I bought it back in the 1980s or 1990s? I'd be reluctant to pay that much for a book even now.

The Wormwood Interview reprinted with the permission of Mark Valentine.

Index to Short Story and Novel Titles

"Adventure of the Green Skull, The" (Valentine), 156
"After Dark in the Playing Fields" (James), 32-33, 215, 218, 238, 239, 252, 254
"All I Ever See" (Chinn), 346-349, 352
All of a Winter's Night (Rickman), 66
"Almanac, The" (Valentine), 151-152
"Ancient Lights" (Blackwood), 222
"Antioch Imperial, The" (Valentine), 155
"As Blank as the Days Yet to Be" (Valentine), 83, 158
"Ash Track, The" (Valentine), 151
"Ash-tree, The" (James), 30, 37, 117, 193, 196, 201, 211, 233, 238, 245, 251-252, 264
"Assizes" (Ward), 246
"At the Heart of It" (Harrison), 45-46
"At the Mountains of Madness" (Lovecraft), 108
Avilion (Holdstock), 366
"Axholme Toll, The" (Valentine), 155-156, 157

"Beast with Five Fingers, The" (Harvey), 154
"Beneath the Overground" (Portals of London), 176
Black Fox, The (Heard), 162
"Blue Boar of Totenhoe, The" (Allen), 272, 273
Boneland (Garner), 83

Box of Delights, The (Masefield), 51
"Brass Tombstone, The"/"P Aia Johns Blak" (Boston), 137, 138
"Breakdown, the" (Johnson), 72
"Burden of Dead Books, The" (Gray), 46

"Cambridge Beast, The" (Allen), 104, 273, 275
"Canon Alberic's Scrap-book" (James), 16, 37, 41, 191, 194, 212, 229, 231
Carbonel (Sleigh), 132, 133, 134
"Carnival Horror, The" (Fanthorpe), 139
"Casting the Runes" (James), 18, 30, 111, 207, 212, 214, 216-217, 232, 233, 244, 251
"Cathedral at Humberfield, The" (Thomas), 350
"Chalk" (Haynes), 340-342
"Chauffeur, The" (Allen), 273, 275
"Coffin of Lissa, The" (Derleth), 191
Cold Calling, The (Rickman), 63
"Conkers" (Rowlands), 272, 277
"Conservation" (Bell), 278
"Copper Bowl, The" (Eliot), 191
"Count Magnus" (James), 26,

30, 195, 211, 212, 229, 238, 239, 252

Dark is Rising, The (Cooper), 51
Daughter of Time, The (Tey), 23
Death of Anton (Melville), 170
Demons of Ghent (Grant), 101-105
De Nugis Curialium (Map), 34-35, 162-163, 207-208, 380
"Diary of Mr Poynter, The" (James), 111, 195, 205-206, 214, 216, 237, 238, 239
"Dog, The"/"The Interruptions" (Johnson), 70
Dracula (Stoker), 187, 192
"Dream of Dead Eyes" (Thomas), 351
Dream Quest of Unknown Kadath (Lovecraft), 190-191
"Drud, The" (Fanthorpe), 139
"Dug Out" (Longhorn), 246

Earth Abides (Stewart), 377
"Eldritch Chair, The" (Fanthorpe), 139
"Episode of Cathedral History, An" (James), 194, 199, 202-203, 209, 213, 229, 238, 245, 378
"Evening's Entertainment, An" (James), 179, 184, 214-215, 229, 238, 243, 252, 328-331, 332, 334
"Ex Libris: Lufford" (McGachey), 235
"Experiment, The" (James), 179, 211, 232

"Fall of the King of Babylon, The" (Valentine), 156
"Faraway islands" (Portals of London), 176
Fear in the Sunlight (Upson), 27
Fen Runners (Gordon), 51, 325
"Fenstanton Witch, The" (James), 193-194, 211, 245, 252
Fever of this World, The (Rickman), 66-67
"Figures on a Hillside" (Duffy), 334-337
"Fire Companions" (Valentine), 155
Five Jars, The (James), 32, 33, 127, 133, 201, 205, 206
"Folly, The" (Valentine), 151
Franchise Affair, The (Tey), 24
Frequent Hearses (Crispin), 258-259
Friends of the Dusk (Rickman), 66

"Game of Bear, The" (James), 213, 228
Ghosts of Blacklode, The (Gordon), 52-54, 56
Giant under the Snow, The (Gordon), 51, 234-235
Gobblecock Mystery, The (Austen-Leigh), 171
"Go to the West" (Valentine), 152
"Gravedigger and Death, The" (Allen), 272, 274
"Grave of Anir, The" (Valentine), 150, 151
"Great God Pan, The"

(Machen), 50
Green Man's Challenge, The (McKenna), 326-327
"Grip of Fear, The" (Fanthorpe), 137-138
"Guardians of the Guest Room" (Valentine), 152
Gypsy, The (Lindholm/Brust), 83
"Gypsy's Curse, The" (Tyrrell), 246

"Hampstead Horror, A" (Portals of London), 176
"Hatchment, The" (Allen), 272
Hatful of Sky, A (Pratchett), 346
"Haunted Dolls' House, The" (James), 212, 218, 238, 239
Hazel Wood, The (Albert), 83-88, 89, 91
"Herald of the Hidden" (Valentine), 83, 152, 153
"Heritage of Fire, The" (Valentine), 151
"Hermit's House, The" (Valentine), 151
Hobby Horse Cottage (Read), 84
Hoebury Hill (Daniels), 369-372
"Hold Fast" (Allen), 272, 274
Hollowing, The (Holdstock), 83, 170, 366-369
"Horror at Red Hook, The" (Lovecraft), 190
"Hound, The" (Leiber), 58, 207
House on the Brink, The (Gordon), 52, 54, 378

"Idol House of Astarte, The" (Christie), 268

Illuminatus! (Shea/Wilson), 378
"Incomplete Apocalypse, An" (Valentine), 154
Incredible Crime, The: A Cambridge Mystery (Austen-Leigh), 171-174
"Interruptions, The"/"The Dog" (Johnson), 70
"In the Bag" (Campbell), 70
"In the Walls of Eryx" (Lovecraft), 257

"Joan" (Allen), 272, 274
"John Humphreys" (James), 21, 54, 215, 253
"Judderman" (Budden), 124

Kingdom of Carbonel (Sleigh), 134

"Lane, The" (Warburton), 254
Last Battle, The (Lewis), 101
"Last of the Scarisfields, The" (Duffy), 265, 269
"Last Post, The" (Valentine), 154
Lavondyss (Holdstock), 83, 90, 91, 366
Legends of Croquemitaine, The, 94-96
Lion, the Witch and the Wardrobe, The (Lewis), 51
"Lost Hearts" (James), 16, 46, 193, 214, 238, 243, 244
Lost Journals of Benjamin Tooth, The (Crook), 128-129, 133-134
"Lost Maze, The" (Grant), 104-105
"Love, Death and the Maiden"/"Mädelein" (Johnson), 69

"Madberry Hill" (Valentine), 151
"Mädelein"/"Love, Death and the Maiden" (Johnson), 69
"Madness of a Chalk Giant, The" (Insole), 331-334
"Malice of Inanimate Objects, The" (James), 20, 212, 231, 271
Man in the High Castle, The (Dick), 377
"Marcilly-le-Hayer" (James), 212
"Margaret and Catherine" (Allen), 272, 274-275
"Martin's Close" (James), 19, 111, 193, 214, 238, 245, 246, 252
Masquerade (Williams), 71
Mean Spirit (Rickman), 63
"Melodrama, The" (Johnson), 69-70, 71
Melwerther Hall (Daniels), 370
"Merfield Hall/House" (James), 215, 228
"Mezzotint, The" (James), 26, 37, 41, 110-112, 146, 195, 211, 215, 231, 232, 233, 235, 244, 252, 340-341
"Midnight Museum, The" (Fanthorpe), 139
Midwinter Watch, The (Gordon), 52, 54-56
Mischief Acts (Gilbert), 159-160, 161-163
"Mist Shrouded Cities" (Portals of London), 176
"Morpheus House" (Valentine), 157
"Mr Humphreys and His Inheritance" (James), 184, 196, 199, 214, 229-230, 238, 239, 241, 252, 258-261, 262, 264-265
Murder Must Advertise (Sayers), 173
Mythago Wood (Holdstock), 83, 85, 90, 170, 366

"N" (Machen), 223
"Nameless City, The" (Lovecraft), 69
"Neighbour's Landmark, A" (James), 20, 21, 29, 193, 216, 223, 238, 239, 252
"Ne Resurgat" (Allen), 272
Ness (Macfarlane), 167-170
"New Corner" (Rolt), 222
Night After Night (Rickman), 63-66
Night Country, The (Albert), 88-91
"Night in King's College Chapel, A" (James), 211-212
"Nine Green Men, The" (Fanthorpe), 138
Nine Lessons (Upson), 23-27
"1909 Proserpine Prize, The" (Valentine), 154-155
"Number 13" (James), 17, 212, 238, 243

"Oddities Investigated: Tales from a Hero's Casebook" (Johnson), 69
"Oh, Whistle, and I'll Come to You, My Lad" (James), 26, 30, 37-40, 41, 114-115, 123, 181, 183, 185, 211, 212, 232, 253
"Other Salt, The" (Valentine), 156
Our Lady of Darkness (Leiber), 57-62

"P Aia Johns Blak"/"The Brass
  Tombstone" (Boston), 137,
  138
Pale Brown Thing, The
  (Leiber), 58-62
"Pale Man, The" (Briggs), 353,
  363-366
"Pharisees' Glass, The"
  (Russell), 337-340
"Pickman's Model" (Lovecraft),
  190-191
"Pool, The" (Johnson), 72
"Prince Zaleski's Secret"
  (Valentine), 156
"Prize, The" (Johnson), 70, 71
"Pull Devil, Pull Baker"
  (Harrison), 49

"Quantum of Darkness"
  (Kidd), 246
Quick Curtain (Melville), 170-
  171
"Quis est Iste?" (Harman), 231

"Rats" (James), 29, 30, 38, 65,
  211, 238, 239, 253
"Residence at Whitminster,
  The" (James), 21, 55, 195,
  196, 198, 208-209, 212,
  213, 237, 238, 239, 251,
  253, 330
"Return of Kala Persad, The"
  (Valentine), 156
"Return to the Runes"
  (Sutton), 229
"Right Through My Hair"
  (Boston), 137
"Rockery, The" (Swain), 377
Roofworld (Fowler), 104
"Rose Garden, The" (James),
  17-18, 196, 211, 238, 241,
  243, 253
"Rude Woman of Cerne, The"
  (Bulstrode), 342-345

"Scarecrow, The" (Johnson),
  70
"School Story, A" (James), 17,
  212, 214, 215, 232
"Scouring, The" (Niveau), 353-
  355
*Scouring of the White Horse,
  The* (Hughes), 321
"Sea Citadels" (Valentine), 83
"Searchlight, The" (Johnson),
  70
"Seer of Trieste, The"
  (Valentine), 155
"Seventeenth Hole at Duncas-
  ter, The" (Wakefield), 222
"Shadow in Georgian London,
  A" (Portals of London), 176
"Sheelagh-na-gig, The" (Allen),
  271, 273, 276
"Signalman, The" (Dickens),
  114
Silent Saturday (Grant), 103
"Smoke Ghost" (Leiber), 58
"Snow Queen, The"
  (Andersen), 51
"Soldier, The" (Johnson), 44,
  71-72, 177
"Some Very Odd Happenings
  at Kibblesham Manor
  House" (Harrison), 46-48,
  49, 379
Spanton Industrial Estate
  (Daniels), 370
"Speaker Lenthall's Tomb"
  (James), 197-198, 215
"Spinney, The" (Ward), 254
"Stalls of Barchester Cathedral,
  The" (James), 18-19, 26,
  162, 201, 212, 213-214, 238,
  243, 253
"St Michael & All Angels"

(Valentine), 150-151
Stormhound (Fayers), 131-134
"Story of a Disappearance and an Appearance, The" (James), 195, 203-204, 215, 237, 238, 239
"Strange Story, A" (Jefferies), 346
"Striding Folly" (Sayers), 267-268

Tale of the Tailor and the Three Dead Kings, The (Jones), 9-14
"Tenant, The" (Derleth), 191
"Their Special Glee" (Valentine), 153
"There was a Man Dwelt by a Churchyard" (James), 193, 212-213, 218, 238, 243
"Thing from Boulter's Cavern, The" (Fanthorpe), 139
Thornley Mill Shopping Precinct (Daniels), 370
"Tontine of Thirteen, The" (Valentine), 156-157
Too Near the Dead (Grant), 103, 105
"Tower, The" (Laski), 266-267
"Tractate Middoth, The" (James), 26, 30, 195, 196, 211, 212, 238, 239
"Transmutation of Base Metal, The" (Jakeman), 246
Treacle Walker (Garner), 346
"Treasure of Abbot Thomas, The" (James), 212, 215, 232
"Tree Worship" (Valentine), 152-153
"Turn of the Screw, The" (H. James), 187
"Twelfth Night" (Harrison), 49-50
"Twelve Medieval Ghost-stories" (Anon), 9, 207
"Twilight at Little Brydon Cricket Club" (Valentine), 152
"Two Doctors" (James), 33-34, 179, 214, 229, 232, 237, 239, 253

"Uncommon Prayer-book, The" (James), 111, 192, 193, 195, 196-197, 205, 214, 216, 218, 238, 239
Undying Monster, The (Kerruish), 322
Urban Legends (Grant), 103

"Vale of the White Horse" (Thomas), 349-352
"View from a Hill, A" (James), 21, 215-216, 217, 233, 238, 243, 253, 356
"View from a Hill, A: A Christmas Ghost Story" (Lee), 356-359
"Vignette, A" (James), 31-32, 34, 35, 211, 232, 253
Villager (Cox), 159-161, 163
"Voice in the Wall, The" (Fanthorpe), 138

"Wailing Well" (James), 193, 204-205, 209, 215, 231, 253
"Wall-Painting, The" (Johnson), 70, 71
"Walls, The" (Lamsley), 254
"Wandlebury Eyecatcher, The" (Allen), 272, 273
"Warning to the Curious, A" (James), 21, 26, 30, 40-41, 42, 123 184, 185, 186, 195,

INDEX TO STORY AND NOVEL TITLES

205, 210, 211, 238, 239, 243, 244, 253
"Watchman, The" (Johnson), 70, 71
Wee Free Men, The (Pratchett), 83, 85
Weekend at Thrackley (Melville), 170
Well of Loneliness, The (Hall), 172
Wench is Dead, The (Dexter), 23
"Wendigo, The" (Blackwood), 15
"We Pass Under" (Budden), 124
"What Goes Down" (Tumasonis), 267
"Whispering Wires" (Portals of London), 176
White Dragon, The (Garnett), 325-326
"William Sorrell Requests..." (Valentine), 151
Windvale Sprites, The (Crook), 125-129, 133-134
Witch Hill (Sedgwick), 323-324
"Without Instruments" (Valentine), 157
Wittley Holt Station (Daniels), 370
Wizard of the Pigeons (Lindholm), 83
"Woken by Candlelight" (Valentine), 153
"Wren's Restless Sanctuary" (Portals of London), 176-177
Wylding Hall (Hand), 141-148

"Yogh" (Valentine), 155

"You Walk the Pages" (Valentine), 155

Also available from Shadow Publishing

Phantoms of Venice
Selected by David A. Sutton
ISBN 0-9539032-1-4

The Satyr's Head: Tales of Terror
Selected by David A. Sutton
ISBN 978-0-9539032-3-8

The Female of the Species And Other Terror Tales
By Richard Davis
ISBN 978-0-9539032-4-5

The Whispering Horror
By Eddy C. Bertin
ISBN: 978-0-9539032-7-6

The Lurkers in the Abyss and Other Tales of Terror
By David A. Riley
ISBN: 978-0-9539032-9-0

Worse Things Than Spiders and Other Stories
By Samantha Lee
ISBN: 978-0-9539032-8-3

Tales of the Grotesque: A Collection of Uneasy Tales
By L. A. Lewis (Edited by Richard Dalby)
ISBN: 978-0-9572962-0-6

Horror on the High Seas: Classic Weird Sea Tales
Selected by David A. Sutton
ISBN: 978-0-9572962-1-3

Creeping Crawlers
Edited by Allen Ashley
ISBN 978-0-9572962-2-0

Haunts of Horror
Edited by David A. Sutton
ISBN 978-0-9572962-3-7

Death After Death
By Edmund Glasby
ISBN 978-0-9572962-4-4

The Spirit of the Place and Other Strange Tales:
Complete Short Stories
By Elizabeth Walter
ISBN 978-0-9572962-5-1

Such Things May Be: Collected Writings
By James Wade
Edited by Edward P. Berglund
ISBN 978-0-9572962-6-8

The Black Pilgrimage & Other Explorations
Essays on Supernatural Fiction
By Rosemary Pardoe
ISBN 978-0-9572962-7-5

Shadmocks & Shivers
New Tales inspired by the stories of R. Chetwynd-Hayes
Edited by Dave Brzeski
ISBN 978-0-9572962-8-2

Bloody Britain
By Anna Taborska
ISBN 978-0-9572962-9-9